I dedicate this novel to my five children,
Nancy, Alexander, Heather, Christine, and Reginald,

eleven grandchildren,
Noreen, Graham, Annette, Julie, Janet & Jessica
Casey, Joshua, Kristen, Kurt and Amy

and

eight great-grandchildren,
Colby, Brian, Noah, Jack, Isaac, Madison, Lily and Hannah

In loving memory of their
grandmother, great-grandmother & great-great-grandmother
NELL
Upon whose life it was based

Uncle John's words echoed in my head...
"The big thing to remember in this life is,
that no matter who forsakes ye,
ye are never alone.
God is always near ye.
God knows your problems.
He loves ye, and in the long and the short
of it all,
He is the one that will always stand by ye
no matter what happens.
Just believe and trust in Him."

Contents

Prologue

It had always been my ambition to travel to Scotland to see my mother's birthplace, and now at long last my dream was being fulfilled. The plane touched down at Prestwick Airport early in the morning, and the sun came streaming in the window to give me a glorious welcome. How often I had heard from my Mother's lips about the beauty of her homeland. How often my mind had imagined the hills and glens, the lochs and heather. I felt an excitement I had never known before rushing through my veins as I gathered my belongings together and slowly descended the stairs of the aircraft. I was in Scotland at last.

My husband, also a Scot, accompanied me on this trip, and it was wonderful to meet his family for the first time. His brother, Alex, met us at the airport and decided to take us on a short trip to see the city of Ayr and Burns' Cottage on the way home. The weather was unusually warm as we made our way down the west coast to the home of the famous Scottish poet, "Robbie Burns." We visited the humble cottage where the bard was born. It made me stop and ponder that such beautiful poetry, and greatness of thought, could spring from such a quiet, small, and humble dwelling. I loved Ayr, the old church, the old bridge, and the atmosphere of history.

I would soon discover that this atmosphere prevails everywhere in Scotland. History is on every doorstep. Songs from long ago resound from every hill. Every glen has a story, and the more I saw, the more I thought of my mother's life and wanted to see her birthplace. That night, snug by the hearth of my sister-in-law Jessie's home in Moodiesburn on the outskirts of Glasgow, we made plans to visit East Kilbride, my mother's village, the next day.

Morning dawned just as beautifully as the day before. It was handpicked, warm and sunny, and our trip to the old village was a lovely one. When my mother had lived there, East Kilbride had been a village, but now it had grown to be a town with a population of over 67,000 or more, and was the largest of Scotland's five new towns. How was I going to find my mother's little cottage?

As we entered the town, I glanced eagerly from left to right, trying to picture what it might have looked like back in Mother's day. Suddenly my eyes fell on a sign, a sign that read, "Whitemoss Rounda-bout."

"WHITEMOSS!" I shouted without restraint. "That was the name of my mother's home! They called it 'Whitemoss Cottage!' Oh, how thrilling it would be, if I could find someone who remembered the family."

First, we went to the museum to see if they could tell us anything. My mother's name had been Helen Sweenie, and she had lived in a cottage called Whitemoss, on the Whitemoss farm, almost eighty years ago. This was the only information I could give the woman at the museum, and she merely shook her head sadly and said, "No, I'm terribly sorry, but I can't help you."

Slowly getting back into the car, I felt keenly disappointed. We wheeled the car around and were heading out of the driveway when the museum door suddenly swung open and the lady waved us to a stop.

"It's not much help," she apologized, "but there is a 'Whitemoss Round-a-bout' here and I believe they called the new bowling green and tennis courts by that name."

She proceeded to direct us to these places, and then suddenly thought of two brothers who lived in old East Kilbride who just might be able to give us some information, as they had known most of the people years ago in the old village.

Off we went to see them. Their names were Peter and Paul Marshall, and we were lucky enough to catch Peter just as he was returning home from a walk. He was a likeable old gentleman, and I was overwhelmed with joy when he remembered my grandfather.

"Great man he was!" he said as he stamped his cane on the sidewalk. "Great man, alright! How well I remember him. So, you're his granddaughter, from Canada! Is your mother still living?" he asked, eyeing me up and down in a typical Scottish manner.

"No, I'm sorry to say she passed away quite a few years ago."

"Oh, I am sorry to hear that, Lass. Did ye ken your grandfather built most of the houses in auld East Kilbride? Aye, he was a gid builder! Could build a house quicker than ony man the day. He was also known as the Pansy King of here about. Beautiful pansies, that man had! Aye, beautiful garden tae!

"He married three times, ye ken. Tae bad he lost his first yin. She was a gem, I understand. I did'na know her. She had ten bairns, ye ken, but only five lived. It was your mother's brother, Frank, I was friendly with. I only remember your mother as the youngest of the family, a wee thing with bonnie red hair that fell down her back in beautiful curls and she always had a delightful smile for everyone.

"She had a hard life after her mother passed away, with one step-mother after another, but I lost track of her after she grew up a bit. I heard that she had gone to Canada but nothing after that.

"Your grandfather lived a rather quiet, lonely, and unhappy life at the last, I felt. Kept pretty much to his garden. Family pretty much left him alone. No one wanted to visit him and put up with the old bisom he'd married. Can't say as I blamed them.

"Well, here I am rambling on and on and I know you want to see the wee cottage. Well, it's over on Whitemoss Grove. It's the cottage, not the big house across the lane, and it was part of a farm then.

"Now, it's the bowling-green attendant's house. I think you might find it empty at the moment. A new attendant has just been appointed and I don't think he has arrived yet."

I couldn't thank him enough, and after a warm handshake I returned to the car to start the search for Mother's cottage.

We soon found the 'round-a-bout' again and Grove Lane. Then we got out of the car and began walking up a county lane lined with trees that led up to a cottage on the one side and a farm house on the other. As I walked it seemed, as if by magic, I had left the hurrying and scurrying of the twentieth century behind, and was entering the quiet and more placid age of the late nineteenth.

Suddenly, Mother's cottage, 'Whitemoss' appeared between the trees, looking much as it must have looked eighty years before when Mother had lived there. I slowly walked toward the picket gate. The house was empty, just as Mr. Marshall had said the gardener hadn't arrived yet and the place was rather badly overgrown with weeds. I opened the gate and walked up to the front door, staring at it as though I expected someone to open it and welcome me. I crossed to the window and peered into the living room, then walked around the house to the garden where my Mother had played as a child. Again, I felt drawn to the old house. I peeked through the kitchen window and could see a sink, complete with an old-fashioned pump, and over to one side of the room was a closeted bed. I then looked into the backyard living room window, because the room stretched from the front of the house to the back and I could see a large open fireplace.

My husband, with his brother and sister, said they were going to look at the bowling- green and tennis courts that lay just beyond the back garden gate, but I wished to linger in Mother's garden.

Slowly, I walked around the garden, thinking how wonderful it must have looked when my grandfather took care of it. Then, I went around to the front of the house again and tried to picture my mother, a bright, light-hearted girl of eight, skipping out of the house with her long red ringlets bouncing beautifully up and down on her back as she made her way to the gate, swinging it open and skipping down the lane to play with her hoop. I had once seen a picture of Mother (when she was a child) playing with her hoop, so it was easy to imagine.

Slowly turning for one last look at the house, I was strangely drawn towards the living room window. It was then that it happened, as though in a dream, I seemed to see a wee girl about eight years old with a huge tear running down her cheek as her nose pressed against the windowpane. Her hair hung in a cascade of long red ringlets, and as I stared in amazement, I could hear a voice. The little girl was talking. The voice was so familiar.

Transfixed, I watched and listened.

Chapter 1
My Life Changed

I can still remember that gray November day when my mother lay in her bedroom, deathly ill, and I stood by the living room window with tears rolling down my cheeks. I was afraid that she might die, and I loved her so very much. I just couldn't imagine what life would be like without her. She was everything to me, she loved me dearly and was so good to me. God couldn't take her away from me, could He? I needed her. I was only eight years old.

My father seemed beside himself with worry as he paced the floor beside me, wringing his hands in a desperate gesture of despair. My sister, Jean, had taken time off work to help at home and she was in the bedroom with Mother. My two-day-old baby sister had died two weeks ago and mother had become deathly sick since then. She had developed pneumonia and we were all waiting for Dr. McGregor to arrive.

Finally, the doctor came and father led him down the hall to mother's room. Then all was silent!

I felt so alone, and I didn't like being alone. I remember crawling up into the big old arm chair by the window and wrapping a shawl around me as I watched the storm that raged outside. The trees were swaying violently and I thought that a large branch on the old maple tree would break off. Even the little white picket gate that led to the lane was swinging back and forth on its hinges, making a mournful creaking sound.

In the horrible quiet that followed, I prayed to God to make my mother well. The old clock on the mantle struck four and I was reminded that they had been in Mother's room for almost an hour. Suddenly, the deadly silence was broken by the sound of weeping. Jean reappeared first in the doorway, and whispered in a voice scarcely above a whisper, "Mother just died, Nell."

• • • • •

My life changed that gray rainy day in November. Mother had died and never again would I feel her warm embrace, or hear her beautiful, lilting voice as she told me the stories of the Bible. She was gone and all my wishing or praying couldn't bring her back. I knew she was with her Heavenly Father and that she must be happy to be with Him because she loved Him so, but I couldn't help wondering what would happen to me.

I also worried about Father. He missed Mother so much. He no longer seemed like himself. He would just sit for hours in his rocking chair, staring at the fire.

He was a builder by trade, but now that it was winter he didn't have the same amount of work. Other years, he had kept himself busy planning new houses, and working well into the evening hours at his desk. I always remembered my father busy, without a moment to spare; but now all that had changed.

Mother used to scold him for having no time for the family, to which he would hastily reply, "Well, you have to eat and have clothes, woman. What would you have me do, be lazy and sit around the house all the time? While there's work to be done, I'll be at it."

How different he looked. His head bowed and his shoulders bent, staring at his hands as he rocked ever so slowly back and forth.

He was a handsome man, with sandy brown hair and blue-gray eyes. When Mother had been living, his eyes would twinkle and his lips curl into a grin, which Mother claimed she couldn't resist. Now all this was different. He never laughed and joked anymore. He didn't seem to even want the family around to disturb his thoughts.

Father's greatest hobby had always been his garden. It was a wonderful relief from his building, just to be able to work with a delicate flower, such as a pansy, and produce new varieties. He had become known far and wide already for his pansies. He enjoyed showing them at the Flower Show and winning prizes.

Now things were different. Even the garden drew no interest. He usually spent much time in the winter planning his garden to make it even more beautiful than it had been the previous year, but now he just sat silently meditating.

My father was a man of many talents, and one was a singing voice. He sang in the church choir for years before that fateful autumn day, but now no one could persuade him to go back into it again. He used to sing the old Scottish songs at the local dances and 'get-togethers' of the village, but now he wouldn't go out.

My sister Jean had been working out in 'service' as a maid before Mother took sick. She was ten years older than me. Now, at eighteen, she had come home to look after the family. Frank, one of my older brothers, aged eleven, had taken Mother's death very hard, but unlike me he tried to hide all his emotions. Perhaps it was just as well with Father the way he was.

Frank, often called 'Wee Frank' because he was small of stature and frail of body, had always been a sickly child, but in spite of his frailty he had managed to get into more scrapes than one would believe possible.

I remember my cousin Elizabeth, the past September, running into the house frightened silly saying, "Frank's down in the deep well deeded."

My Mother, although pregnant at the time, had jumped up with fright in her heart and ran to save him. He had managed to catch a large stick that his older chums had held down to him, and with the help of Mother, our cousin, and neighbors, he was finally rescued. It was possibly the fright and the stress and strain of that experience that helped to cause the death of the baby.

Something was always happening to Frank. He had fallen out of a tree once and broken an arm and he had almost been run over by a horse in the lane but he was a very lively loveable exciting person and everyone loved him dearly. Another person who was very close to me was Uncle John (Mother's brother), whom I loved very much. He owned a grocery store in the village and we often visited him there. He would always let both Frank and me sample the sweeties. He had been kicked by a horse when he was younger, so was lame and walked with a limp.

Wee Frank used to love to sit near Uncle John and listen to his stories. We used to visit Uncle John a great deal when Mother was alive, in fact, almost every time we went to the village to shop. Often on Sundays, too, we would call around for a short visit after church. Sometimes Uncle John and Aunt Jane would come to our cottage for dinner on the weekends or on Wednesdays when the shop was closed.

Uncle John saw my Father's deep sorrow and tried to get him to come out of it. One day I overheard a conversation between them.

"Do you no' think it's about time to start your planning for the spring, John? Several people have talked to me at the store about having you draw up plans for new houses, but they say you haven't been to see them yet to discuss their ideas. What's the matter, John? I know how deeply you have been hurt by Jean's death, but you must think of your family. They need you, too, you know. Young Jean's doing a splendid job and all, but they need to know they have a father. You need to get back out into circulation yourself, too. It's not good for a man to keep himself shut off in sorrow. How about going back into the choir again or joining some of us in a wee card game now and then?"

All of Uncle John's pleas seemed in vain, for they fell on deaf ears, and Father remained in solitude, cut off from the world in his sorrow.

My older sister, Jean, who was now at home and had taken on all Mother's work, was a wonderful housekeeper and cook. I found her pretty nice to have around, except that she pulled and tugged at my hair dreadfully when she combed it every day. She didn't seem to have the patience Mother had, but in most things she was very kind and thoughtful to Wee Frank and me.

Our older sister, Maggie, had been married for the last two years, and as she didn't live too far away, managed to visit us quite often.

George, my oldest brother, was very busy those days courting a very attractive girl and his head seemed to be in the clouds. Of course he came out of them long enough to eat a considerable amount at meal time and to demand that my sister Jean clean his boots and have his tie and shirt out ready and his suit pressed for his big night — which seemed almost every night lately.

Jean, too, had her eyes on a young man. He was the son of a blacksmith and was really very nice-looking, with black wavy hair and a twinkle in his eye that had all the girls at the church dreaming. Jim had never made any advances towards Jean, but she was hopeful because he was always very polite and courteous and often teased her about her freckles. Needless to say, she never missed a chance to be at the church functions where he might attend, and used every excuse imaginable to pass by the Smithy whenever she was in the village.

When the Christmas Pageant at the church was cast, Jean was asked to be an angel and Jim was one of the three kings. After the performance Jim said she really looked like an angel, which made Jean blush to the roots of her hair.

For days, she went about the house in a dream world after that conversation, coming out of it just long enough to say to me, "Isn't he handsome? Do you like him? Do you think he really likes me? Oh! I wish I didn't have freckles…"

Sometime in February, Jean was approached by the choir leader, Mrs. Kennedy, to become a member of the choir.

"We need new members for our Easter music, you know," chirped Mrs. Kennedy enthusiastically, "and I do need young people. Jimmy Young is coming in, and so are Johnny Walker and Betty Wilson, so why not you?

"Do you think you could bring your Father along too? We need good tenors. We always need tenors and he has such a beautiful voice. We are getting a new alto in the choir next week, a Miss Bowman from Hairmyers. She is a librarian and has come here to stay with her aunt, as her mother just passed away in January. Poor thing, she seems so lonely."

It didn't take Jean long to decide that she wanted to be in the choir now that Jimmy was going to be in it. She asked Father if he'd care to join, but in his usual manner those days he replied. "Oh, I'm not interested anymore now your mother isn't with us. She was always so interested in those things that it makes me feel lonely even sitting in church, let alone trying to sing. One has to feel in the mood to sing. One has to be happy. Besides, how could I go to practice? I will stay home with Nell and Frank on Thursdays while you go, I couldn't leave them alone. You go, I'm too old for that kind of thing. I've had my day. Go and enjoy yourself."

I found myself looking forward to Thursday night now, as I thought Father would put me to bed and I'd get him to romp with me and tell stories, but it didn't work out that way. Jean would get me all ready for bed before she left for choir and Father only came into my room long enough to hear my prayers and kiss me good night. I can remember burying my head in my pillow and sobbing quietly after he left the room the first Thursday evening. Father hadn't said a word to me since Mother had died. He seemed to be in another world, and his children were not a part of it. My young heart ached for a pat on the head or a warm embrace in the rocking chair, the way he used to when he told stories or read to me. He had always been very busy and never had much time for such things before Mother died, but he had always found a little time. Now he had more time and never did it at all. I began to feel deep down in my heart that he didn't love me very much, or he would show me a little more affection.

Late one Sunday afternoon, after Uncle John and Aunt Jane had gone home and Father was sitting staring at the fire as usual, the Rev. Albert McKinnon came to see us. I guess he really came to see my Father, as he asked to be alone with him and they talked for a long time.

No doubt the Reverend really placed things on the line to Father, as the following Sunday found Father back in his pew with us, like old times. It was good to have him there. George did a good job of making Frank and me, behave in church, but Father was much better at it.

On the way out we were filing past the Reverend McKinnon and shaking hands with him when a woman suddenly appeared at our side from out of nowhere and said, "Oh, Reverend McKinnon, your sermon was simply wonderful. I don't know when I've heard such an inspiring message. I am so looking forward to being in your congregation, and meeting everyone here in East Kilbride."

With this overture sweetly ringing in his ears, the Reverend McKinnon turned to Father, who was by this time talking to some old friends and said, "Mr. Sweenie, please excuse me, but I want you to meet one of our newest members, Miss Bowman. She comes to us from Hairmyers, and will be our new librarian here in East Kilbride." Turning to Miss Bowman he went on. "Mr. Sweenie is an old and faithful member of the church who just lost his wife recently, and is finding it rather difficult to adjust. Miss Bowman just lost her mother last month, too, so you have something in common." Then, with a smile he turned to greet the next person in line.

That was about all it needed to get Miss Bowman started. She talked to Father like a long lost cousin all the rest of the way out of the church, and said she hoped she would see him again soon, as they said goodbye.

The next Sunday, Miss Bowman was in the choir and we were just leaving the church to walk home when I heard her call cheerily, "Hello, Mr. Sweenie. How are you, and how have you been this week?" Then the tone of her voice changed to that of a sad, heavy-hearted individual and her eyes sought his for the sympathy she craved. "I have had a dreadful week. I'm so lonely here. I miss my friends and it takes so long to make new ones…"

On and on she talked, and as they began to walk, Frank and I wandered along behind, discovering a new route home via Miss Bowman's aunt's house.

Another week or two of similar unintentional, or so it seemed, meetings on Sunday mornings and Father was convinced by Miss Bowman that he should join the choir as she was doing now, so that he could help out for Easter. Another thing we noticed was that Father no longer used the name Miss Bowman, but Beatrice.

Thursdays now were different again for Frank and me. Father asked Mrs. Gillespie, who lived across the road in the big house, if she would come and stay with us while Jean and he went to choir practice. Being a staunch church woman and happy to see Father coming out of his sorrow, she readily agreed.

Life seemed much happier at our house now. Father was more cheerful, and Jean anxiously waited for Sundays and Thursdays when she would see Jimmy Young.

I remember well the wonderful weather we had on Easter Sunday that year. Everyone arrived at the church looking their best and Father wore a new suit he had bought just before Mother died. He looked very elegant, with his sandy hair greying slightly at the temples and a new glow of excitement in his eyes as we began our walk toward the church.

Jean created quite a striking picture, too, in her new beautiful green satin dress with her lovely red curls bouncing on her back as she walked.

"I'm sure Jim will pay special attention to you this morning, Jean," I laughingly jibed. He had treated her very much the same as all the other girls lately, and she was worrying a bit about it.

As we rounded the corner near the church we suddenly beheld Miss Bowman. She was wearing a very attractive outfit in a brilliant blue, which brought out the color of her eyes. I felt that although she wasn't really a pretty person, her ensemble plus her gushing personality as she lavished attention on Father made her appear attractive even to me. She actually glowed as she approached Father, and like a young school girl rushed over to him saying, "Oh John, I'm so excited about this morning. I do hope everything goes well. Don't you? My, you look handsome this morning. Is that a new suit you're wearing?"

Glowing with the satisfaction of being noticed he answered her with a smile. "Yes it is, as a matter of fact; and while we're on the subject, you look very beautiful yourself, my dear."

"Oh, do you really think so? I did so hope you would like it. I knew you liked blue that is why I chose it. We must hurry now or we'll be late, and that would never do, would it?" She smiled into his eyes as she took his arm.

Father didn't bother to turn and say goodbye to Frank and me as he usually did, but bending over slightly and looking straight into Beatrice's blue eyes, he took her hand in his and turned to go around to the choir door.

At that moment I had a strange feeling rip at my stomach. I really couldn't stop it and I really couldn't explain it, but I felt it nevertheless. I clutched Frank quickly by the hand, only to discover how cold my hand was compared to his. What was that strange feeling? I didn't like it. I wanted to cry but I didn't know why. Slowly, we made our way into church and slipped in beside George, who had gone on ahead to see someone.

The choir sang beautifully and the service was rather special, even for me; although I couldn't understand half of the Rev. McKinnon's sermon. I kept myself busy, however, looking at the choir, and especially the members I knew best. Jean and Dad looked great up in the choir loft in their new black robes and mortar boards, and even Miss Bowman looked good, though for some reason I wished she didn't appear so attractive. I seemed to have mixed feelings about her as a person. What was she really like? Was all this sweet talk a front?

The sermon was over and the minister was pronouncing the benediction when my thoughts stopped long enough to observe what was going on around me. I hoped I would understand more about sermons when I got older, but right now I always got lost in thought somehow when the meaning became blurry after some large words were used.

After the service, Frank and I waited at the front of the church, as we had always been instructed to do, and after a while Jean appeared, looking very troubled and upset.

"Well let's go home for dinner," she abruptly announced in an irritated manner.

"Where is Father?" I questioned. "Aren't we supposed to wait for him?"

"Not this time," she snapped with anger erupting from her voice. "He's been asked to dine with Beatrice," and she gave my arm a tug as she sarcastically continued, "and of course, he didn't refuse."

Jean's angry mood grew even more as she busied herself about the kitchen getting dinner. George had been invited to a friend's house for dinner, so that just left the three of us, and of course Uncle John would be over as usual.

When Uncle John arrived, Frank and I ran to greet him and he hugged us each in turn, and finally sat down in the big sofa with one of us on either side. Even though he was lame, he didn't seem to mind our childish fussing. He asked us questions and we laughed and joked with him until dinner was ready. Aunt Jane hadn't felt like joining him, as she was tired. She often took Sunday to rest after working in the store all week.

At the table, Jean couldn't hide her anger and it came out in many little ways. Finally, Uncle John asked her what the trouble was, only to get a tart reply that nothing was the matter. However, as soon as she had served dessert and served Uncle John his tea, she excused herself and left the room.

"What's bothering Jean the day, Nell?" Uncle John asked, and I just shrugged my shoulder. "She seems mighty upset for it to be nothing, I'm thinking" he replied. "Maybe you'd better go and see if you can help."

I made my way out of the kitchen and along the hall to our bedroom, and upon opening the door very quietly saw Jean lying face down on the bed sobbing as if her heart would break.

"Jean," I whispered. "Jean, what's the matter?"

"I can't tell you," she snapped, but went right on crying.

"Can you not tell Uncle John either?" I queried. "He thinks you're not doing all this crying for nothing." I hesitated before continuing. "Perhaps Uncle John could help. He always seems to help me with troubles," I pleaded.

Finally she looked up. Her tear-stained face looked directly at me and she mumbled, "What will it be like for you?" She seemed to study me for a while without saying a word, and then burst out in another torrent of tears.

I slipped out to Uncle John and asked him to come in to her, as I was sure he could help where I had failed. After all, I was only little. Leaving Frank reading a book at the hearth in the kitchen, Uncle John put his arm around my shoulder and walked back with me.

After a few minutes, Uncle John was able to quiet Jean down enough to talk to her. As young as I was, I could understand quite a bit of what they said.

It all came pouring out of Jean in one loud outburst, like a river bursting a dam. "It's Father, that's what's bothering me. He's gone clear out of his mind on that Miss Bowman. You should see the way they look into each other's eyes. He's very attentive to her, holding her arm when they walk together, and opening doors like Sir Galahad. He didn't want to join the choir until *she* asked him to, and now this! She's asked him for dinner and he didn't refuse, did he! Oh, how could he?"

"Now there, Jean, I think you're jumping to conclusions," Uncle John soothed. "I'm sure your father just wishes the companionship of an interesting woman. After all, the aunt will be there, too, you know. I'm extremely glad your father is coming out of himself and taking an interest in people again. I don't mind saying, I was worried for a while. Your father is a good man, and he loved your mother, and I don't suppose the thought you're proposing has even crossed his mind."

"Well it's crossed *her* mind. You can count on that. Uncle John, you should just see her lavish her attention on him. She's out for a man and Father's available, that much is very obvious, and I don't like it one little bit. Why doesn't Father start visiting some of our old family friends if he needs companionship?"

"He will. Give him time, Jean."

"Well why does he have to start with a woman, a single woman, and one we know nothing about?"

"Well, I still wouldn't be worrying my pretty head about it, if I were you. Your father can take care of himself, I'm sure. You're imagining things, building mountains out of mole hills and I'm sure you have nothing to worry about. Now, I must run along. I'll see you next week, and stop worrying about all these things which will never happen."

Jean composed herself finally, and was busying herself with the evening meal while Frank and I sat playing a game before the fireplace in the kitchen when Father arrived home. He was beaming, full of life and fun, pulling Jean's hair and toying with my curls.

He swept me up on his knee as he sat in the rocking chair by the fire, and we were all laughing and enjoying ourselves more than we had for months, when Father laughingly said, "Now, I have a surprise for you. We're going to have a guest for dinner next Sunday. Beatrice Bowman is coming over, and we must be on our very best behavior because we want her to like us. Don't we?"

There was an awkward pause but he soon continued.

"You'll have to prepare something rather special, Jean. She is an excellent cook, you know. The meal today was a sheer delight just to look at, never mind the taste, but the proof of the pudding certainly was in the eating, it was superb. I guess she has been doing the cooking at home all along for her mother. I do hope you'll like her. She certainly likes all of you from what she's seen of you at church. We must begin a clean-up, tidy-up project this week. Right Jean? The house must be in tip top condition."

As I looked up, Jean was twisting the dish towel around and around in a mechanical sort of way and suddenly she turned to Father and said, "I'm sorry, but I don't feel well. May I be excused? Would you please serve the supper for me?" Hurriedly she left the room.

Father just smiled, and putting me down answered, "Of course, all girls feel down once in a while, you run along."

Father served us with dinner and was in excellent spirits. Jean reappeared later to wash up the dishes, and I couldn't help noticing her red eyes and nose. Her nose always got red when she cried. I'm afraid I was somewhat bewildered by this time. Could something that made Father so happy be so bad, and why should it make Jean so unhappy? At my age, I figured the best thing to do was to forget it and play with Frank. I'd let the older folk work this out and not worry my head about it; after all, it was only a guest we were having next Sunday, and Uncle John would come too, and I loved his visits.

Chapter 2

A Dinner Guest

The week passed quickly, and Jean had the house as neat as a new pin – of course she always had it that way — but she was worried and tension ran high.

"I don't know what it is — perhaps its woman's intuition or something, but I just don't like her," she muttered when I came home from school one day. "She just doesn't ring true. She never speaks to you and Frank unless Father is there, and then she is trying to create a good impression. Surely an intelligent man like Father will see her falseness through the thin veneer of concern and love which she tries to portray."

Sunday morning found Jean up long before Father, with the meat in the oven and Wee Frank and me dressed and ready for church extra early. The table was set for dinner before we left and the whole house looked spotless and beautiful. It crossed my mind that maybe Jean and Miss Bowman were having a competition of some sort in cooking and good housekeeping, but I also remembered Father's insistence that everything be just right for Miss Bowman's visit.

The walk to church was a lovely one, with the fresh spring flowers blooming everywhere. As we sat in church, watched over by George, the light came streaming through the stained glass window and fell on some of the choir members. It gave a lovely rosy blush to Miss Bowman's cheeks, and I thought she looked rather pretty today, something like someone I knew, but I couldn't think who it was. Father was smiling at her across the choir. If Father liked her, she must be nice. Oh well, we'd soon find out.

The Rev. McKinnon was delivering a good sermon that day, I guess – everyone seemed to be listening. It was all about love and how we should love one another as ourselves. He said we should love all people and be concerned for their needs. *That was it*. Now I knew what was happening. Father was concerned for Miss Bowman's needs. He had said she was lonely in a new place and he wanted to show our concern for her in her loneliness. Now, why couldn't Jean understand that?

With that settled in my mind, I enjoyed the rest of the service, the long walk home, and the fun of singing and reciting a poem for Miss Bowman and Uncle John in the living room while Jean was getting the dinner on the table.

The meal was a fabulous success as Jean had prepared a scrumptious stew with dumplings and a delicious display of desserts, and I stuffed myself far too much, as did everyone. Pleasantries were exchanged across the table as Miss Bowman complimented Jean on her excellent meal, and Jean paid a compliment to her about the pretty blouse she was wearing.

At one point during the meal Father said, "Don't you think we're being just a little too formal? Now that we know each other better, I would like you children to call Miss Bowman, Aunt Beatrice."

"Why don't you just call me 'Aunt B' for short? That would be easier, wouldn't it?" she offered, looking first at Frank and me and then giving a wink towards Father.

"An excellent idea," Father replied. So it was settled for all time.

After dinner, Aunt B offered to help Jean with the dishes, but Father insisted that she rest herself on her day off and retire with him to the living room to look at the latest books he had purchased on the designing of houses.

"George and Nell can help Jean quite well, I'm sure." he said as he led her out of the kitchen and down the hall to the living room.

In a second he was back at the door, which was always kept shut to keep the kitchen warm, saying, "Do come along, Uncle John. I'm sure you will enjoy it, too."

Uncle John gave a wee short cough, straightened his tie and said, "Oh, of course if you wish me to, John." He glanced around the room, his eyes resting for a moment on Jean, then he slowly made his way towards the door carefully closing it behind him.

Silence fell upon the quartet in the kitchen. Wee Frank, who was not well, sat near the fireplace reading a book Uncle John had brought him from the store. Jean washed the dishes and George and I dried them. George dried all the big plates and pots while I dried the cups and saucers and spoons. It wasn't long before Uncle John reappeared in the doorway and said he thought he'd go now and call on old Mr. Love, who had taken a stroke about a month ago and didn't have many visitors.

After a little while I turned around to speak to Wee Frank and saw him sound asleep in the rocking chair. Noticing him at the same time Jean said to me, "Away and get a cover to put over him, Nell, and I'll get him to move over onto the couch. I think he is running a fever and the sleep will be good for him."

I quietly slipped out of the kitchen and along the hall to the left, to the bedroom, to get a quilt. I was returning with the quilt a moment later when I heard Aunt B laughing in the living room and saying, "Now John, you know I can't stand to be tickled. No John, not here, what if the children should… Oh!" and silence.

My curiosity raced to the fore. I knew it wasn't right to peek, but in that instant I just simply couldn't help myself. What was happening? Why the silence? Questions had to have answers, and I intended to have them.

The door to the living room was ajar ever so slightly, and the kitchen door was closed tightly, so I dropped the quilt near the kitchen door and slipped along the wall to the living room door. They were talking again.

"Beatrice, you look just beautiful, and I love you. Will you marry me? Please say yes. I need you so. You'll never know how badly I need you."

"Oh darling, I love you too, and there is nothing in the world I'd rather do than marry you."

I had restrained myself up until this point but I could not anymore, so I looked, and saw them in each other's embrace kissing rapturously.

My heart pounded in my breast, I wanted to cry out *"Stop, no, don't,"* but I remained silent. I wanted to run to Father and say, *"Remember us, your children? What about us, what will happen to us?"* but I remained rigid. I looked again and saw them staring into each other's eyes, completely lost in each other, the light from the fire dancing on their profiles as they gazed at one another, and then suddenly I knew *why* Father liked her, *why* he felt possessed, *why* he had such a burning desire for her. She looked like Mother. Yes, that was it. Oh, not really like Mother, but the resemblance was there, and to a man as hard-pressed by sorrow as he had been only a few short months ago, she looked like Mother.

Slowly, silently, I crept along the wall to the kitchen door again, picking up the quilt as I went, and as I quietly slipped into the kitchen I closed the door firmly behind me.

"I thought you were never coming with that quilt, Nell. Just put it over him on the couch. I suppose you thought you could dodge a pile of dishes that way, did you? Well, I wish I could think of a way too. Hurry up, George, and finish drying, so I can finish my work and put everything away. They call it a day of rest, but I fail to see that Sunday is a day of rest for the women folk.

"What's the matter, Nell? Are you not feeling well? You look mighty white. Probably coming down with whatever it is Wee Frank has, or did you eat too much dessert? You make a proper pig of yourself sometimes. When are you ever going to learn that you should stop eating when you're still a wee bit hungry? If you put on too much weight now, you'll have a hard time taking it off when you're a young lady in your teens, when it really counts."

As Jean finished her excited ranting, the door swung open and Father and Beatrice stood framed in the doorway arm in arm smiling at one another. With a gleam in his eye and a beaming smile, Father announced to all of us as he stepped forward into the kitchen, "Children, I'd like you to meet your new Mother. Beatrice and I have decided to get married, and we wanted you to be the first to know."

Chapter 3
Big Family Problems

Father's announcement was a very startling one for all of us, and our first reaction was to stand still in shock and bewilderment. Jean was the first to move. She slowly took off her apron and hung it up at the side of the cupboard, all the time staring first at Father, and then at Beatrice. As she moved back towards the window, the sun's rays set her golden hair aflame to match the anger, which was quickly rising in her heart and mind, and then with her hands clenched and her eyes narrowing she stated flatly to Father, "My Mother is dead, and *she*," pointing her finger accusingly at Beatrice, "cannot replace her." With her voice trembling and her body visibly shaking, she glared at Father and continued. "I can see now your love for Mother wasn't strong enough to warrant your staying loyal to her memory for very long. All that great display of emotional upset was just a camouflage for your own self-pity. You cast Mother's memory and our lives aside in just a few short months for the pleasures of another woman. Well, I sincerely hope you get what you deserve. I'm fairly certain you will."

Her glance went to Beatrice, whose face was turning an understandable red. Father, leaving Beatrice at the door, walked over to Jean. I couldn't tell from where I stood whether he was angry or understanding.

"Jean," he said with a gesture of his hand. "You don't understand. You're very young and you were so very close to your mother, but it takes time. Give Beatrice a chance, and I am sure she will prove a very loving wife for me and a good mother for the little ones. You must think of them, you know. You had a mother during your tender years, what about them? Would you want to deprive them of a normal healthy childhood?"

Jean jerked away from his outstretched hands, and tossing her head haughtily in the air, returned her fiery answer, "I'm too young to understand, am I? Oh no, Father, you've got it all wrong. I understand everything clearer than you do, at this point. I understand that this woman has chased you from the day you first met her, and you have *pretended* not to notice. I understand that to her you represent the safe security and fulfillment that she has been looking desperately for and couldn't find. Perhaps other men became wise to her little game in time, but she has managed to trip you up quickly while you are still reeling from the horrible emptiness that has hit you because of Mother's death."

The tears were now swelling up in Jean's eyes and I stood rigidly beside George, waiting to see what would happen.

She continued, "Call her 'Aunt B,' or 'Mother,' should I? She will never be anything to me but 'Beatrice,' the woman you marry, and as for the part about her being a loving wife, why don't you open your eyes? It's evident she couldn't love anyone but herself if she tried."

At that moment, Beatrice walked angrily across to Father, her eyes flashing with rage.

"How long are you going to take this outrageous display of behavior, John? Isn't a child supposed to honor her father?"

Father just stared at Jean, anger slowly taking the place of understanding and sympathy, now that he was aroused by Beatrice. Jean, however, was of no mind to stop. She had had her feelings bottled up inside too long, and out they must come. Spitefully she retorted, "A child should honor a father, yes, if he is worthy of that honor, but if a father falls short of the child's respect, what then?"

The words hardly left her lips before Father's hand was drawn swiftly across her face. Father's patience had reached its limit and he ordered her sharply, "That will be enough, Jean! Go to your room!"

Jean however, slumping against the sink and caressing her cheek with the back of her hand, glared at Father in utter contempt for a moment, then straightening herself to her full height and tossing her head haughtily, she started towards the door. With tears streaming down her cheeks she turned for one last rebuttal and sarcastically remarked, "A mother for your children is it? I have tried to be that. I promised Mother on her death bed that I would stop work, and come home to look after Nell and wee Frank, but I guess that doesn't count, either. Very well, if that is the way you want it, that's fine, I'll go back out to service and neither of you will have to worry about me, ever again."

With her face buried in her hands, she ran crying from the room. Silence reigned for a moment, and then it was broken by Father's voice as he turned abruptly and faced George.

"Well, George, are these your sentiments too?"

"Not exactly, Sir." George stammered, "I must admit it came as a shock or perhaps surprise is a better word. I just never thought for a moment that there was anything between you two. Anyway, it won't matter to me very much as I won't be around much longer. I've been meaning to tell you, but you've been so busy and I wasn't absolutely sure until this morning."

"Sure of what, my son?"

"Well, Mr. Henderson up on Briarcliff Road wants me to learn the plumbing trade with him. He has no sons, you know, and he would like me to go into partnership with him with the idea of working up a good business together. I'd thought I'd give it a try. He wants me to live over at their place, but I thought, up until now, that I was needed here."

"Well, I hope this is what you want. I could and would like to take you with me into the building trade, but that is entirely up to you."

Putting down the dish towel that he had been nursing all this time, George made his exit quickly, saying he was going to visit a friend.

Wee Frank, unnoticed, still lay on the couch. We didn't know until later that he had awakened, saw the commotion and decided to fake a sleep. Nevertheless, he miraculously missed the whole miserable experience and now it was my turn.

While Jean had been getting upset and George had quietly bowed out of the picture in his usual calm manner, I had been doing some serious thinking on my own. I believed, in fact I knew, that much of what Jean had said was true. Aunt B had chased Father until she managed to catch him. I had watched it happen in a very casual but subtle way for weeks at church. On the other hand, Father was a man of strong will and personality, and he must have wanted to be caught. He must have been desperately lonely without Mother. Aunt B could fill that emptiness and make Father happy again. She had proved this point already. Father played with us again and read us stories and took us for a ride now and then with the horse and buggy. In my small mind, I reasoned that if Aunt B made Father happy she must be all right so it was not hard to answer, but with some reservation in my voice, when Father approached me.

"Now, Nell! How do you feel? You like Aunt B, don't you? She will be good for Frank. Beatrice took a course in nursing when she was younger, so she will be just wonderful to have around should Wee Frank have a sick spell or have an accident, as he is so prone to do. What do you say?"

"Yes, I'm sure she will," I said bravely, not knowing whether I was or not, but not wanting to get into either of their bad books.

"Good! I wish the older ones were as sensible as the younger ones," Father mused.

"Yes," replied Aunt B. "I'm sure you do." Then summing it all up, she continued, "Perhaps it will be much better in the long run with both Jean and George going away. They are the ones that would resent me and cause trouble. The little ones I am sure I can handle."

"They'll love you in no time as I do," Father assured her, placing his arm around her shoulder and squeezing it as he led her back to the living room.

That night, in spite of my bravery in front of Father, I lay awake long into the night thinking about the events of the day and their consequences on my life.

Jean was going away. She tugged my hair every morning and was a little impatient with me for being so slow, but I loved her and understood her and I knew she loved me and wee Frank. Mother had asked Jean to look after us, wasn't this going against Mother's wishes? The fact still remained though, Jean was going away.

George was going away, too. He always seemed so strong, so handsome, and I was always so proud of him. If I fell, he always picked me up and made my sore better with a kiss. He took me for a ride now and then on the back of the horse from Green's farm. We often romped in the garden together when George was helping Father. I knew I'd miss him horribly, but I could do nothing about it. George was going away, too.

Aunt B was marrying Father and would soon be my stepmother. I had heard many nasty things about stepmothers. What about Cinderella and Snow White? "No!" I told myself. They were just fairy stories and life wasn't like that. Aunt B didn't look like a witch, why, she was very pleasant looking; not pretty or beautiful, but pleasant. Why, she even looked a bit like Mother. This time, a cold chill went down my back. No, she didn't look like Mother, either. She wasn't near as pretty as Mother had been. She didn't seem as warm and loving as Mother had been, either. Oh, how I missed my mother. Why had God taken her from me? I buried my head in my pillow and cried. I didn't want to lose my sister and brother, either. I was losing everyone, it seemed. Why had God let this happen to me? Finally, in complete exhaustion from crying, I fell asleep.

Chapter 4
The Wedding

It was a beautiful spring that year, and everything seemed full of promise. The trees burst into bud and then into leaf very quickly. Life at home was bright and full of promise too, except for the two dark clouds that hung over the house. Jean and Father scarcely spoke to each other now, and Jean was looking for a good position to go to.

June 30th was set for the wedding. It was to be a quiet wedding in the manse with a reception held in the Church Hall. Father had said to Uncle John one day, "There is absolutely no reason to wait, John. After all, we are mature adults and know what we want in a mate. I know people will talk, since it is only seven months since Jean passed away, but they will just have to talk; after all, if they're busy talking about me, they'll leave someone else alone, and I have broad shoulders." He laughed as he slapped Uncle John on the back. "We only live once, you know, and I see no reason to postpone our marriage."

Uncle John had queried, "But, do you know her, John? Do you really know her? You've given yourself very little time to discover what she is really like. Do you know anything about her, her past, her family, or friends? The only things you know about her are what she herself has told you. You'd want to know more about the pedigree of a horse before you bought it, wouldn't you? Have you given any thought to wee Frank and Nell? They're losing their sister and brother now, after having just lost their baby sister and mother. Will she make a good mother for them? What experience has she had with children? John, this is for life, I wouldn't rush into it so quickly if I were you."

Father's sharp stinging words hastened to force yet another breach in the family that day. "Well you're not me, and I don't believe you have a say in my life any longer."

George left for his new position at the Henderson's in May, and Jean had found a place of employment starting in July. During May and June, Father tended his garden and redecorated much of the house. Odd jobs that had been utterly ignored before suddenly were done cheerfully within minutes. Life was always happy when Father was around. He sang while he worked. Often he brought Beatrice around to see the improvements he was making. He asked for her advice and accepted it. He acted like a little boy with a new toy.

I liked seeing Father so happy and contented around the house, and I wished he would stay like this forever, but I feared the changes that would soon take place. George and Jean would be gone after the wedding, and then there would just be wee Frank and me, and Father and Aunt B. I wondered what that would be like. I would miss my brother and sister terribly, and I wondered what Aunt B would be like in my mother's and sister's place in the home. I was afraid, but I had heard Father say once that "one is always afraid of change." Anyway, why shouldn't everything be all right? Hadn't God seen fit to make Father happy again after his terrible loneliness and sadness? Mother had always said that God would bring forth good out of all evil or trouble, and here it was. Maybe the dark troubled times were over for us now and we could be happy again.

It seemed no time at all until the wedding day was upon us. It was an exciting day for me. Jean had bought me a lovely new blue dress with frilly lace up the front and over the shoulders. My hair was a gleaming cascade of red curls flowing down my back, caught by a lovely large blue velvet ribbon. I even had new shoes for the occasion. I felt terrific, and couldn't help wondering why Jean still felt like crying and hadn't bought a new outfit for herself.

The Rev. McKinnon conducted a short service in the manse while we children all sat stiffly in a row along the side of the living room with Beatrice's aunt, Uncle John, and Mrs. Gillespie. Following the ceremony, we all went straight to the Church Hall, where there were some people from the choir in attendance, and a few of Father's old friends from the village, who he had neglected for the last year. There were very few friends of Beatrice's from Hairmyers, a few relatives, of course, and a few couples whom she had worked with over the years.

Father's only brother and his wife, and sister and her husband were present, although we very seldom saw them except for weddings and funerals. Mother's people were conspicuous by their absence, all except Uncle John, who graciously told me how nice I looked and did his best to keep wee Frank out of mischief.

The bride wore a navy suit with a flowered hat in pink, and seemed to be in her element as she greeted the guests at the door and sat at the head table for dinner. The center of attention seemed to suit her completely, and she was indulging in it quite freely. The gentlemen present at the wedding had the right to kiss the bride, but on several occasions I saw her throwing her arms around them and kissing them before they had made the gesture. Most of the men seemed to enjoy the experience, but most of their wives seemed to be annoyed.

Soon the laughter and speech making was over, and we were heading home in Uncle John's buggy.

"Remember, bairns, I'm no far frae ye. If ye ever need me, I'll be there. If ye ever need a listener, I'll listen, but I'll no be coming around tae see ye sae often. I don't think I'll be wanted around the same somehow, but please come to see me as often as ye can, for I'll miss ye."

Turning to me, he continued, "You're a young lady now, aren't ye, Nell? Was it nine you were on your birthday last week? Frank, you'll soon be twelve. You'll have to watch over your wee sister. She'll be need'n ye." Turning to George and Jean, he continued, "I wish you the best in your position George and in yours Jean, but no matter how you feel about things try to come home now and then for the young ones' sake. Will ye?"

The horse had stopped in the lane by the gate of the cottage and we all seemed to hesitate before going in to face the last short night that would be ours as a family together.

• • • • •

Thus ended one chapter of my life and the new one that opened was to be a far different world in many ways.

Chapter 5
Life was Hard

Early the next morning, Jean packed and got ready to leave for Glasgow. She would be living-in with a fairly well-to-do family who had a cook and a maid, and she would have one day and evening off a week. The couple was past middle-age and had two children away at University. It seemed like an ideal situation for Jean, and I was happy for her, but cried when she left just the same.

It was hard to sleep that night knowing that neither Jean nor George were at home and that a strange woman lay beside Father in his bed, instead of Mother.

I jerked myself up on that one. Mother is dead, I told myself, and I mustn't forget it. There was simply no reason why Father shouldn't marry again.

I wished Uncle John hadn't said that about not coming around much to see us anymore. Slowly, the door opened and Frank peeked into the shadow of the room. "Can I talk to you, for a wee bit? I can't sleep." he asked in a low, choking voice.

"Yes, come on in," I answered in a whisper. I felt much better having someone to confide in. He was missing George every bit as much as I was missing Jean, and he too, felt cut off from Father.

The days that followed during that summer were endurable; in fact, they were even happy in some respects. Father certainly seemed happy and Beatrice appeared happy as well, although working in the kitchen bored her quickly. Nevertheless, she had to have things immaculate at all times, so turned to me for a helping hand more and more. She found many an excuse for going out of doors to Father while he worked in the garden. Father's pansies were wonderful again this year as usual, and he named a new variety after Beatrice and another after me and entered them in the flower show.

Beatrice's favorite pastime was reading, however, and this is what she spent increasingly longer periods of time doing, especially when Father was not at home. When he was home, all was sunshine and light and she hastened around the house looking very busy, indeed, and looking after all his needs. I couldn't help feeling a slight resentment creeping over me, which I didn't like but couldn't deny, because I always seemed to be left behind in the kitchen with orders to wash the dishes or just take a mop over the floor, etcetera.

In the evening, Father and Beatrice almost always played cards. It was Beatrice's favorite game and she was a whiz at it. Often wee Frank would beg Father to play with him, but Father wasn't always inclined to teach a youngster.

As the summer progressed, Mrs. Gillespie, our neighbor, was asked to stay with us more and more in the evening while Father and Beatrice went out for a game. One night as Father left, he turned to Mrs. Gillespie and said, "Beatrice needs to get out once in a while, you know. She's cooped up here all day while I'm at work and she just isn't used to it. It's the least I can do to take her out in the evening. Thanks ever so much for staying with the children."

I grew to enjoy the nights they were out even more than the ones when they were home. Mrs. Gillespie was a warm-hearted motherly woman who was a bit on the plumpish side and whose hair was graying, but she was always in a good mood and would tease and fool with wee Frank and me before bedtime, often taking time to talk about school and getting us to talk about our lives and what we wanted to become.

When Father and Beatrice were home we were nearly always rushed off to bed with Beatrice directing, "Come now, children, you must get your sleep," and Father would grunt, "Good night," as he poured over plans for a new house or a garden book.

On the odd occasion when Father did have time to spend with us as he had often done before Mother's death, Beatrice always intervened. "Your Father is much too busy. You must understand that he is a very busy man."

Father would usually back her up with, "Yes, that is correct, now off to bed with you, your mother and I have something to discuss."

By the time September had rolled around and school had resumed, I could see a definite pattern taking shape in our lives. Father, always a determined and headstrong man before, was now reduced to putty in Beatrice's hands. She got first choice in his life in everything. If she wanted something, he bought it for her. If she wanted to go somewhere, they went. Nothing was too much trouble for him if Beatrice wanted it. If she had scolded us about something, he reprimanded us also without ever trying to discover the ins and outs of what had taken place. A pat on the head now and then was all we got by way of love or understanding.

It was as though wee Frank and I were part of another world which he didn't want to be reminded of. Although in his fifties now, he wanted to pretend he was just beginning again with a new lover and he didn't want the faces of two children spoiling the illusion of youthful love. We reminded him of ties, and his new selfish nature didn't want to be reminded, so we gradually sank further and further into the background of his life.

If Father was resentful of our presence, Beatrice too by late fall was showing outward signs of her own hatred of our presence. We reminded her that her husband had loved someone else before her. We represented work in her life that she had never before been expected to do. Feeding, clothing, and mending for two children were not things she enjoyed doing. Looking after a husband was one thing, security came with that, but why did she have to cope with these two brats?

It gradually became evident that she had decided to tolerate wee Frank and make me a personal maid. I found myself washing most of the dishes, scrubbing floors, and ironing clothes most of my hours at home. I even had to forego playing games with wee Frank by the hearth in the kitchen because there was always a job to be done.

After school, I often met Frank and we dashed off to the store to see Uncle John. It was one of the few things we could do together. Uncle John always greeted us with hugs and kisses, and then gave us samples from the candy jars or some choice morsel from the baked goods counter.

One day during one of our visits, Uncle John asked us how things were at home. Trying to be brave, I began listing all the good things that were happening, but Frank soon blurted out the truth. "We aren't happy! Nell often cries at night and I often wish I was a girl too and could cry a little myself. They don't want us there. Dad doesn't love us anymore, he only loves her and she loves only herself."

Tears came into Uncle John's eyes as he drew young Frank close to him and patted his head in a loving gesture. "Ye need to be brave son, ye need to be brave. It's no easy tae take, but since there's no way oot, you'll need tae be brave."

He circled his other arm around me, and looking upwards out of the window to the wee patch of sky that could be seen from our position, continued, "The big thing to remember in this life is, that no matter who forsakes ye, ye are never alone. God is always near ye. God knows your problem. He loves ye and in the long and the short of it all, He is the only one that will stand by ye no matter what happens. Just believe and trust in Him, my lad, and ye'll no need to be frettin'."

Home in the quiet of my room that night, I searched deep in my drawer and found Mother's Bible. It had been underlined in many places and bore many a mark of wear, but it was still in fairly good condition. I caressed it tenderly, knowing it would help refresh my memory of the stories my mother used to tell me going to bed at night.

I could still remember her clearly, sitting beside my bed. She would cuddle me down under the covers, and then taking the Bible she would glance at it, and thinking of a story, tell it to me in her own words, explaining in detail, if I wished her to. After the story came prayers, in which I remember praying for everyone, including aunts, uncles, and cousins, and then a loving kiss and cuddle came my way before the final 'Good night' was said. She was never too tired or too busy to go through this little private time with us each night.

As I recalled our quiet time, tears flooded my eyes and I wept into my pillow. I guess I fell asleep and went into a dream, for I pictured Mother sitting rocking in her favorite rocking chair in front of the fire in the kitchen, telling me about God. She seemed to be saying, "What you cannot change there is no use worrying about, child. Do your best under the circumstances, respect your elders and love your God with all your might."

I woke up in a cold sweat. I had a terrible ache in my inner self to be loved and cherished at that moment, so I rushed out of the room calling, "Father, Father." Beatrice met me at the door of their room. She was dressed in her robe and held a cup in her hand, obviously she hadn't been able to sleep and had made herself some tea.

"What on earth are you doing calling out like that at this hour of the night? Your Father is sleeping."

"I must see him," I pleaded, "I had a dream —"

"Go to bed this instant," she directed. "No child of mine should be afraid of dreams in the night."

"But it was a dream about Mother!" I blurted out.

Instantly I felt the sharp sting of a hand drawn across my face and I reeled in amazement and pain. Blindly, I turned back to my room. I didn't cry now, strangely enough. I felt something new and different gnawing at my stomach. Could it be more loneliness? I had never been as lonely before. Could it be jealousy? I had never experienced jealousy before. Perhaps I was jealous of Beatrice, now that she seemed in complete possession of Father's love. Or could it be — could it be — oh no — but yes it could be — it could be —HATRED. I had never *hated* before.

I lay tossing in bed most of that night wondering what I felt. What I had done wrong? How I could face life and what it would all lead to?

My tossing and turning ceased as the dawn began to break on a new day. I knew some of the answers. I could associate my dream to my life. The dream of Mother could help me. There was no doubt about it, I couldn't change things, so I must put up with things as they were – but to do my best under the circumstances must mean my school work. Yes, of course this would be what Mother would want me to do, and if I worked very hard at it, Father would let me further my education at the end of grammar school. That could mean I might teach school, or perhaps become a governess. I would work very hard towards this goal, and just as soon as I could, I would get a job and leave home. Right now I had Frank to talk to, but before long he would be leaving home to work and I didn't want to be too far behind him.

The more I thought of it, the more I knew that this was indeed the answer and God had given it to me in a dream. I bowed my head in prayer and thankfulness and soon fell asleep.

Chapter 6
School Filled My Needs – Until

As time went on, things didn't get any better at home. Beatrice had now become lazy in every sense of the word. She did nothing she could possibly get someone else to do. She read most of the time and complained of her leg bothering her. She had always limped a little, but now her limp had increased and the extra weight she was putting on these days wasn't helping any.

I did most of the cleaning in the house, except for Beatrice's room, where I was forbidden to enter. I really didn't mind, as it was one less room to look after. Strangely enough, it was "her' bedroom now, and Father slept in Frank's room while Frank slept in the kitchen wall bed.

School completely filled my needs in life now as I strived towards higher and higher marks, and helped the teachers all I could after classes, hoping to have fewer hours to put in at home. My greatest joy was still visiting Uncle John, although I always felt pressed for time, as I was expected home promptly to help with the evening meal and chores.

During the winter, Frank and I both had the flu, but the great nursing skills that had been attributed to Beatrice earlier didn't materialize. If we needed anything we got up for it ourselves, otherwise we just stayed in bed until we were better.

That summer, Father worked with great zeal in his garden. His pansies were particularly pretty and he entered many in the flower show, winning the first and second prizes for them. He busied himself with his building projects and we saw very little of him at home except for the card games at night, although even these were getting further and further apart. Reading between the lines, it seemed to me that Father was trying the same scheme as I was. From something you can't escape, just bear up under it and busy yourself as much as possible so you don't have to face it any more than absolutely necessary. I began wondering where that great love and devotion had gone that previously enveloped the two of them.

Conversation at the dinner table seemed to be reduced to "pass me's" and weather. Jean, who had tried to come every two weeks to see us all, had had such cold receptions that her visits were now reduced to once in two months or so, and I hadn't seen George for almost six months now. Father saw him in the village once in a while, but he never came home.

Life went on. We existed. None of Mother's old friends ever visited anymore, and it was only by a chance meeting in the village, or occasionally at Uncle John's store, that I saw my Mother's relatives.

I asked Beatrice once if I could have one of my cousins over to stay with me for a few days for a holiday but she would have none of it.

In the fall things got even quieter and Father started going into the village on his own more often at night. Beatrice grew stouter and more miserable. She was no longer the attractive person she had appeared to be at the church a year and a half ago. On Sundays, she tried to improve her looks for the choir, which she kept going to but from which Father had dropped out, claiming he no longer had time.

On Sundays, Father sat with us near the back of the church and hustled us out promptly after service, as he didn't seem to want to talk with many people now. Beatrice took her time coming out as usual, flattering this one and that one and always making the Rev. McKinnon feel good at the door. She really had a way with people. She could make everything sound so real, so genuine, and in spite of her own plumpish appearance she still had a way with men. She would look at them straight in the eye, take a hold of their hand, squeeze it and roll her eyes saying something complimentary to them and you could see them gloat with satisfaction, their ego completely taking over their common sense.

As winter settled on us again, it found Beatrice becoming more and more interested in outside activities, only now she always went alone. She was in a play the church was putting on, and she portrayed a wealthy, middle-aged widow with countless suitors, all after her money. Beatrice literally threw herself into the part. Practice was called for twice a week and Mr. Bromly, a widower and in his sixties, called to take her to the church each time. His reason was that he passed that way and it would save Father going out.

Father, Frank, and I all went to see the play when it was presented, and Beatrice really played her part well – which was only natural, since she was well-cast. She fluttered and fussed over each man in turn (one of whom was Mr. Bromly), but outwitted them all, gaining financially in each case one way or another.

As I was putting my coat on and waiting for her to come home with us, I overheard a conversation between two ladies of the church who were standing on the other side of the coat rack and couldn't see me.

"Well, Beatrice certainly suited that part. Did you see the way she flirted with those men?"

"Of course, I did. It comes naturally with her. That's how she got Mr. Sweenie – with sweet talk."

"Aye, and have you noticed the way she's flirting with Mr. Bromly lately?"

"Frankly, I can't see what they see in her. She's a sly one. She can appear so sincere and loveable when actually she's anything but. I'd hate to have her as a stepmother, wouldn't you?"

Father must have overheard part of it too, as he quickly hustled Frank and me out the side door and then left us to get the horse and buggy. I felt sorry for him. He had thought Beatrice the answer to all his dreams. He had been gullible to all her flattery, and now he must feel like a fool. He had thought she'd be another Jean, and she didn't remotely resemble her, but a man doesn't admit his mistakes easily. It's easier to remain silent and endure than admit even to yourself that you could have made a poor choice.

At school my hard work was paying off. I won honor marks and Mr. Tom, our school principal, had much praise for me. I acted in the school play and played Mary in the church Sunday school pageant. Now, things seemed to be improving slightly at home, since Father had wakened up a little and demanded a little more work from a certain party and no more trips out with Mr. Bromly.

Then, one cold brisk snowy day in February, after a short stop to see Uncle John, I raced home covered with snow and very anxious to tell Frank, who was home with a cold, about my newest achievement: the winning of an oral contest. Just as I came up the lane, I saw Doctor McGregor's buggy in front of the gate and naturally wondered if Frank's cold had developed into pneumonia. I raced into the house and Mrs. Gillespie met me with, "Your stepmother's fallen and hurt herself badly. I don't know just what is going to happen."

Later that night, Father told me I would not be able to attend school for a little while, but must remain home to look after Beatrice. I felt a combination of resentment, pity, and bewilderment all at once as I answered.

"Of course I will."

Later that week, as I attended her in bed, I clumsily dropped a spoon off the bed tray. It fell with a clatter to the floor near the edge of the coverlet and as I bent down to pick it up, something protruding out from under the coverlet drew my attention. At that instant, my curiosity got the better of me again, so I lifted the coverlet to see what it was.

To my utter amazement, I saw a wooden leg lying under the bed, and I gave a little scream. I'm afraid it upset both Beatrice and Father. It seems Beatrice didn't want me to know about it, and with her long dresses she was able to hide it quite well. I did known that she had had an accident, years ago, and had suffered an injury to her leg at that time, which had caused her to limp a little, but I hadn't dreamed of a wooden leg.

After this revealing fact, I took on a new attitude towards both Beatrice and Father. I thought I could see it all more clearly now. Beatrice hadn't only been lonely, but she had needed a man to fend for her and Father had felt that he could help her in this way too. So he married her, not just because she looked like Mother and he was lonely, but for sympathy as well.

About this time, one night in particular stands out in my mind, it was in February of that year. Father had asked three other men over to play cards and one hadn't come, so I had been asked to sit in and play the other hand, as Frank had an assignment to hand in for school. I had often looked over their shoulders and practically knew the game, so it wasn't very difficult to do.

While we were playing, it must have been around ten o'clock that the bell in the village square rang out. We all stopped and looked at one another. "It must be the death of the Queen!" Father said. "Queen Victoria has died! She was a great lady! It will be a long time before another one as great fills her shoes." I can remember feeling very sad and crying just a little. It was like losing a very close friend.

When Beatrice began to get around a little again I begged to go back to school, but she didn't think she could manage alone, so that meant I lost my year at school and would have to return in the fall. I felt very depressed. It just didn't seem fair somehow, but I could do nothing about it. I had hoped Father would let me further my education next year and perhaps train for my career. Now all must wait yet another year.

During the summer, Beatrice improved greatly but didn't return to her old self completely. I was allowed to go back to school in the fall, provided I came straight home each day and took on no extras at school. This cut out my visits to Uncle John's store, and I missed them terribly. Life was fairly humdrum, that fall and winter with school and housework occupying my whole time, but I dreamt of the day soon when things would be different, when I would earn my own way and so could Frank, and we could get away from it all.

We often talked about our future and all the things we would do. Frank was getting along fine at school considering, he was absent so often as his illness seemed to persist now. He had an irritation in his throat that would not give him peace. It hadn't even left him last summer and it worried me, although he said it was alright and nothing to bother about. Neither Father nor Beatrice seemed to be concerned, so being a mere child myself, I too, kept silent.

Now that Beatrice was off her leg so much and just sitting around most of the day reading, she seemed to be putting on still more weight. I had become used to her cane tapping on the floor as she summoned me to come and do this or that for her. I had become used to the never-ending chores that she had ready for me to do and the list she presented to me when I arrived home from school, but I never quite got used to the snide remarks that were often made for my benefit. I never quite got used to her changing moods or her quick temper and her sharp words that could cut so deeply. She resented both Frank and me as though we were thorns in her flesh, and yet now she needed us and this was very frustrating for her. She also realized that Father wasn't around as much as he had been and she often went off in a rage about him.

"Your father isn't what I thought he was. Here I am, sick and lonely, and does he care? Of course not He's off with the men without a thought or care, probably drinking too. He said he wanted to marry me, and while I was well and strong it was fine, but now when I'm sick and need him where is he?"

Dr. McGregor often got this outburst when he visited the home, and I heard him one day telling her to calm down and watch the blood pressure, as it wasn't good these days due to her terrific increase in weight. "This weight problem just isn't good for you," he stated. "You'll never be able to walk properly on your leg if you don't try to lose some weight. I'll put you on a diet, and see what happens."

Now it became my job to try to cook for her diet. She was very fussy — nothing pleased. She liked fried foods and she would insist upon them. "After all," she reasoned, "the only thing left for me to enjoy in life now is food."

Father and Beatrice now snapped quite openly at the table and life was generally rather miserable. Frank and I stayed out of it whenever possible and left the scene of the quarrel as promptly as it was practical to do so.

As winter wore on, things got worse rather than better. Father made himself scarce more frequently now, and this angered Beatrice no end. Frank's cough irritated her also, and my school work or reading frustrated her terribly. Unless our full attention was on her, she was just plain miserable.

At night I often went to bed and cried. "Why, oh, why, Lord, have things turned out this way? What can I do to help Father? I know he is going into town to be with his old buddies, but I worry that he is drinking too much, and he has never done this before. What about Frank's cough? Will he be all right? What about my career? Will I be able to attend senior school next year? The way things are going, perhaps Father won't allow me to. Oh, not another year of waiting, Lord. Please," I pleaded.

Winter turned into spring, as it has a way of doing regardless of all our human problems, and with spring came new hope and lightness of heart. I found myself skipping up the lane like a child, although I carried myself more like a young lady now. My hair was cut to the nape of the neck, but I still had light curls that bounced. I was just beginning to feel and look like a young woman. I was beginning to feel the glances of the boys as I walked into the school yard. I liked that, and I liked to bounce a little and make my hair flip up and down in a saucy manner. I knew my red hair was my shining glory, and I determined to make the most of it.

It was on one such lovely spring day that I came walking up the lane, with Billy by my side on his bicycle. He was in my class at school and seemed attracted to me, which pleased me no end, although I wasn't particularly interested in him. He had carried my books home on his bicycle while I had freedom to walk, skip, or run if I wanted. We said our good-byes at the gate and I burst into the house quite jubilantly, ready to talk to Beatrice and tell her about Billy, because if there was one subject she still enjoyed discussing, it was men. I glanced into the living room and saw no one. I called and looked into the kitchen and got no reply, and finally I called hesitantly outside her bedroom door but still received no answer. The door was ajar, so I pushed it open slightly, and still calling, peeked in.

Much to my horror I saw Beatrice flung across the bed with her eyes staring and her mouth open. I ran to her and tried to shake her and talk to her, but could get no response, although I could hear heavy, heavy breathing. I ran as quickly as I could to Mrs. Gillespie's house across the road. She said she would go over to our house immediately, and that I must run into the village for help.

As luck would have it, Billy, being more interested in me than I had given him credit for, had turned back down the lane just to see if he could see me again. He found me all right, running as quickly as my legs could carry me, so he put me on the cross bar of his bicycle and rode me into Dr. McGregor's. The doctor soon had his horse and buggy out and I rode back with him while Billy tagged along to see if he could help in any other way.

As we approached the cottage, Mrs. Gillespie met us at the door with, "She's gone, doctor, she's gone. It must have been a stroke." The doctor went in to see Beatrice and Mrs. Gillespie asked Billy to ride me back to the village to find Father, who was working on the row of houses on Maxwell Drive and could be easily found.

As we approached the house where Father was laying stone, I saw him look up just in time to see us arrive. His immediate reaction was anger and he told me to get off that boy's bicycle and never to do such a shameful thing again, for if he caught me doing it again, I'd not sit down for a week, and the boy would be wearing a black eye.

I stood rigidly waiting for him to finish admonishing me, and then slowly made my way closer with my head bowed and tears in my eyes. I hated to have to tell this news to Father, much as I had grown to dislike Beatrice, I knew death was always a shock. This was my first experience with death since Mother had passed away, and I was beginning to feel ill. Billy quietly said good-bye and left me. Father slowly lowered the scaffold and approached me.

"What on earth are you crying for, lassie? I said never to do it again. You've had your warning, now state your business and let me get back to work."

"Beatrice is dead," I blurted out, feeling that it would only prolong the agony to say it any other way. Father stood stock-still, his steel-gray eyes blank of expression and then disbelief.

"What are you saying, child? Beatrice is dead? She can't be, she was fine this morning when I left. I ate my lunch on the job at noon. What happened?"

"They figure a stroke took her," I ventured. "I went for Dr. McGregor. He's there now."

Slowly, his arm slipped around my shoulder, "Come then lass, we'd best be on our way home." Turning to the other men he said, "Tell Mr. Aikenhead that my wife has just passed away with a stroke."

Silently, we rode home together.

Chapter 7
"A Woman's Place is in the Home"

I finished the remaining two months of school and passed in a blaze of glory. My marks were exceptional and the principal couldn't praise my achievements enough.

The day school closed, I waited anxiously for Father to come home from work. I wanted to tell him my good news and ask him about next year, and if he thought I could attend grammar school. I had never mentioned the subject of my future to him, only to Frank, and I trembled a little with excitement just thinking about talking to him.

While I waited I prepared his favorite meal, fillet of sole and French fries with green peas and salad, and his favorite dessert, vanilla custard over peach preserves. When everything was well under control, I started setting the table, being careful about every detail, as today just had to be perfect.

Frank arrived home first. After placing his books on the hall table he walked into the kitchen smiling.

"Well how did you get along, Nell? With flying colors, I'll wager, I can tell by your face. Tell me all about it," he urged, straddling a chair with his legs and hugging the back with his arms as he waited with rapt attention for my answer.

"Oh Frank, I was at the top of the class and Mr. Tom was ever so pleased with me. He wants me to go to grammar school for a few years and become a teacher. What do you think Father will say? I do so want to go."

Before Frank could answer we both heard Father at the door and Frank's answer became, "You'll soon know now."

Father walked into the kitchen and straight to the fire place with his head down and his hands clasped behind his back in thoughtfulness. "I met Mr. Tom down the street, Nell," he said without looking up from the fire. He now turned and faced me. "He says you've been very clever at school and he would like to see you go on." Straightening up and squaring his shoulders, he continued, "You realize, of course, that that is impossible. I need you at home. Both Frank and I need you here to keep house, now that Beatrice is gone. It's one thing to educate a son for his life's work, but quite another thing for a daughter. I believe men should teach school anyway. A woman's place is in the home. Let us not discuss it any further."

I stood stunned and confused. I couldn't believe what I had heard. I wanted to run from the house, to escape, out into the open air where I could breathe. Instead, I managed to stammer, "But Father!"

"No 'buts' about it, Nell. I have made my mind up and it is final. Now let us have our tea, I'm very hungry."

The shock had held my tears back until now, but I suddenly lost my calm, and bursting into sobs, I ran for the kitchen door.

"Come back, young lady, let's have no such scene around here. I want my tea served, *now!*" He banged his hand down on the table.

Suddenly there sprang up something inside me. I didn't recognize it, or did I? Yes, I'd felt it before, I'd known this stunned reaction before. It felt like *hate*. Surely I couldn't hate my Father, or could I? How could he do this to me if he loved me? Slowly I turned, and with eyes glaring but emotions calming, I regained my self-control, returned to the stove, and served him his tea.

That evening, Mr. Tom called to see Father, and I again found myself creeping out of the kitchen and along the front hall to listen at the living room door, and again I heard things I didn't like and couldn't understand.

Mr. Tom argued with Father for over an hour. He said it was a sin not to allow a young lady such as Nell to further her education, but as strong as the argument was that Mr. Tom presented on my behalf, my Father's was still stronger.

"I cannot afford to send her into Glasgow like Frank and hire someone at home to do the work."

"You could if you wanted to John," Mr. Tom argued. "Besides, Nell has been doing all the work for the last couple of years or more and doing her school work besides and you know it. I'm sure she could handle both."

"She's not going. I need her at home," was always Father's answer.

That night I cried myself out. I cried until I felt I would never cry again because I would have no tears left. I cried for two reasons. Because of my great disappointment and the seeming end to all future for me except housekeeping and secondly because of the horrible feeling inside me that told me that Father really didn't love me if he would not think of my future. It was true that most other girls in my class would either go out to housework or stay at home until they married, but Mr. Tom had spoken so enthusiastically about my future and the possibilities that could be open to me. I recoiled at the thought of housekeeping all my life. If Father's only thought was to have a housekeeper for himself, I had been reduced from a daughter to a slave to do his bidding. I resented it bitterly.

For the next few months I acted according to the dictates of my bitterness. I was surly around the house, and sarcastically "yes sir'd" Father all the time. I had lost all my feeling for beautiful things. Even the garden made me rebel inside, as I felt Father had more love for it than for me. I made myself most efficient in the house and my meals were superb, but Father's compliments only made me sneer and feel resentment, for I felt sick inside.

Being very spiteful and on edge, I often had words with Father. On one such night, when I had stalked from the room in hot anger, Frank met me in the hall. He had come from the living room and he was holding out Mother's Bible. "Read it, Nell," he pleaded. "I know that Father was wrong, but bitterness and revenge never helped any situation."

I snatched the book from his hand and glaring at him said, "It's full of history. History, that's all, do you hear? Only history, what could this possibly have to do with me and my future, my life, my — everything?"

"Read it and try to find an answer, Nell. It has helped me many —" He coughed and coughed again and again. Then, gasping out one word at a time continued, "Oh, Nell, please promise me you'll read it!"

"Of course, Frank, I'd do anything for you," I answered, but my mind was on his coughing. He didn't look well. Could he possibly have tuberculosis?

That night I read the Bible when I climbed into bed. I read Paul's letters saying one must be contented with the situation God places one in and make the most of it in God's sight, even if it doesn't please one.

I discovered that Jesus and I had something in common. He too had lost all his friends and felt rejected and indeed was even betrayed, but it hadn't made Him bitter, nor did he seek revenge. Why couldn't I try to be more like Jesus and Paul?

Why couldn't I forgive Father and accept the inevitable circumstances in which I found myself? If I changed my way of thinking it would definitely be a happier home for Frank, and for Father. My thoughts raced ahead of me. If I changed my attitude towards things I could make our home a very happy place. I could take the place of Beatrice! I knew it wouldn't be hard to make it happier than when she had been with us. I could make Father happy and contented and more like his old self when Mother had been alive.

Resolution and determination are very strong forces, but when you add faith in God alongside of them you are bound to notice a change in your life, and it was no exception in mine.

I remembered Uncle John's words, "You are never alone. The Lord will be with ye." Now, after a quick prayer to the Lord to help me, I resolved to have a new attitude. I determined to do my best at home and make Frank and Father happy.

Our home soon changed from a very miserable one to one full of joy. This didn't take place over night, of course. It was a long hard struggle, mainly inside of me. One of the most difficult things in life to do is to make a good situation out of a bad one. Without the Lord's help and the encouragement from Frank and Uncle John, I would never have made it.

Night after night I prayed to God to give me courage to be nice to Father and not hold resentment in my heart. I found myself working hard to please him, cooking his favorite meals and stimulating conversation at the table about his work or garden.

That summer I helped weed and water the garden and pored over house plans with him. Gradually, he took me into his confidence and treated me more as an equal, not a child. I was growing up, I was maturing, and life was slowly becoming more enjoyable at Whitemoss.

I asked Father if I could have a dog, as I felt the need of it for protection while he and Frank were away all day. Much to my utter amazement he consented, on the grounds that I keep the dog out of the garden.

I chose a beautiful highland collie pup. He was a delightful dog, with flashing eyes of devilment and the long nose of a thoroughbred. His markings were very commendable too. He had a large white bib or dickey on his chest, a long white nose and four white paws with just a hint of white on his tail while the rest of him was a gorgeous golden brown color.

Frank and I loved him dearly, and during that first summer on our own again, much time was spent loving and training him for his duties. Many an evening we would romp in the lane together. Just the three of us, Frank, Laddie, and me while Father worked in his garden.

It was a happy time. Frank had always wanted a dog, but up to this point Father had always refused. Now Frank was completely thrilled. Laddie really took to Frank, and by fall he had learned when to run down to meet him coming from school. He slept by his feet in the kitchen as Frank pored over his books in the evening and he looked sad and wagged his tail good-bye every morning as Frank left for school.

That was the summer that Father tried growing tomatoes in his green house for the first time. He was very fond of them and he would sit at the table eating them and smacking his lips with great satisfaction saying, "Nell, you really should try them. They're simply delicious. They're much better than any you could buy. Will ye no try one? Ah! Come now! Just try a slice." Finally his persuasiveness paid off and I did try his tomatoes, and by sheer determination I managed to get to like them and later to rave about them too.

Another thing that happened that summer was a visit to Edinburgh. With no warning whatsoever, Father announced one day that he would like to take Frank and me to Edinburgh.

"It's a shame that you live in a land as beautiful as Scotland that simply bubbles with history and never get a chance to see any of it," he stated one day with that old twinkle in his eyes that I hadn't seen for a long time now.

I was ever so pleased with myself. I felt a complete victory over my previous bad feelings about my Father. He showed me his love and I showed mine to him. I was so happy that it had all worked out so well, and I quietly thanked God for hearing my prayer and helping me over the rough spots.

When the Saturday arrived we found ourselves going into the station at East Kilbride, taking a train into Glasgow, and then getting another one for Edinburgh. The sun broke through the clouds just as we arrived in the city, and the weather stayed good for the rest of the day.

It was a thrilling experience for me to see Princess Street for myself and take the tram along it to see the Royal Mile. To visit Holyrood Palace with all its splendor, and mount the hill to Arthur's Seat, casting my eyes to the right to behold the blue Firth of Forth, and below to see Edinburgh spread out beneath us in all her glory. I could see it all at a glance, the castle gloriously situated upon the Castle Rock with the Royal Mile joining it to Holyrood, while to the left in the far distance loomed the purplish-blue mountains of the Highlands. Scanning the horizon again, my eyes rested upon the castle.

"Oh, Father," I pleaded, "please hurry, and let us visit the castle. I can hardly wait to see it."

It was indeed a thrill for all of us to visit Edinburgh castle sitting majestically on the top of the rock in all her splendor, dominating the entire landscape by her beauty and grandeur. All three of us enjoyed the day immensely and grew closer together because of it.

Another day that summer was spent on a trip to Stirling Castle. Stirling, magnificently perched on a spectacular rock, still keeps her steadfast vigil, guarding the only route to the Highlands via Bridge-of-Allan.

As soon as I approached the castle I could feel a sense of awe. I imagined I could see history unfolding before me as the Kings and Queens of old played out their parts on the stage of time. The guide who showed us around had a vivid imagination, and made the stories of Bruce and Wallace dance before our eyes.

A chill ran up my spine as I approached the spot where Douglas' body had fallen out of the window when he was killed by James. We visited the dungeons and stared over ramparts to see the mountains off in the distance to the north, the mighty Grampians, including Ben Lomond, Ben Venue, Ben Ledi and Ben Vorlich, the giants that guard the North.

With a sweep of the eye we could see the Wallace Monument standing proudly against the blue sky. The man that was a giant of his day was still the silent giant guarding the castle and people of Stirling, or so it seemed.

To the east, the ribbon-like loops of the river Forth twisted and turned, making its way to the sea through the lush green plain.

We saw the Palace with its symbolic figures of stone sculpture gracing the outer wall. We saw Queen Ann's garden, and of course Father loved the roses. It was a truly wonderful day for all three of us, and as we made our way home we all held a deep and hallowed love for our heritage.

Summer soon passed in this carefree and happy way, and soon we had settled into a long cold winter again. Wee Frank, who was not 'wee' anymore but about five feet nine, went back to school. He was now a young man of sixteen, and very handsome indeed. Successful at school, he looked forward to his last year and then a teacher training course. His cough persisted though, and it bothered me. He seemed to have almost a rattle in his throat most of the time, and he was very thin. Father didn't think it too serious, so time went on.

Father busied himself with his house plans and went out playing cards quite often. I busied myself with the chores at home. Keeping the home fires burning, clothes ready for everyone and the meals on the table was quite enough to keep me out of mischief, and I read a great deal.

I really enjoyed the companionship of Laddie during the long cold winter days alone in the house. Laddie would lie sleeping under the kitchen table, coming out every so often to see me and nuzzle up to me for reassurance of my love.

One wet, chilling, winter day, a knock came at the door, and as I opened it I saw a very rough-looking character standing on the threshold. I became frightened at once and my hands turned icy as I told him he couldn't come in, but that I would make him something to eat and a hot drink. No doubt he sensed I was alone, and suddenly his foot was in the door and he was trying to force his way past me. I made an attempt to close the door in his face, but his foot wouldn't allow the door to close, and with one easy thrust of his heavy shoulder he forced the door open.

"You'll let me in, all right," he growled with an ugly smile that showed his all-but-toothless mouth.

"So you're all alone and you're afraid, aren't you? Eh! Well there's nothing to be afraid of, nothing at all."

His hands were touching me. Horror had taken possession of me. I wanted to scream, but I knew no one was close enough to hear. I could feel his strong, cold, clammy hands on my shoulder and I shook, and he laughed.

As I struggled to push him away from me and out the door, my mind was a blank except to utter a quick prayer. "God, PLEASE help me!"

"There's no one can help you now, girl - no one." The grip of his hands tightened on my arm as I painfully tried to free myself. He had a wicked glint in his eye, and inwardly I knew his intent. I struggled. Laddie was barking wildly in the kitchen but the door was closed as usual, and it was too far away for me to open it.

I could feel my strength waning and I wanted to cry, but my fighting words to myself were, "God CAN help me! I know He CAN!" I defiantly argued as I felt the man envelope me with his strong arms.

Suddenly, there was a click of the latch door and out bounded Laddie. He took a flying leap at the stranger and bit his arm while his claws hit the man's unshaven face, and a red gash appeared on his cheek. The dog held on to his arm like a vice, so in order to fight it off, I was released. A torrent of filth flowed from the man's mouth as he struggled to kick Laddie or force him out the front door.

Quickly I picked up the wooden umbrella stand and brought it down firmly on the stranger's head. It broke, but dealt him a good blow, stunning him, and as he reeled, I pushed him out the door.

Laddie released his grip on the man's arm long enough to let him fall out the door, but soon caught hold of his pant leg as the man struggled to get to his feet again. I quickly bolted the door and ran to the living room window to see what was happening. I could see Laddie holding on to his pant leg with all his might while he growled in anger and put up a very good fight. The man responded to it all with loud cursing and shouts of pain.

Finally the man called out in desperation, "Call you're damn dog off me, and I'll go away."

I felt now, after the terrific fight Laddie had put up, that the man would go away, and if he didn't, that Laddie would attack again, so I opened the window a little and called to Laddie to stop.

Laddie seemed to realize that I was now safely inside the house so he let go the pant leg, but accompanied the limping stranger through the gate and part way down the lane, barking and snarling all the way. Only when Laddie was sure of no further danger did he return to me for his reward of loving, which he so richly deserved and which I so happily gave.

Only days before, Frank had taught Laddie how to open the latch on the kitchen door, in case of fire, and now that trick had been used by Laddie to save my life. God had answered prayer.

It was a good winter, taking everything into account. Father seemed contented and happy, and Frank and I were happier than we had been for many years. Laddie was a wonderful dog and a great companion for me during the day. He was like the icing on our cake of happiness that winter.

I found myself wishfully thinking that perhaps life could go on and on like this until Frank and I were old enough to marry. Even Jean came to see us more often these days, and on one very joyful visit she brought her shy young beau along — none other than the same one she had had her eyes on years before in the choir, Jimmy Young. Jimmy had missed Jean when she went away to work in Glasgow; and absence sometimes really does make the heart grow fonder, so he had ventured after her into Glasgow. They announced their wedding for February.

It was a quiet but very beautiful church wedding. Jean looked every inch a dream girl in her bridal gown. Her red ringlets were tied with a white velvet bow and her bridal veil fell in a gorgeous cascade down her back, making a lovely picture as she walked up the aisle. I was her bridesmaid and enjoyed the excitement of it all very much. Frank stood tall and handsome beside Jimmy as best man. Father gave the bride away. The differences that had existed between Father and Jean had melted away completely, and Jean was her free happy self again. Even brother George was at the wedding in the capacity of usher, with his very attractive fiancée close by him most of the day.

Life was good, but even as we laughed, loved, and celebrated together again as a family, the dark clouds of trouble began to gather over our clear blue sky.

Chapter 8
Wedding Bells Again

$\mathcal{I}$t was at the wedding, on that happiest of days that I saw the first signs of the storm approaching.

She was approaching Father. She was dressed in a brown tweed suit and stood tall and serene, with her graying-red hair neatly pulled back in a bun, showing her sharp features off to advantage. Her strong character immediately projected itself the instant she spoke.

"So you're Jean's Father. I've heard so much about you. Now I can see where Jean gets her good looks from," she purred.

"And what *did* you hear about me? Sorry, I don't believe I caught your name," Father questioned.

"Why I'm Miss Margaret McIntosh. Just call me Maggie like everyone else does. I work in the same house as Jean does in Glasgow. I've been with the family for ten years now. Do you really want to know what I've heard about you?" she laughed into Father's eyes.

"Well, perhaps not, now that you put it that way," Father evaded.

"I've heard," she continued as she slipped her arm through his and led him over to the couch in front of the window, "That you are quite a builder around these parts, and that you are considered the Pansy King at the Flower Competitions. I was over on Maxwell Drive just this morning and was told that you built all the houses down that street. It is a magnificent street, the houses are beautifully designed —" On and on she went during the rest of the wedding reception. It was the same old story. Flattery, a cunning way, a quick mind simply gushing with sentimental dribble, but Father was drinking it in again as though he had an unquenchable thirst.

A couple of months went by after the wedding and Father didn't make a move to visit her, but a woman as strong willed as Maggie wouldn't let time or anything else stand in the way of her getting what she was after, so she decided to come to East Kilbride to see Jean and Jimmy.

Quite uninvited, she arrived at their door one day and spent part of the day with Jean. However, early afternoon found her saying she'd like to see Jean's Father about getting some pansy seed. Jean could see through her immediately and tried to put her off, saying her Father wasn't at home today and couldn't be reached, as he was away inquiring about building supplies.

Fate and Maggie worked hand in hand that day to put temptation directly into Father's path. They met at Jean's gate just as Maggie was leaving and Father was arriving. He drove her to the station for her train. His doom was sealed by that little act of kindness and the romance blossomed from then on.

Father went to visit her in Glasgow every weekend all summer. His eyes sparkled when he spoke about her. He often sat at the table, musing to himself as he went over in his mind things that had been said or would be said upon their next meeting.

Again, Frank and I found ourselves out of things. This summer was not like last summer. This summer, Father was in love again – or was he? Was he just in love with love, or enjoying flattery? No matter what name it went by, the end result would inevitably be the same - another marriage - his third.

How would this one turn out, I wondered? Would she fulfill his every dream? This time there was no use arguing with Father about it. In fact everyone, including Uncle John, sat back this time and never uttered a word of protest. There were a few raised eyebrows here and there when the wedding was announced but the general consensus was, "He's been there before and he certainly is old enough to know what he's doing."

The wedding took place quietly in the manse, followed by a short honeymoon, and then Maggie was living with us.

I asked Father if I could go back to school now that Maggie could do the housework, but he wouldn't hear of it. "A woman's place is in the home, and that is what you should train for. Maggie can give you excellent training in this."

I spent the first few months at home trying to carry on as usual, but whereas Beatrice had sat reading for hours handing out orders to me, Maggie was of a different breed altogether. She was stubborn, immaculate, and bossy. She demanded instead of asking, summoned instead of calling, and her worst trait of all was to criticize instead of praising. To her way of thinking, many things had been neglected for a few years and she intended putting them straight.

As I look back, I imagine her secret desire was to outdo the first stepmother and prove to Father how much better she was. I think it must have been quite a strain on her, trying to compete with a first and second wife. Even at best she would realize that Father must have loved them in turn and I would think there would always be an uneasy feeling of competition, even though the other wives were dead.

Whether it was this strong urge to please Father no matter what happened I don't know, but she soon turned the house upside down. She claimed her training gave her a much better insight into housework than a mere girl could have and proceeded to show me.

Literally everything was changed. No doubt this was an effort to destroy old memories Father might have had. She began by rearranging the living room, painting and papering it and talking Father into getting rid of most of the old furniture, even his old comfortable easy chair in favor of a new one. The kitchen was next, and on through the house she went.

Everything became perfect in her wake. Windows shone, cupboards glowed with pride of neatness, curtains hung magnificently, and the house in no time looked like a beautifully wrapped Christmas present.

The most important ingredient of a Christmas present, however, is the love that goes into buying it, wrapping it and giving it but I am afraid 'that kind' of love was missing. Father, Frank, and I were supposedly the receivers of her art of cleanliness, but we were never allowed to enjoy it. If a hand mark appeared near a door handle we were told about it. If a picture was crooked she noticed it. If Father didn't put his pipe on the pipe rack he was reprimanded for it. If he or Frank left their reading material or house plans around on a table or chair, that was a fault.

Only one discrepancy was permitted however, for when Maggie moved in, her cat moved in with her, and strangely enough it could do no wrong. It sat in the best chairs, ate the best meat and enjoyed the only sign of love I could see Maggie giving out.

It wasn't long before Fluffins (as the cat was called) and Laddie came to grief. Or should I say, Laddie came to grief. One day shortly after the wedding, there was a knock at the door and Maggie went to answer it. I was in the bedroom at the time, but both Fluffins and Laddie occupied the kitchen. Maggie had just finished cutting a thick slice of meat off the roast for Father's supper, and it was lying on a plate on the table. Coming along the hall I glanced into the kitchen just in time to see Fluffins dragging the slice of meat off the table, and Laddie pouncing on it as it hit the floor, but unfortunately for him, Maggie reentered the room at that precise moment, and she naturally blamed Laddie for the whole incident. She hit Laddie cruelly with the broom until he stood whimpering and cowering at the door. She continued to beat him until I opened the door and let him out. No explanation in Laddie's defense would be listened to, and that was the last time Laddie was allowed into the house.

Poor Laddie, his sad look spoke volumes to me about his feelings. Laddie and I had much in common that winter. I felt much like a dog and I was treated like one. I worked from early morning until night, doing many humdrum jobs that Maggie didn't particularly care to do, such as painting, peeling vegetables, washing dishes and mending socks. Even these jobs always rated criticism such as, "When you paint you leave streaks. You should have scrubbed those potatoes instead of peeling them. Why didn't you take the skin off the tomatoes? You pile the dishes far too high in the drying pan, why don't you dry some first. You really should have known enough to have used a darker colored thread on that sock." In no way could anything be done right.

In order to preserve my sanity, I turned my situation into a game, now realizing that I mustn't allow this horrible feeling of inferiority to overcome me. The game I played with myself was to guess what fault she would find in a job I had completed. After a while, I became an expert at this guessing game, and it helped to take the sting out of her constant and damaging criticism.

I well remember one bright spring day when Maggie went to town with Father and I washed up the lunch dishes and piled them in the dish pan to dry. The day was so gorgeous that I couldn't resist the temptation, so I lifted up the kitchen window a little higher than usual and placed the dishpan full of dishes on the wide window sill to dry. I had often done this the previous summer and found the dishes dried beautifully in no time and I could put them away without drying them.

That particular day I left the house and went for a quick visit to Uncle John's, but it wasn't my lucky day. In my absence the cat jumped up onto the window sill and hissed at Laddie who was lying just under the window. The dog jumped up in an effort to catch the cat and knocked over the dishes. Picture that happening just as Father and Maggie came around to the back door. It was quite a mess and quite an expense to replace the dishes, I suspect, and both Father and Maggie were furious at me for being so lazy, careless, and stupid.

I grew more and more restless, more and more upset. I felt treated more like a child than I had been at a much earlier age. I couldn't do this, I couldn't touch that. I was too old to be treated like a child or be given special privileges, and too young to be treated like an adult. I was in that no man's land of teens.

I can well remember my fifteenth birthday. It had been a particularly hot day in June and Maggie was on one of her cleanup sprees. This time it was washing the windows. After finishing a window I climbed down the ladder to pat Laddie, leaving the pail of water sitting on the cross-section of the ladder. Dear old Fluffins, being a little jealous, jumped from the window sill onto the ladder and the ladder, which was precariously situated, tipped over, thus knocking the pail of water over right on top of Maggie, who happened to be walking by. I couldn't help laughing, she looked so funny all dripping wet, but she didn't think it was funny and soon went into a torrent of abuse.

For days I took this verbal abuse, but then as more and more resentment kept growing in my heart, I finally decided to consult the one person I knew could help me, Uncle John. Tears streaming down my face, I told him what had happened and I also told him what it was like at Whitemoss now Maggie was there. I was sobbing, and he knew this was a serious matter. Taking me in his arms to comfort me he asked me to come and work for him in the store for the summer at least. He needed someone as his leg was acting up again and he found it very hard to manage. He said he would speak to my father, and if my father said no, he would think of something. It wasn't a very happy birthday, but perhaps I had a solution to my problem.

I can't imagine what Uncle John said to Father to convince him to allow me to work in the store. I only know Father said 'yes'.

Chapter 9
Wee Frank is Very Sick

*L*ife now took on a new perspective. I lived to work in the store, and endured the hours at home. I met many new people. I talked with them and became their friend quickly. I saw many families in the course of a week as they came to pick up their groceries, and I saw the happiness on the faces of many children and young girls my age that enjoyed the luxury of two parents. Oddly enough I wasn't jealous of them, only depressed at times as I pondered my own situation.

Uncle John was a gem to work for. He laughed heartily and often, and enjoyed a good joke with his customers. PRAISE OTHERS FOR THE LITTLE THINGS THEY DO seemed to be his motto. It was a good philosophy, for one tends to strive harder and harder to do bigger and better things after a little praise has been received.

Life at home went on as before, with Father spending more and more of his time in the garden, and not just because of his love for it, but because it kept him out of the house which was now so perfect nothing could be disturbed.

Frank got work at the local market for the summer and seemed happy enough, although his persistent cough seemed to gurgle in his throat more than ever now and his color was pale.

Summer passed and autumn greeted us with a sorry blast that warned us to prepare for the bleak winter that was fast approaching. Frank attended teacher training school now. I was so proud of him. I envied him a little, or was it envy? Perhaps it was just an aching desire still within me to do big things with my own life, but I was just a girl.

Christmas time is usually a happy time. A time to give gifts, visit people, and have people in. It is a time to attend church and praise God for the gift of His Son. It is also a time to love one another. This Christmas was no such time. Frank lay sick in the kitchen bed, his face white against the bleached white pillowcase. He had collapsed at a function at the school and had been brought home. The doctor said it was a bad case of over-exhaustion and flu, and that we must watch out for pneumonia.

"But, what about the cough, that has been plaguing him for so long?" I queried as the doctor made actions of leaving.

"Well his T.B. hasn't improved any. However, it's nothing to get alarmed about, provided he is kept warm and can pass off this bout of exhaustion," The doctor replied. "Perhaps in the spring he will have to take some time off and go to France or someplace to be in the right climate to overcome the tuberculosis."

Springtime found Frank still in bed most of the time, making a desperate attempt to recover, but the tuberculosis had a firm hold on him now. The doctor now suggested a trip to southern France and the sun of the Mediterranean to help him. Father agreed to save up and send him there in the summer, while Maggie frowned and said all he needed was our own good summer sun.

Life became very hard for Frank at this point. Harder than I realized for a long time, as I worked every day and was away for many hours at a stretch.

One day when I returned from work and was helping to put the dinner on the table, Frank called for a drink of water. I turned immediately to the pump at the sink to get him one but Maggie stopped me dead in my tracks by ordering.

"Don't you dare, give him a drink. He is always wanting something always bothering me for this and that and it isn't necessary."

"But it's only a glass of water he wants," I pleaded.

"You heard what I said!" was her inhuman reply.

That night when Father and Maggie were out I had a long talk with Frank.

"I'm dying Nell, and I'm too young to die," he spoke, his voice quite clear of emotion.

"You mustn't speak this way, Frank. You mustn't," I ordered, my voice quivering and shaking as I tried desperately to stay calm and unemotional for his sake.

"It's true, Nell. I know. It's only a matter of time and I want you to do one thing for me if it's possible."

"Oh! What is it Frank? What is it?"

"Talk to Uncle John and see if he would mind if I went to live with him for a little while."

"Oh, yes, Frank, I know he'll want you. It's *her* that's making you unhappy isn't it?" I couldn't even give *her* a name. At this point I didn't feel she deserved it. She was an animal, and a selfish one at that.

"Yes, Nell. I know I could die in peace at Uncle John's, for he really loves me."

"Oh, Frank, you just can't die. You can't," I pleaded. "I need you."

Frank was taken to Uncle John's house the next day, much to Father's utter amazement and displeasure, and died in Uncle John's house among friends and loved ones a month later.

An empty void filled my life at this point. I felt my life fall apart. I heard and saw everything that people said and did, but it was as though I was in another world looking on in a state of numbness or shock. I functioned well enough. I had disciplined myself for years to carry on, despite all situations, and that helped to carry me through at this trying point in my life. I served in the store by day, I ate my meals, I went for long rides into the country on my newly acquired bicycle and "lived" with Uncle John and Aunt Jane. I had only gone home long enough to gather together my clothes. I felt desperate, alone, resentful, bitter, even hateful at times.

Often on my long bicycle jaunts in the beautiful countryside of Lanarkshire I would ask myself the question -"why?" Why had Mother died? Why had Father married again? Why had he fallen into the trap twice? Why was I a woman? I would now be close to finishing my training if I had been a man, but then Frank was a man and why had he died so young and with so much promise for the future? Why God, why?

I stopped attending church because I wasn't sure I understood religion anymore, or was it because I didn't want to run into Father and Maggie? I now saw their attendance at church as pure, unadulterated, hypocrisy. How could a woman be so cruel as to refuse water to a dying man, and yet call herself a Christian and attend church regularly? The question lying heaviest on my heart, however, was why Father even yet couldn't see Maggie for the self-centered, cruel person she was, and couldn't see what he had done to his family.

Sixteen is supposed to be a very romantic period in one's life. A time when a girl is having her coming out party in some circles, attending dances, singing, laughing, and even loving a little. My sixteenth birthday passed by unnoticed, as had all my others. I was one year older, that was all. I was one year more desperate and lonely. Frank and I had been close, and I missed him dreadfully. I resented his death and felt God had dealt an unkind blow. Then again, I would reason that it was not all God's fault, if indeed any of it was His fault. After all, hadn't God given all human beings freedom of action, we are not puppets on a string. It was really Father's fault for neglecting his son. It was Maggie's fault for influencing Father and taking Father's attention away from his sick child. I realized again that Maggie probably had the same motive with Frank and me as Beatrice had had with Jean and George to get rid of us, get us out of the house because of the competition we presented to her. Well, now she was rid of both Frank and me for good, no longer would we compete with her for Father's love or attention. I felt that I never wanted to see Whitemoss again.

Father made two or three feeble attempts to see me at Uncle John's, but I refused to speak with him. He went to see Jean to ask her to speak to me, but she refused to intercede. In fact, she too had become very curt and awkward in his presence again, and she never made visits back to Whitemoss.

I felt alone, completely and utterly alone. It was true I still had Uncle John and Aunt Jane and sister Jean fairly close, but nevertheless I was indeed alone. As the summer passed, my mind tried to sort out the problems of my life, and I came more and more to the conclusion that God, instead of being my enemy, was my only true and trusted friend.

I read my Bible often during those days, trying to make sense out of it all and many passages helped me immensely.

"Ye believe in God, believe also in me."

"I go to prepare a place for you. If it were not so, I would have told you." John 14:1-2. Frank was there now with Mother, and both were well again. I seemed to feel this truth to be a fact beyond a doubt. Then I realized I could no longer feel sorry for them. Bereavement is a time of feeling lonely and sorry for oneself when a loved one dies, and it is at a time like this that we must turn to God and ask for his help to keep us going and take us out of this lonely despair that we have fallen into. For if we are truly Christian, we believe that the deceased are now out of all their pain, misery and unhappiness, and dwell with their Father in Heaven.

"God is my refuge and my strength, an ever-present help in trouble." Psalm 46:1

The passage that I grew to love most of all however was — "For God so loved the world that He gave His only begotten son that whosoever believeth in Him should not perish but have everlasting life." John 3:16.

God had been distraught over the pain and death of a beloved son, just as I had been for a beloved brother. God knew what it was to see a loved one suffer at the hands of his enemies. The difference between God and me in this case was that God, in all his majesty and power, could have stopped it all with a gesture of His hand, or just by willing it not to happen; but He didn't stop Jesus' death because he wanted to forgive everyone their sins, including me, and that was the only way He could succeed in His purpose. It was the only way people would believe completely in Christ, and in a life hereafter, gloriously demonstrated by the resurrection.

God knew my problems. He had always helped me through difficulties in the past, and I knew He wouldn't let me down now. He was the One I could always depend on to guide me, and because of His love I could pick up the pieces of my life again and carry on.

The first thing I decided to do was talk to Jean about going out to service. I loved it at Uncle John's, but I felt that he was creating a job for me, as he really only needed part-time help. Besides, I wanted to feel my wings a little. There was no use even thinking of any career now, so why not make some money the only way I knew how, housework. I'd save and save. I'd buy nice clothes and attend the theatre, but mainly I'd save, and I'd let God lead me. "Perhaps I'd even go to America or Australia someday," I kidded as I talked to Jean.

"Not on a maid's salary you won't," she chided. "Perhaps you could go as a companion with some rich person though, if you're lucky. One never knows in this world what turn our lives will take."

Jean got an interview with Mrs. MacKlintock for me a week later. She ran an agency for the hiring of domestic help. She placed me first in a home in Glasgow with six children, and I was the only hired help. It was a fairly large house, and much as I loved the work with the children and got along splendidly with the mistress of the house, I felt I had had enough hard work and struggle to do me a lifetime already, and I began to feel a strong desire to change my position. I didn't want to cook at all, so I applied as a table maid.

This time, with a good reputation to back me up, Mrs. McKlintock was able to place me in a lovely home. I was to be the table maid.

I was to attend guests, serve table, make beds, dust, answer the door, and by all means keep the silverware clean. I must be immaculate at all times, but attend to the hearth and the thresholds and keep them spotless. Also my manners and bearing were to be of the upmost importance.

It was really quite an order, for the doorbell was constantly ringing as many guests were invited to this home. Mr. Summercomb was out a great deal due to his business as a stockbroker, but Mrs. Summercomb carried on with a string of guests regardless.

"I get so lonely and bored just sitting in this big house by myself, I just have to be on the go," she often said to me as we planned a party and fingered over her many dresses to decide what she should wear. Every now and then the two of them went away together and the help got a holiday with pay, or so it seemed, as the work was cut in half.

"So many of you domestics are going to America these days, I don't want to come home and find you gone." Mrs. Summercomb often commented.

It was truly a wonderful set up. I didn't have to work too hard and the work was interesting and even exciting at times, as we got ready for important guests, or some gala affair. I visited Uncle John's and sister Jean's homes quite often on my days off, but never Whitemoss.

In the spring of that year my brother George got married and I attended his wedding. Of course, Father and Maggie were there, but we only talked very formally to save embarrassment.

Father gingerly approached me.

"I hear you're making out fine in Glasgow, Nell."

"Aye"! I abruptly replied.

"Will ye no visit us once in a while when you're in town?"

"No. Not as long as my stepmother lives there," I curtly answered.

"What about me! Ye could come to see me, ye know," he questioned.

"I'm sorry, Father. I've had enough."

That ended the conversation, and as Maggie sidled up to him I stared straight at her in contempt and moved away to talk to other friends. That was the last time I saw Father for a couple of years.

My mistress, Mrs. Summercomb, had a brother, a bachelor, and he had often visited his sister at her home. He was a very kind and understanding man and everyone liked him. In the early spring he had taken a heart attack and was confined to hospital for a long time.

He passed away in June, much to the upset of the entire household. His body was brought to his sister's home until the funeral. It was the custom at that time to place the coffin near the fireplace or the focal point of the room, and this was where the body rested.

Mrs. Summercomb, a very immaculate woman at any time, became extra finicky at this point as she was naturally emotionally upset. She called me into the large living room and instructed me to clean the hearth and make it immaculately clean for the visitors that night and the funeral the next day.

I had seen death now three times and should have been used to it, but I found myself extremely uneasy as I knelt at the hearth cleaning alone in the room so near the corpse.

I began imagining things I guess, and out of the corner of my eye I thought I saw movement. I adjusted the lamp, and rebuking myself inwardly for acting so foolishly, I turned my back resolutely on the corpse and continued my cleaning. Suddenly I heard a loud thud behind me, and turning white as a sheet, I ran towards the door of the room, glancing over my shoulder, as I went. Too excited to see where I was going, I ran right into the arms of Mr. Summercomb, who was just entering the room. I guess I remained there for a few seconds to regain my composure. I was so grateful to feel a real live person. Then very quickly I came to the realization of where I was and backing up, with the feeling of horror and foolishness I could feel my face turning red.

As soon as I could catch my breath I blurted out, "Oh, Sir, I'm sorry."

"No need to apologize," he smiled. "You got a fright. It could have happened to anyone. It was only the poker falling over there on the carpet. Someone was careless and didn't put it on the stand correctly. Come now," he said as he lead me by the arm back over to the fireplace, "you finish your job and I'll stay with you."

"Oh, sir, I'm ever so grateful," I muttered. "I really shouldn't be afraid, you know, I've seen death many times before but somehow this is different."

"You didn't know him very well, that's why," he casually replied. His understanding made me relax and I continued my job and he continued to talk.

"You have beautiful hair. Has anyone ever told you? I've been watching you for some time now. You really are extremely well-mannered and mature for a person in your lowly position," he commented as he fingered the figurines on the mantle.

The flattery pleased me and I smiled and worked all the harder. Soon the hearth was gleaming and I was proud of my work and so very glad it was done.

"There now, I'm finished," I sighed with relief. "Thank you ever so much for understanding and staying with me. I feel much better now."

"Think nothing of it, the pleasure was all mine, believe me," he said, taking hold of my arms and turning me around to face him. "I have wanted to get to know you better for some time now."

For some reason a warning signal went through me. I believe it was the look in the eyes, but whatever it was, I felt uneasy. He couldn't, no, he couldn't, or could he? No!!! It was preposterous to even give room to such a thought, and yet, I felt something. He liked me, and not in a fatherly or brotherly sort of way. Not in an ordinary friendly way either.

I smiled appreciatively and with a quick turn released myself from this involved position and made a quick exit.

Chapter 10
Life's Realities

*A*fter the funeral, Mr. Summercomb went away on another business trip and my thoughts about him seemed more and more ridiculous as the days and weeks passed. My, was I fond of myself to think that he would even look at me. His words, 'your lowly position' rang in my ears and I resented them. How crazy could I be, I rebuked myself. He thinks I'm the lowest of the low and was merely trying to be nice to me when he mentioned my hair. With this kind of reasoning I was able to dismiss the whole thing from my mind.

About a month later I was out in the garden for a breath of fresh air. I had worked hard all morning getting ready for visitors that were coming that evening, and I was taking a well-earned rest. The large oak at the foot of the garden beckoned me to come and sit under its shade and I didn't resist. Spreading my black uniform under me neatly and straightening my white apron, I leaned my back against the large tree trunk as I looked up the garden at the huge expanse of lawn and thought how lovely it would be to be mistress of a home and garden like this one.

I was startled from my dreaming by a rustling of leaves in the corner of the garden by the summer house, and turning abruptly to look around the tree trunk I saw Mr. Summercomb emerging from the house. I quickly tried to hide myself behind the trunk of the tree, gathering my skirts closer to me to make myself less conspicuous, but it was all in vain as he had seen me walking to the tree and he came straight over.

"Well hello there! Out for a siesta?"

"Just a rest: Sir."

He quickly nestled himself down beside me at the foot of the tree.

"A pleasant spot: Isn't it?" he queried.

"Aye, it is that, Sir."

"Please consider it proper to call me Max when we're being informal, and what is your name?"

"Helen, really, but everyone calls me Nell."

"Nell, I like that," he continued as he began to play with a blade of grass, nipping it off every so often. "I wouldn't like 'Nellie,' you understand, but Nell has a lovely ring to it. My, you have pretty hands, Nell." He continued talking as he reached out to take my hand. "Why, your hand is freezing. Let me warm it for you. You know some girls have everything, and you're one of those girls. What color are your eyes?" His one hand left my hand and wandered up my arm to my neck. "My: what a lovely neck, Nell." He placed the knuckles of his two first fingers under my chin to raise my chin up as his eyes penetrated mine. "You have beautiful hazel eyes haven't you? They're deep as the ocean and beautiful as ..."

"Mr. Summercomb!" I exclaimed. "Please excuse me, I must get back." I wrenched my arm away from him and twisted my head as I spoke, making an attempt to stand all at the same time.

"Not before we have a little kiss," he replied as he caught me roughly in his arms and pulled me down on the ground for a long hard kiss on the lips as I struggled to escape.

Managing to obtain my release at last, I glared at him for a second and then raising my voice in protest breathlessly I reprimanded.

"Mr. Summercomb you are forgetting you're a married man?"

"No, but don't try to tell me you're that naive."

"Oh, you devil!" I retorted, and turning abruptly, ran up the garden path towards the house with his low devilish laugh ringing in my ears.

Safe inside, the first person I saw was Mrs. Summercomb busy arranging flowers for the evening guests. Thank God she was in a room that had no windows facing the back garden. Her face was radiant. She glowed with femininity and her charm was outstanding. I stood for a moment studying her. Here was a woman among women, as far as I could see, in beauty and every detail, a prize for any man, yet her husband had just made love to the maid in the garden. Why? How could he do this to her? It just didn't make sense.

"You like flowers, don't you, Nell?" she spoke as she worked with the bouquet. "I often see you rearranging and watering my flowers with a love and concern not shown by most people."

"My Father is a gardener and I do love flowers, Ma'am," I replied, making my exit to the kitchen before she would look up and notice the red cheeks I possessed and wonder why.

Mr. Summercomb tried to get friendly one more time. It was in the upstairs hall and I had just come from Mrs. Summercomb's room after fixing her up for the night, and was about to enter my room at the opposite end of the hall when Mr. Summercomb appeared at the top of the servants back stairs about three feet from me.

"You're not thinking of going to bed already are you?" he ventured.

"Yes indeed I am, Sir," I sharply retorted, all the while trying to remain calm and collected, but actually shaking violently from head to toe. He had taken me by complete surprise, I just hadn't pictured him trying to get my attention inside the house and so close to his wife's room.

"The night is young, let's go out on the balcony for a little bit," he said as he guided me down the hall, his one hand on my elbow and the other around my waist.

For a moment I couldn't gather my wits together to believe what was happening, and then I regained my presence of mind.

"Just a minute, Sir," I stalled. "If you pull me any further, I'll cry out."

"I doubt that very much," he laughed.

"Very well," I said, summoning all the courage and strength I could muster. "Just watch me!" I took a long breath and opened my mouth to scream. His one hand quickly covered my mouth while he held me tight against him with the other arm.

"I believe you would, not that it would do you any good," he retorted, nodding towards his wife's room. "She'd never believe you." However, I must have frightened him a little because he released me at that moment, and my arms were sore from his grip.

"You really have spunk, haven't you? I like that in a woman."

"Well, I detest your qualities in a man," I spiritedly answered as I turned and made a dash towards my bedroom, closing the door in his face and quickly turning the key in the lock.

That was the last episode of that kind, for the very next day when he took off on another of his business trips I gave in my notice to Mrs. Summercomb.

She was very disappointed to hear I was leaving and hoped my sister would get along fine with her pregnancy, and she certainly would give me a good recommendation.

Jean actually *was* expecting a baby, and I would go and stay with her until I got another job, but by telling Jean's need I didn't have to give even a hint of my real reason for leaving, and in this way Mrs. Summercomb would never have the misery of knowing what her husband was truly like. That is, if she didn't already know from previous experiences, which was highly likely.

I stayed with Jean for six months at this time, and it was fun to plan for the baby. Jean's face shone with a radiance only worn by pregnant women. A radiance that says, "I have one of God's own creations within my womb and God has chosen me to be its mother. What a blessing and honor has been heaped upon me." I helped her around her home, as she wasn't in the best of health, as her time approached. I watched her stomach slowly grow, and often felt the movement of life. I had never had anything to do with a tiny baby before, and the prospect of having a dear little niece or nephew of my own was a wonderful one.

Once in a while, however, a black cloud crossed my mind as I thought of the many wee ones Mother had lost. I prayed desperately and unceasingly that everything would go well for Jean and her little one, and it did.

In May, wee Jean was born. She was a bonnie wee lassie, with blue eyes and golden hair and she was called Jean after her mother and grandmother. It wasn't long though before she was nick-named 'Wee Jean' to differentiate from her mother.

In the late spring I went back to work, with Mrs. MacKlintock getting me a position in a very wealthy home in Glasgow. It was a beautiful home nestled back in the trees, and had quite an estate surrounding it. The couple often went abroad, so the help were not called upon to do extensive entertaining. I was to be the table maid again and also keep the house tidy. The size of the house swamped me a bit at first, but after I worked out a schedule, I found it quite easy to keep on top of it, because there wasn't anyone coming behind me to mess things up.

Mrs. Fraser was a dear, loveable lady. A real gem! She spoke very frankly about everything and could size a person up in one scrutinizing glance. Often she would take me into her confidence and say such things as, "Now, Mrs. Williams is coming this afternoon and she is extremely fussy, so please use our best china and serve it in the most conservative way and then kindly exit from the room, as servants waiting around for trays etc. upset her no end."

These little bits of information made it much easier to wait on the table for guests, as I knew a little of their idiosyncrasies and how to deal with them.

Now and then she would pull me aside and ask me if I had a young gentleman friend. She was interested in my family too. When she discovered that my brother and my two sisters were married and Father was married again for the third time she smiled and said, "Well, if you have any questions you would like to ask me, such as what to do in any given situation, don't hesitate to come and ask. I'll do my best to answer you. My daughter died at the age of seventeen and I miss her very much. She actually looked a little like you with golden hair and hazel eyes. Perhaps we can help each other a little in this way."

She was as good as her word, and we often had quite intimate talks together. We sometimes even discussed the birds and the bees and she would always end *that* conversation with, "Just remember, tell them that if they want you intimately they'll have to marry you, and stick to it! It's the only way to keep your self-respect, and theirs."

It would be a year before I would learn from one of the other members of staff that her daughter who died had committed suicide when she had discovered that she was pregnant and the young man had gone away and left her.

That summer I turned nineteen and I decided to see as much as I could of Scotland, my own homeland, but one I had seen very little of except for Edinburgh and Glasgow.

Each time I had a day off and was shopping in Glasgow I wandered around to the travel bureau and inquired about their train and boat trips. One day long ago I had gone with my Sunday School class on a day's outing to Dunoon by boat and I had had a wonderful time. As I fingered over the folder about the Clyde Sails, I noticed that there was still time to catch the boat to Tighnabruaich. Should I just go and buy a ticket now or wait for another day? As I stood there undecided, I felt a tap on my shoulder and there stood my cousin Elizabeth. I hadn't seen her for a long time, years in fact, but I felt the sudden warmth of her friendship envelope me again as it had done years before when we had been closer to one another, before Mother's family had stopped visiting us.

Elizabeth was now a young lady and we stood staring at each other in utter amazement at the change time had made in each of us.

"I'd always know that gorgeous red hair of yours, Nell," Elizabeth said as we stood, hands clasped admiring one another. "You haven't grown very tall. You must have taken after your Father in that respect. As for me, I feel like a giant. I wish I was small and petite like you. It must be nice when it comes to dating the young men. What are you doing now? I heard you weren't living at home anymore. Is that old hag of a woman still living with your Father?" Her questions went on in a steady flow with never a pause for an answer. "Oh Nell, give me your address quickly. I've just got to see you sometime when we can talk, and I've just bought a ticket for a sail down the Clyde. A few girls that work at the mill decided to have a sail today."

Quickly I wrote out my address, and as I handed it to her I hesitatingly inquired, "Would — would, you mind if I joined you on this trip, Elizabeth? I'd love to go for a sail, too. I have the day off and it is such a lovely one."

"That would be wonderful, but hurry if you want to get a ticket, the boat sails in five minutes."

Soon we were sailing up the Clyde past the ship yards, docks, and harbors, past ocean liners docked waiting to sail to many countries. The thought occurred to me again. Perhaps someday I'll sail to America, Canada, or Australia in one of those — maybe in that new one being built now right over there.

Past St. Patrick we sailed, where the Saint was born and had his well to prove it in Old Kilpatrick. He also has a rock in the River Clyde near there called St. Patrick's Stone.

Soon, we saw a huge rocky island that looked like a miniature Gibraltar, and was easily recognized as Dumbarton Rock. As we sailed past this majestic rock, our history lessons flashed across our minds. The Romans had taken this rock but that was about as far north as they had gone. The fierce warriors and weather to the north of this point were too much for them. The Knights of the Round Table once met here, and Dumbarton castle at the foot of the Rock had been in possession of both Mary Queen of Scots and her enemies.

We saw the mansion Finlayston House, where the Earl of Glencairn, the first Scottish noble to turn Protestant, brought John Knox to preach.

"Remember our adventure on the train to Helensburgh for a family reunion?" Elizabeth questioned. "That must have been the year before your mother died. You do remember don't you?" She went into great detail about our picnic, but I could only remember it in a sketchy way, as I had been only seven years old at the time.

The boat passed Greenock, the birth place of James Watt, and docked at Gourock. Many passengers got on at this point, but the boat lost no time continuing its journey across Cardwell Bay to Dunoon. Dunoon, that great holiday resort! We could see Highland Mary's statue just left of the pier and one fancies she is looking across the Clyde towards her lover's home at Ayr. On to Innellan, and we now could see the Islands of Great Cumbrae and Little Cumbrae to the south. Around Toward Point we went, where we saw the little village of Toward, Toward Lighthouse and Castle Toward built for Glasgow's Provost, Kirkman Finlay, in 1832. We also saw the ruins of Toward Castle nestled among the trees to the southwest, where the battle between the Campbells and Lamonts was waged, which the Campbells won through trickery.

Then we saw the glorious site of the Isle of Bute and the Rothesay Castle, built by a Viking king in the eleventh century. Ever onward we came to the Kyles of Bute, one of the most magnificently beautiful parts of Scotland, and on through the Narrows to Tighnabruaich, meaning 'The House on the Brae,' that was once an old inn.

It was a glorious trip, and I felt simply wonderful standing at the railing of the boat, viewing all God's beauty and feeling the warmth and companionship of a good old friend and relation beside me. The boat stopped for a while at Tighnabruaich and we went for a walk along the shore to the little village shops. Elizabeth was talking and laughing with her friends all the way, but always brought me into the conversation. I felt wonderful right to the very marrow of my being. Our trip back was a little wet as the rain came on, but after such a glorious trip down the Clyde how could anyone complain.

When we arrived back at the Glasgow pier I told Elizabeth how much I had enjoyed myself, and she said she had too.

"We do this often, just the three of us. You must join us again sometime. It's always fun. I'll get in touch with you the next time we plan something, to see if you can come."

I smiled, and with a kind embrace we left each other, much blessed by the wonderful day together.

About three weeks after that Elizabeth got in touch with me again.

"We're taking the train to Ayr this weekend to see Burn's cottage. Like to come?"

Again we had a grand day of fun and laughter, and again I learned much about Scottish history.

Another trip was back to Edinburgh to see the things I had missed on my previous visit with Father. St. Giles Cathedral, John Knox's home and Sir Walter Scott's monument, and of course we couldn't resist another visit to the castle.

When summer slowly changed to autumn, our planned trips changed also. We now went sightseeing in museums and art galleries, and for a change, we sometimes went to Edinburgh or just stayed in Glasgow and went on a shopping spree. Occasionally when we all had a night free we took in a 'Pantomime' but the main thing was that we were all together enjoying ourselves.

When I didn't have any plans with the girls I often went home to East Kilbride to see Jean and Jim, and of course Wee Jean. She was the prettiest baby imaginable and I loved her dearly. She too had the red hair of her mother and beautiful hazel eyes. Her chubby little legs and arms were a delight to behold in their perfection, and her complexion was flawless. I sometimes wondered if I would ever have a child of my own like her. I wanted to be a mother someday, but I was determined not to be hasty about any young man, as I had a strong feeling that they were rather fickle in their love life. I didn't want to be hurt, either before or after marriage. I had to have the right one to start with. I didn't want to be another Mrs. Summercomb, wondering what her husband did all the time on his trips or indeed at home.

As often as I went home to East Kilbride I never went near Whitemoss. I just couldn't bear the thought of seeing, let alone talking to Maggie. I saw Father occasionally at Jean's home, but never got into conversation with him much. He didn't strike me as being very happy, but perhaps I was reading things into his facial expressions which were really not there.

My cousin Tom got married that spring. All the relations attended the wedding and chatted and outwardly enjoyed the occasion, but with Maggie present there was the usual tension in the air. She didn't stand as straight and haughty as before, but now her bossy nature was showing even on her sharp-featured face, and strange as it may sound, there was a slightly browbeaten look about Father which was new and different in place of his former self-reliant, efficient self.

I didn't have too much trouble avoiding Maggie at the wedding, as it appeared that she was avoiding me. Ever since the day I had walked out of the house with Frank and went to live with Uncle John, she had hated me. For in that act I had exposed her to everyone. Naturally, there were questions asked on every side about Frank and why he had gone to Uncle John's home to die. People are not easily fooled and it didn't take many questions and half answers to put two and two together and come up with the solution, that of a miserable home life. My moving to Uncle John's too confirmed their suspicion, and there was quite a heyday for the gossips of East Kilbride for a while at Maggie's expense.

Jean announced to me that spring that she was expecting again and I was very happy for her. It appeared that she had found a truly good man in Jim and that she was very happy. One of my most enjoyable pastimes was visiting Jean's home and playing with Wee Jean. She was the dearest wee baby I had ever set my eyes on and her red hair and hazel eyes endeared her to me very much. Many of my shopping sprees ended up with a dress or toy for her. Just to watch the childish delight, as she saw something new coming out of my bag for her, made it well worth my effort.

My married sister, Maggie, of whom I knew very little as she had been married and lived in Blantyre since I was the age of six, took ill that year and died soon after. It was in childbirth, and her husband was very broken up about it. The loss of wife and child so suddenly really was a hard blow.

Except for the death of Maggie, I was very happy that winter, with my girlfriends, my visits to Jean and my talks with Mrs. Fraser. Mrs. Fraser treated me more and more like her child than her maid. She often asked about the family and enjoyed talking to me about my excursions with the girls. She was planning a trip abroad with her husband that summer, and it was exciting just to hear her talk about the places they would visit during their travels.

Chapter 11
Seeing Scotland with Ian

Until this point in my life I hadn't had much time to think about, let alone go out with, many young men. There had been the occasional flirtation with one here and there and that queer little sensation that flashes through a girl when a boy pays particular attention to her, and she suddenly feels prettier than ever before, but nothing lasting or serious. Therefore, I was a little unprepared for the sudden impact one particularly handsome man was to have upon me.

As spring slowly changed to summer the girls and I decided to take a week-long trip and enjoy a real adventure. We would take a train to Oban the first day, then a day cruise on the two funneled paddle steamer Grenadier, across to the Isle of Mull and hopefully around the island to visit the famous sacred island of Iona. A day or two shopping in Oban, returning via Glencoe would complete the week. It sounded like a lovely trip. The girls had the week off, and the Frasers' were away; so as long as I had my work caught up, my time was my own.

Monday started out a fairly nice day with fleecy clouds in the sky as we left Glasgow by train, heading north via Stirling and Callander past Loch Lubnaig and Glen Ogle, and running along Glen Dochart to Crainlarich. The scenery was beautiful and we just sat and admired the magnificence of the passing peaceful countryside and rolling hills. The train made a ten-minute stop at Crainlarich, so we had time for a spot of tea before beginning the last lap of our journey through Glen Lochy to Dalmally, and through the Pass of Brander to Connel, and finally to Oban.

We were really ready for refreshments and rest as we pulled in to the station, and after inquiring around a bit we found a lovely little cottage with a bed and breakfast sign at the gate and were made most welcome by the middle-aged lady who owned the cottage. She treated us like daughters, insisting on serving us tea and scones before turning in for the night, and with the help of a bed warmer we were made very comfortable and had an excellent night's sleep.

The next morning, after a very filling breakfast of porridge, bacon and eggs, and more scones and tea, we made our way to the Oban pier for the steamer to the Island of Mull and Iona. Many people were making their way up the gangplank to the Grenadier. Some would be planning to go to Tobermory. Some would be heading for places like Salen and Staffa, but still others were making their way to the sacred Isle of Iona. The day was beautiful, and for this we considered ourselves extremely lucky. We made our way to the upper deck as the boat slowly turned out of the harbor heading northwest into the Firth of Lorne, skirting the northern shore of the Island of Kerrera. We stood near the railing and the seagulls followed in the wake of the boat. The deck was crowded with people and some of them were feeding the gulls while the huge birds sat on the railing here and there.

Dorothy and Janet decided to go down to the lower deck to get some tea and pastries and Elizabeth and I were to keep their place at the railing. It was about this time that I first saw Ian. He was standing near the railing a little further along and he was pointing out the scenery to a friend. He had blond hair with adorable waves and stood straight and tall, although he was of medium stature. His smile was particularly charming, and his eyes were an attractive blue. I saw all this in one glance over Elizabeth's shoulder, but before I could draw her attention to him, Dorothy and Janet were back on deck with the scones and tea. The tea just hit the spot and we were fairly enjoying ourselves as we sipped it and took in the scenery. Dorothy and Janet chose to move further up the deck, but Elizabeth and I liked our chosen place.

I was talking to Elizabeth quite intently while holding my tea in my left hand and pointing out the scenery with my right hand in which I held my scone, when I suddenly felt someone touching my left elbow ever so gently.

"Don't you think you should be kind and give that poor bird some?" A man's voice mockingly laughed as I turned to see who was talking to me. It was the same young man I had seen a few minutes before, further along the railing. He was smiling down at me in a most charming way and it was only natural for me to smile back and say.

"I think you're right — but — Oh!" Before I could finish my sentence, the bird had nipped a piece of the scone right out of my hand.

"I told you so," he chuckled. "I've been standing watching you and every time you moved your hand out and in, the bird followed it about an inch away. They really are beautiful creatures aren't they?" he continued as I proceeded to feed the bird the rest of my scone. Elizabeth winked and, quietly excusing herself, moved further down the deck.

"He can have my scone but not my tea," I replied as I sipped my tea again. "Isn't the scenery beautiful on this sail?"

"It most certainly is. Have you ever been to Iona before?" he queried as he moved closer to the railing and the seagull flew away, realizing he wasn't going to get any more.

"No, I haven't, but I've heard about it all my life and I've always wanted to see it."

"I've been to Iona several times before but I love it so, and my friend hasn't seen it, so here I am."

He studied me for a moment and then hesitatingly continued, "I've been studying the history of the Island. Would you like me to show you around when we get there?"

His sincere smile and gentleness of manner convinced me of his kindness, and I assured him I would be delighted. He then introduced me to his friend and, I in turn introduced him and his friend to Elizabeth. As good fortune would have it, Elizabeth and Richard liked one another at first sight, too. Two other boys had become interested in Dorothy and Janet and although we all stayed together for the rest of the trip, Ian always stayed at my side.

As the boat docked at the pier of Salen on the Sound of Mull, we stayed at the railing and watched as a few passengers made their way down the gang plank and some got into coaches that had been waiting for the arrival of the boat. These coaches would make their way to different points on the island for the local passengers.

By late morning we were heading north to Tobermory, keeping close to the shore of Mull. When the steamer docked at Tobermory, much activity took place as passengers got on and off at this important dock. We then got on our way again around the northern shore of the island past Quinish Point and Caliach Point to the entrance of Calgary Bay.

At noon we all went below deck for lunch, and I thoroughly enjoyed the fellowship of our group, now grown to eight.

Back again on deck, we managed to find seats for the next lap of our journey south, past the Treshnish Isles heading towards Staffa, the last stop before Fionnphort and Iona. It had grown a bit chilly, but we didn't mind as we were sitting close together with our knees wrapped in a blanket.

"It would be a real thrill to take a trip across the Island of Mull someday," Ian mused as we watched the picturesque shore unfold before us. "I'd love to visit the rugged Glen More. They say there is always a wild and romantic atmosphere about that Glen with its high mountains, gorgeous lakes, and beautiful valleys.

"Have you ever heard the story of the battle that took place halfway through the Glen where a cairn stands in memory of Ewan MacLaine? They say his head was struck off during a battle as he rode downhill and his headless body was carried for some considerable distance before falling. Then there's the tale of his Father's capture and imprisonment in Duart Castle and his escape. That's another place I'd like to visit, the ruins of Duart Castle, which was built in 1250 but put to fire and the sword by the Duke of Argyll in 1688. It was the stronghold of the Chiefs of Glen Maclean and there is quite a bit of talk that the new chief, Sir Fitzroy Maclean, is soon going to restore it so that it could again be the castle of the Chiefs of Clan Maclean.

"The mountain Ben More itself must be a sight to see, stretching to its complete splendor at a modest 3,000 feet. I imagine one would have to travel by coach or horse back if they ever hoped to see it."

Everything was exciting and fascinating having Ian by my side to describe it all to me. He seemed so well-informed and intelligent, and his eyes sparkled as his enthusiasm grew. Sitting nestled together under the robe with the afternoon sun warming us, I began day dreaming as the boat buffeted the waves off the Atlantic and we headed south towards the southwestern projection of the island.

I wondered how many romances had taken place over the centuries on this island and in its glens. How many other men had reached out to hold a maiden's hand and squeeze it ever so gently, as Ian was doing now? How many other men had reached their arm around the waistline of a young woman for the first time, as Ian was doing now? I was thrilled and I had the desire to stop time, so that I could enjoy this unmistakable feeling forever.

"This is indeed an interesting shoreline but I wish we could visit Loch Scridain just north of this part of the island. There is quite a legend told about that Loch. Do you know it?"

"No, I don't believe I've heard that one."

"Well, they say the Loch was carved out of the countryside by the devil." Ian winked and squeezed my hand as he went on, "Legend has it that the devil and Saint Columba had an argument at the top of Ben More, and when the saint won the battle he pushed the devil over the precipice and everywhere the devil bounced, as he fell down the hillside, ledges were formed. The last fall created such a deep cleft that the sea rushed in and filled it up, creating the Loch."

Ian told his tales in such an interesting way I did not notice the time passing, but slowly the steamer neared the southwestern tip of the island and made its way south into the Sound of Iona to dock at Fionnphort. It was then we saw the red granite that the island is famous for.

"Mull granite has been used in buildings all over the world," he went on. "In London it was used in Westminster Abby, Albert Memorial, and Blackfriar's bridges, to name a few."

"Oh look, Ian, over there, see the rainbow. The dock is wet. They have just had a shower. I love rainbows, do you?"

"I think you should make a wish on it," Ian suggested.

"I certainly will," I answered, closing my eyes tightly and wishing with all my heart that the excited feeling I had for Ian would continue and flourish and that Ian would somehow keep in touch with me after this trip.

We had to wait our turn at the hamlet of Fionnphort to board a small ferry which crossed the Sound of Iona to the Sacred Isle of Iona. The boat was a tiny one and difficult to get into, so Ian got in first and steadied it for me. He sat close to me, putting his arm around my shoulder as we crossed the sound, and one time when I turned suddenly to look at him, I found him studying me with his beautiful deep blue eyes. I could feel myself melting and a contentment coming over me I had never known before. Was this love? Love at first sight? Oh surely not, I scarcely knew him. Infatuation? That was it. I smiled back at him and his eyes thrilled me again, so I decided I wouldn't look at him that closely for a while.

"Well here we are," he exclaimed jubilantly, "on the Sacred Isle of Iona, where St. Columba landed on the eve of Pentecost around 563." He helped me out of the boat again, and up the stony hill and along a path for a distance of about a mile until we came to the ruins of the old Abbey Church of St. Mary, restored in the sixteenth century when rebuilt upon the foundations which were founded and built by Benedictine around the year 1200. That church, having been built on the site of St. Columbia's church of about 560, and before Columba it is believed the Druid's had one of their Druid Circles on the same site.

"The Duke of Argyll presented these buildings to the Church of Scotland about nine or ten years ago, and I imagine that is who is working on them now. They certainly have a huge task to perform."

Everywhere we went Ian explained things to me. It was most delightful and I realized he was very clever and learned, as well as mannerly. He slipped his hand through my arm and guided me over to St. Columba's Shrine. It was a very tiny chapel with a small altar, and on each side of the altar was a stone shelf with a damask cloth upon it.

"I understand," Ian began to explain, "that in days following Columba's death, a sacred bone of the Saint was encrusted in jewels and placed on the left side, while his Book, his Staff and his Bell was placed on the right." We saw St. John's cross standing at the front of the Shrine, and then we noticed two other crosses, the Maclean's Cross of the fifteenth century and Saint Martin's Cross of the tenth century.

We then walked up a little hill of rocks to what seemed almost a lookout, but what proved to be St. Columba's cell. "This was his studying place," Ian continued. "These bluish stones, rising to a height of three or four feet, would form the walls of his hut. They believe the walls would probably have been made of thatch. The slanting gray rock would likely have been his couch, and that set of rocks over there which looks like a fire-place would have been his seat when a wooden board was placed across the two granite ends."

Before we left the island, we visited the St. Oran's Cemetery, a grave-yard of ancient Kings, including England's Malcolm, MacBeth and Dun-can, many kings of Scotland, four kings of Norway, and one king of France. The St. Oran's chapel that sits at the edge of the graveyard had a medieval floor which lay open to the stars. This would be another job for the restorers of these ancient buildings, however, the doorway was intact and it dated back to 1200. The road leading to the cemetery could scarcely be seen, but here and there protruded through the grass. It too would date back to the twelfth century.

Another short walk brought us again to the jetty at the water's edge near Iona Village and as we climbed back into this fragile ferry our eyes scanned the far shore of Mull across the Sound of Iona and saw the village of Fionnphort, our destination, again.

Our journey back in the Grenadier steamer was every bit as thrilling as our afternoon sail had been. After a delicious high tea with the group, Ian and I made our way back to the deck. Slowly, the evening shadows fell across the water and the moon appeared dimly on the horizon, but the stars could not be seen as it had begun to rain lightly. It was while we were stand-ing on the deck in the rain under an umbrella that we had our first kiss.

I knew very little about this man, and yet his touch thrilled me, his eyes bewitched me, and his lips spelt heaven.

"Are you planning to return home tomorrow?" he asked as we docked at Oban.

"Oh, we had planned to stay and see some of Oban tomorrow, and then take a roundabout trip home if we could through Glencoe."

"Would you mind very much if we tagged along?" he hesitatingly ven-tured.

"Well no, of course not, but tomorrow could be a very boring day where men are concerned." I laughingly teased and the apologizing went on, "Buying gifts for those back home."

"Oh that doesn't sound boring at all, in fact it sounds rather fascinat-ing. Perhaps you would help me buy something for my mother and sister. I know they have beautiful Iona stone here, and sometimes you can find a rare piece of jewelry made with it. It is not as plentiful as it once was, and Mother would like a broach made of it if that can be found. My sister has her heart set on a St. Columba Cross on a chain if I can find one.

"Other things we could do, to fill in the day, would be to visit the fish-ing docks as they haul in their catch in the evening, and I'd love to climb to Pulpit Hill to see the city from there and the beautiful view of the Firth.

I'd even like to see the coliseum-like building that McCaig built to relieve unemployment. They call it 'McCaig's Folly,' I believe."

Wednesday proved a wonderful day. I'll never forget it. Everything we did was perfect. I will always think of Oban as a romantic and most interesting town. The following day we caught a train north, following the coastline via Lynn of Lorne, Loch Creran, Loch Linnhe, and finally Loch Leven to Ballachulish near Glencoe. The scenery was beautiful. We had a problem finding accommodation that night, but were made comfortable finally in a boarding house. Next morning we made an early start by coach through the Glen, stopping for a picnic on the way near the Iona Cross, erected in 1883 by a McDonald in memory of his clansmen who died in the massacre of 1692; and Ian wondered if any of his relatives had died in that Massacre.

Arriving in Clifton that night, again we found bed and breakfast and took the first train out of Tyndrum to Glasgow in the morning. At the station in Glasgow, Ian held my hand ever so tightly and said, "I have never met anyone like you before and I have no intention of losing you. Let's meet here a week from tomorrow and we'll take a sail up Loch Lommond together?"

I said I would, and he squeezed my hand and touched my long red hair ever so lightly.

"I'll be living for that day," he said as he waved his hand and walked toward the platform designated for Edinburgh.

After his departure my cousins giggled and teased me, but then they commented, "All kidding aside, I think he really likes you, and I am sure that you will be seeing him quite often in the future. Are you sure you really want us around next week?"

"Of course, silly," I answered and blushed as I waved good-bye.

Chapter 12
Cinderella

The next week seemed never-ending. I thought of Ian day and night. I re-lived the previous trip a hundred times over – I could picture him stand-ing beside me at the railing of the boat. I could feel his gentle touch on my elbow as he began to talk about the seagulls. I could hear his voice describing the Isle of Mull and Iona, but the romantic moment of his kiss was the one I thought of most. Was I in love, I wondered? It was really too soon to tell. I really knew nothing about him. I didn't know anything about his family, his education, or his ambition. Of course, he knew nothing about me either. We hadn't discussed everyday things. We had just reveled in God's beautiful world as we found it and enjoyed each other's company to the full.

Only one fear reared its ugly head in my mind every so often, and that was the fear that he wouldn't be at the station on Saturday. However, every time I had negative feelings, I reassured myself with his last words — "I'll be living for that day." He just had to mean that.

I wondered what his life style was like and who he really was? He cer-tainly was well-educated, indeed quite scholarly and he held himself so proudly. His clothes, too, were immaculate and his grooming perfect.

I felt that I in turn must be perfect to measure up to his standard. I took time on Wednesday afternoon to go shopping for a new suit and pair of shoes. I admit I went a bit overboard on the price, but this was indeed a special occasion and I wanted to look my best.

Friday night found me working hard with the curling irons so my hair would be its prettiest in the morning. My corset was fairly tight, but I fig-ured I could stand anything to make myself beautiful for him.

I was awake before the alarm went off in the morning and imme-diately got dressed, then, combing my hair this way and that I tried to discover the prettiest hair style possible. Finally, descending the staircase almost half an hour later I stopped before the huge mirror on the landing to see how I looked and I was very pleased with the reflection. I felt beautiful at that moment, with a feeling that I could conquer the world, let alone one young man. I had made it a habit of using the front staircase quite often during Mrs. Fraser's absence. I loved the majestic look of the stairs and the imperialistic feeling I got as I descended them, and when I left the house by the side entrance the staff sent me on my way merrily with many good wishes and compliments ringing in my ears.

Confidently, I walked to the tramway and was soon at the pier. Now my pompous feelings were beginning to wane and I felt a tugging at my stomach that spelled fear. I anxiously walked up to the wicket for the Loch Lommond sail, but saw no one there. My heart sank.

Perhaps he had changed his mind. Perhaps something had happened and he couldn't make it. Then, fear taking hold of me again, I thought perhaps he had never intended coming and that he had had a good joke out of me. I turned and looked up at the poster on the wall and the notice board about the sail. My eyes were beginning to blur. I mustn't start to cry here, I thought, it would be too humiliating.

Suddenly I felt two firm hands on my shoulders. "Well, hello, there. I am very sorry to have kept you waiting. I met a friend on the train from Edinburgh and chatted too long. Let's hurry, or we'll be late."

His firm hand was clasping mine now and he pulled me quickly over to the wicket. Then he guided me, with his hand on my elbow, over to the pier and the boat. Finally, safely aboard just before the whistle blew and the boat began to move, Ian looked at me.

"You're a real beauty, Nell. You look just wonderful. It's been a long wait since last week. Has it been long for you?"

"Aye, it has that," I smiled into his deep blue eyes. I felt my body quiver a bit as I realized the effect his eyes had on me. They penetrated, they dominated, they thrilled. I mustn't allow myself to be carried away too fast, I rebuked myself inwardly. His charm was terrific, but I must not show him I felt this way. Be casual, I told myself. Keep calm, I told myself, but as the trip progressed I could feel myself losing this control battle and I realized that I was as a child, standing admiring, loving, and listening most of the time as he expounded on the glories of our history and the beauty of our Scottish landscape.

"You fit in with this landscape, Nell," he suddenly declared, putting his arm around my waist as we stood at the railing drinking in the beauty of Loch Lommond. "You complete the picture. Like a beautiful girl in a painting that adds that perfect touch. You're it. You make the trip worthwhile, exciting, enjoyable - perfect."

I was exuberant as I returned home. He had asked me to meet him and go to a theatre the following week, and then out to dinner after. Another day we went on a trip to Ayr, and on still another occasion we visited Stirling. On those last two trips I said nothing about my previous visits to these sights with my Father and brother, as I felt it would have spoiled Ian's thrill of storytelling.

As we returned from our visit to Stirling he asked me to join him in the sweetie shop next to the station for a bite of supper. He said he wanted to take the later train back, as he had something very special to ask me.

We went inside the wee shop and found a comfortable table in the corner of the room near a beautiful old fireplace. The room was warm, but my hands were like ice as I pondered in my mind what he was going to say.

He ordered and as the waitress left, Ian stretched his hand across the table and reached for mine. "I have never known anyone I have liked as much as you," he began as he took my hand in his two strong ones and drew it to his mouth to kiss my fingertips.

I felt somewhat embarrassed and attempted to pull my hand away from his grip but he would have none of it.

"Tonight is a special occasion for you and me," he continued hesitatingly. "I have fallen in love with you, Nell, and I would dearly like you to consent to marrying me."

"I, I —-" I stuttered, quite dumbfounded by his statement.

"No, no don't make a decision here and now. Think of it for a while and then let me know. I have been thinking that you will have to meet my parents and sister, and I would like to meet your family."

"I love you, Ian," I stated confidently now that I had my second wind, "and I would like nothing better than to marry you." Our eyes met in a solemn and yet exciting moment, then I went on. "My mother passed away when I was only eight, and my Father has remarried for the third time so there is really no one I must consult on my side, but I would love to meet your family."

"Darling, I'm very sorry about your folks, but I'm thrilled you're going to marry me." He smiled, his hand raising my hand for another kiss. "How about coming to see my family at a coming out party that my parents are giving for my sister? I told my mother about you, and she said that it would be a suitable occasion for you to meet them and our other friends. By the way, it is a formal occasion, so I'll see you for the first time in a gorgeous gown. Of course, you don't need a gown to make you gorgeous you look simply scrumptious in that suit. I'll remember you all my life in that suit, sitting at this table when I asked you to marry me."

All through the meal he went on in like manner, not giving me too much time to talk, and I began wondering just what kind of a family he had come from and what kind of a family I would be marrying into. As he continued to talk across the table to me, I began to see him in an entirely new light. He seemed suddenly far removed from me, as if he were a stranger. He didn't seem like the Ian I knew at all. He spoke of his pending visit to France. He spoke of his father's business and how he someday wished to own it himself. He spoke of finishing his course at University, possibly in France. It was the first time he had ever opened up about himself or his family or his plans for life. He was talking continuously about our future together and wrapping me up in a neat bundle with it.

"If you have to go back to University your parents will never approve of a marriage at the present time," I ventured.

"Oh yes, they will," he laughed. "Father has been hoping for a long time that I'd get married and settle down with a lovely young girl. Now I know that you're the one. He also wishes me to finish my course before I go into his business."

Just about that time he noticed the time and said he'd have to hurry to catch his train. "I'll put you in a cabbie first," he said, "and then I'll know you'll be safe." He hailed a passing cab and just as I was about to enter it he said, "By the way, I'll have another surprise for you next week, too. I've just bought myself a motor car. I'll pick you up at your house next Saturday. I'll have Sis send you a formal invitation, and I'll come for you at one o'-clock in the afternoon, as it will take quite a while to drive to Edinburgh. You can change at our house. Mother says it's fine for you to stay over and I'll drive you home again on Sunday. Good-bye darling, I love you," he whispered, giving me a quick kiss on the cheek.

I was slightly dazed as I sat in the cabbie driving home. That stranger back there had asked me to marry him and I had said yes. That stranger back there must be a member of a very wealthy family, for he had spoken of Oxford, business, formals, and motor cars. The words whizzed and blurred alternately in my mind. Only the very wealthy owned motor cars. He must be, he had to be, oh no, oh yes. He was rich! Very rich! Then a cold chill ran over me, I was poor! I was worse than poor, I was a servant in a rich man's house.

As I sat there riding and listening to the clop, clop of the horses' hooves on the pavement, I turned colder and colder inside. I hadn't told him anything about myself. He hadn't asked, he didn't seem to want to know. He just seemed so much in love that he bubbled over with his plans for the future, all of which I was a part. Who had he thought I was?

Obviously, he knew my address. Probably got it from my cousin, and he would know that everyone living in that district of Glasgow was wealthy, so no doubt assumed that I was, too. What would he think about me when he found out I was "a maid." Would I be like Cinderella, would he love me anyway?

Of course he would, I thought. I'll be Cinderella with two stepmothers instead of one, and I had no ugly stepsisters to interfere. I laughed a little.

Then I began to dream. I'll just have to be the prettiest girl at the ball. I'll wear a gorgeous gown and have my hair styled exquisitely. I could just see myself descending a beautiful stairway with Ian at the bottom to meet me.

That night I slept like a baby, dreaming of being a princess in a golden silk gown with my prince coming for me in a motor car.

In the morning I awoke to reality. How could I afford an ordinary gown, let alone a gorgeous one? I had spent far too much on my clothes lately as it was, and my savings were at an all-time low. Oh, horrors! What would people say seeing me going away with a man, bag and baggage in a motor car, and not returning until next day? What if they told Mrs. Fraser when she returned the following week? Indeed, how and when should I explain my situation to Ian? When he drove up the circular drive at the front of the Fraser home and Kitty told him to meet me at the side entrance, he would know I was *a maid*. What would he say? What would he do? The questions pounded in my head all day as I attempted to do my work. I went from a warm feeling to a cold chill, alternately. Finally I decided I'd take things as they came. I'd tell him as soon as I could and I'd hope for the best. After all, he had said he loved me and that he wished to marry me.

Closing my mind to all worries and looking forward to the big occasion coming my way, the week soon passed. The invitation arrived with a lovely note from his mother, inviting me to stay at their home for the night. I borrowed some money from Kitty the cook, whom I had confided in during Mrs. Fraser's absence, and bought myself a beautiful gown. It was made of deep blue velvet with lace trim and had a pompous bustle on the back. The neck line was fairly low and showed off my single strand of pearls to advantage. I bought a pair of dainty dancing slippers and a pair of long white gloves.

Saturday finally arrived and I dressed in my best suit, piled my hair high on my head, and wore my lovely new ostrich-plumed hat and long white gloves. I was pleased with the girl in the mirror in my room, but I figured I'd just slip down the front staircase again and take a full length look at myself. I carefully carried my suitcase down and laid it on the landing as I turned this way and that studying my reflection very critically in the huge mirror.

Kitty came into the hall just then and looking up at me said, "You certainly look a lovely one in that suit, but wait until he sees you in that gown you've bought. We'll all be pulling for you here at home, Nell. Richard! Come and see Nell for a minute," she called as the chauffeur passed along the hall.

"Miss Sweenie, you ought to put his eye out." He mounted the staircase and lifted my suitcase saying as he did it, "He sure is a lucky man. Here, let me help you carry your bag?"

At that precise moment the doorbell rang. Kitty, standing in full maid's uniform did the normal and natural thing. She opened the door. There stood Ian, dressed in his usual immaculate fashion, although more so.

"I've come to call for Miss Sweenie," he politely announced.

"Certainly: Sir. Step right in," was Kitty's chirp reply.

I descended the gorgeous staircase with Richard preceding me, carrying my luggage. He nodded as he passed Ian and Ian said, "Just put the luggage in the back seat, please."

Before I knew it, I was in his arms at the foot of the stairs and his lips were pressing ever so gently against mine as Kitty quietly slipped discreetly away into the shadows.

"Darling, I've something to tell you," I blurted as soon as I had caught my breath.

"Tell me later darling, we must hurry," he replied as he rushed me out of the house and stood beaming with pride pointing to his motor car.

"Oh darling, it's beautiful," I dared to say, wondering all the while if it would hold together, if the tires were all right. I'd heard so much about tire failure in these new auto-buggies.

"Do you really think so?" he beamed. "Well then, get in and we'll give it the supreme test. We'll see if it meets with your approval to ride in. It's the best on the market, you know. It's a Rolls Royce."

"A Rolls Royce!" I stammered while I gathered my sparse knowledge of the auto-buggy machine. Rolls Royce was THE most expensive make of motor cars, wasn't it? Just how wealthy was Ian anyway?

Taking the thoughts right out of my mind, he continued, "Yes, it's the best money can buy."

He had cranked it, and now with the motor running the car shook quite a bit. He soon climbed into the driver's seat beside me and we were off. He certainly knew how to handle it, as we took corners and stops quite easily. It was rather frightening driving through Glasgow in it and many people stopped to look. I felt quite thrilled with the attention and unconsciously took on an aristocratic air. My hat was forever trying to come off so my hand anchored itself on top of the flimsy thing.

"You'll have to get yourself one of those new tie-on hats for riding, my darling," he mused. Honking the horn at frightened and curious people as we made our way through the city seemed to please Ian. Finally, we were out in the country and it was easier driving and easier riding. My mind relaxed somewhat and then my old dilemma came back. A little voice inside me said, "You have to tell him. Tell him now and get it over with. Tell him so that at least he is under no illusion about you at the party." So I ventured forth in fear and trembling again.

"Ian, remember I said I had something important to tell you? Will it be alright to tell you now?"

"Of course, darling, I'm afraid I have been carried away with my car. What have you got in that pretty little head of yours that's bothering you? You should have no worries at all you know, you're just too pretty for worries. Don't you realize that? Worries will give you lines and wrinkles, even gray hair. I'm going to keep you as free of worries as I possibly can when we're married so that you won't grow old too quickly on me. Now darling, what was it you wanted to tell me?"

Haltingly I stammered out, "It's about me — my family — my father — my job!"

"I love you remember, nothing about you or your family can change that," Ian beamed.

"But, you don't understand, Ian. I love you too, but will it be alright? I'm a —" before I could utter the word 'maid' there was a loud bang and then a terrible jerking and bumping. We had a flat tire. Ian got out of the car, and so did I. He took off his jacket and rolled up his sleeves.

"Well, I guess here is where I change my first tire," he laughed as he got out the necessary tools. I thought how wonderful he was not to curse and swear as many a man would have done under similar circumstances.

"I'll spread out this rug under the tree for you and you can watch me," he continued as he prepared a place for me to sit comfortably. "I brought along a little lunch, we'll just eat it here when I'm finished. I had intended eating it further along the road, but this will do fine."

It took a while for him to fix the tire, but I couldn't bring myself to talk about my problem and he had obviously forgotten about it. We ate a delightful lunch and some pastries and were soon on our way again. The closer we got to Edinburgh the more afraid I became, and to mention my plight now seemed impossible.

Before I could believe it, we had reached Edinburgh and were making our way through the traffic. Many people ogled us again as there weren't too many motor cars around, especially the Rolls Royce.

"Well, here we are," Ian exclaimed as we rounded a corner and came up to a large stone gateway with a small stone house adjacent to the gate. A little old, weather-beaten man came out of the house to greet us.

"Good evening, master Ian," he spoke with the utmost respect in his voice and then turning to me continued, "Good evening Ma'am." Then he opened the gate and waited while we drove through.

"Thank you, Robin," replied Ian as he waved good-bye.

The driveway went straight up to the front door. The house was magnificent. It had height and grandeur, dignity and respectability. It stood there, a symbol of what the family stood for. Ian parked over to one side of the large veranda and then came around the car to help me step down.

"Now to meet my mother!" he exclaimed. "Father will not be home until later and Catherine will be too busy getting ready. You won't meet her until the party this evening."

He guided me up the stairway to the lovely veranda, and across the veranda to the double door entrance way. He rang the bell, but walked right in and the butler came to meet us.

"Oh, sir, you're home. Your mother has been quite anxious about you and that motor car. I'll tell her you've arrived safely."

The moment he walked away Ian began to take me in his arms, but I pushed him away. "No. Not now, not here! What would your mother think of me?"

His mother appeared shortly, and I was glad I hadn't been caught in Ian's arms. She was a very stern-looking woman, with hair severely pulled back at the temples, although worn fairly high on the top of her head. Her brow was deep, signifying intelligence and dignity, while her dress was of a stern nature, plain and in dark navy. She held herself regally and seemed to stiffen her chin a little more and lifted her nose on a little higher tilt, as she sized me up and down, while making her way across the reception room and into the center hall.

"So, you're Nell that Ian has been talking so much about. We are happy to have you with us, my dear, on such an auspicious occasion. You must be weary from traveling in that wretched machine Ian has, so I will have Grace see you to the guest room immediately so you can freshen up. It will not be long before the guests will be arriving." Signaling to the maid, she continued. "Grace, do please see Nell —" she hesitated on the name and then repeated it. "See Nell to her room. — Your name must be short for something else," she queried. "Is it Helen?"

"Yes, Ma'am it is," I stumbled.

"Well, would you mind if we called you Helen from now on? Nell sounds so common. I once had a poodle by that name. Probably that's why it doesn't sound right. Would you mind?"

"Not at all, Ma'am, err Mrs. McDonald."

Grace showed me up the spiral staircase to my room, and as I walked behind her I experienced the strange feeling of being in a favored place in a large home. Grace's job was usually my job. What had I gotten myself into? What would Ian's mother say when she found out? What would Ian say? Would I wake up from this dream as from a nightmare, or would it all work out like Cinderella?

I stood staring at my reflection in the large three-sided mirror near the window now. Grace had left the room and I was alone. I was a mixture of tiredness, happiness, uneasiness, fearfulness, and excitement. When would be the right moment to tell Ian who I really was? Obviously, he thought that Mrs. Fraser's home was mine and after my beautiful descent down the stairs into his arms with maid and chauffeur on hand to help me, what else could he think? Oh well, no time to worry about such things now. I must get dressed in my blue velvet gown and be ready to go down stairs when they called. The bedroom was gorgeous, the curtains and bed coverlet magnificent. I felt like a princess, and after I had changed I looked like one.

Soon someone knocked on the door. It was Grace to tell me that the guests were arriving and she would escort me to the library where I would join Ian.

Ian stood near the fireplace. He, too, had changed to his full dress attire, and his swallow-tailed coat gave him an air of elegance beyond description. He came to meet me, and then taking me by the arm to guide me, he proceeded with a host of introductions. His father arrived and entered the room with much dignity and gracious poise as he, too, met a stream of guests.

Finally, it was my turn to be introduced to him.

"Well, how-do-you-do, Helen? My son has been telling me what a fine person you are and how very fond of you he is. I am very happy to make your acquaintance on this auspicious occasion."

There it was, the introduction was over and I hadn't had to say a word, just a smile and hand shake. Finally, Ian's sister made her breathtaking entrance. She was pretty, and haughty, and had many gentlemen at her elbow, falling over one another to do her favors. She was just eighteen, and I couldn't help thinking of the difference between her life and mine, including these birthday celebrations.

Now that all introductions were over, the guests were served punch or wine, whichever they desired, and then we were led into the richly draped high-ceilinged dining room with the elegant deeply carved dining room suite. We partook of a delicious meal, followed by a fabulous dessert, and of course a delightfully decorated cake for Catharine.

After the meal, Ian said he would like to take me out into the garden while things were getting organized for the reception and dance. We walked out on the terrace and down a small flight of stairs onto the lawn. After walking a few steps further to where we couldn't be seen from the house, Ian pulled me to him roughly, and kissed me soundly on the lips.

"I could hardly wait for that one," he sighed. "Darling, I love you."

"Ian," I ventured. "I have something to tell you."

"I have something to tell you, too," he glowed. "Father is sending me to a French University to finish my last years. Won't that be exciting? Just think, we'll live in France. Have you ever been there? Do you know the language?"

"No, I'm sorry I don't know the language and I have never been there," I replied, my head drooping somewhat. "Don't you think we should wait until after your University training Ian? I wouldn't mind."

"Not on your life, Nell, err ah, Helen. Father is going to announce our engagement tonight."

"Oh Ian," I pleaded, tugging at his arm as we made our way up the staircase again towards the dining hall just as the music began. "Do you not think we should talk a little before any announcement is made?"

Ian's father met us at the doorway and taking hold of my arm firmly and reassuringly, asked for the dance. Ian protested losing the first dance, but his father made light of his protests and declared he wanted to get to know his new daughter better.

As we glided over the floor, my thoughts raced. Dare I say the truth to Ian's father, when Ian himself didn't know?

"You dance divinely, my dear. Do you come to Edinburgh often? I can't tell you how glad I am to see Ian taking an interest in you as he has. He has been somewhat of a gadabout up until he met you. You know, the usual thing, one girl after another but never settling on one, but you're different. He's acting differently. He speaks much more about the future now than before. Tell me, has he told you about France? I have a little home on the outskirts of Paris which you will be able to live in while he finishes his studies. It's not very large, you understand, but ample. Tell me what does your Father do for a living? 'Building,' well, well! Now, that's a good trade to be in just now. He must have a good business head. Well, my dear, you dance divinely and now I must escort you back to Ian, or he will be very unhappy."

The conversation and dance had both gone beautifully. I had answered all questions with yes or no and a few non-committal sentences. Even the question about my father's work I had simply answered with the word "builder." How long could I keep my secret?

I danced most of the dances with Ian until an hour later, when Ian's father stood near the orchestra and began to make an announcement. "I should like to announce the engagement of my son Ian to Miss Helen Sweenie." All eyes were on me, and Ian was leading me over to the platform for all to see and shake hands with in congratulations. He slipped the engagement ring on my finger in front of everyone, and my head began to swim in the sea of faces before me. This just had to be a dream. Any moment now I'd wake up to find it was all my imagination and that I was safe in my own bed. Cinderella had had a bit of magic worked out for her, but here I was all by myself. No fairy godmother in sight. I didn't even have to run away at the stroke of midnight.

The evening finished as lovely as it had begun, with Ian kissing me at the foot of the stairs before I made my exit to retire for the night. I climbed the curved staircase, turned and threw a kiss to him and then made my way along the hall to my elegant room. Once inside I primped and bowed and curtsied before the triple mirror, looking admiringly at myself from every angle. I did make a pretty picture with my long golden hair flowing down my back in gorgeous curls that bobbed ever so little as I walked. The blue velvet suited me too. Even my party shoes were exquisite as I made them peek out under my long skirt. I was the "Belle of the Ball." I had captured the prize of the night. I was happy, I was in love. Eventually, I realized that even that gorgeous creature in the mirror needed rest and tomorrow would prove a very big day too, and so to bed.

In the morning, when I awoke with Grace knocking on the door, things didn't have quite such a glow to them. Grace announced I was to have breakfast with the family in the breakfast room off the dining room in half an hour. I quickly dressed and brushed my hair. In my dark green suit, I was ready to travel right after breakfast.

As I entered the breakfast room Ian's mother sternly said, "Good morning, Helen. Did you have a good night's rest?" Scarcely waiting for a reply, she continued, "I must say I was a bit perturbed about the announcement last night. I do not understand why someone didn't tell me about it."

"But, mother, you were feeling ill last evening and went off to bed early so we were unable to tell you beforehand."

"That seems like a pretty weak excuse, Ian. What is it about this girl that you don't wish me to know?"

"Nothing, Mother, nothing!"

"What is your Father's business, Helen?"

"A builder," Ian's Father interrupted before I could get a chance to answer.

"A builder of what? — - Ships?"

"No, houses," I replied.

"And where do you live in Glasgow?"

I was becoming hot and flustered. My heart was pounding in my breast. My hands were becoming clammy. What if she found out the truth here and now before I had a chance to tell Ian? I cleared my throat and answered, "On High View Street." It was the truth, I did, but it was not my father's home, as she would think.

"Next Wednesday I am going to visit friends in Glasgow. I will also visit your home, Helen, and have an interview with your parents."

"Oh, I'm sorry but my mother passed away when I was only eight."

"Very well then, I'll speak to your father."

"Well he, he's away this week."

"Very well, I'll speak to your guardian. You must have one or someone who looks after you and the household when your father's away. Haven't you?"

"Yes, Mrs. Fraser," I blurted out before I could think of anything else to say.

"Good, I'll visit you on Wednesday at three o'clock sharp."

"Yes ma'am, I mean, Mrs. McDonald."

Ian drove me home that day but my conversation was very spasmodic.

"What is bothering you, Nell?" he questioned. "Didn't you like my folks - my house – the party? Have I said anything? Did Mother say anything? She is a bit curt at times, but you'll get used to her after a while. She's not as bad as she seems."

"When we stop for lunch I'll tell you, Ian. It's a long story." Then returning to my moody quietness I tried to figure out how I could tell him the truth without incriminating myself. My thoughts ran deep. How could I possibly tell this man of wealth, education, position, and distinction that he was in love with a *maid*? What reaction would the news have? Tell him I must, though, and it might as well be now.

Chapter 13
We Live in Two Separate Worlds

The car chugged to a stop at the side of the road where a lovely stream was lazily making its way to the river. We laid the white linen cloth over the grass and I proceeded to empty the contents of the picnic basket Grace had packed for us onto the linen cloth, as Ian spread a blanket under a tree for us to sit on.

"I'll eat my meal first," Ian joked. "I receive bad news just a little better on a full stomach, and somehow by the look of your face it's *very* bad. How about letting it out, Nell, you're not eating anyway."

I almost choked on my sandwich and tears came to my eyes, as I somehow knew the game was over and I must confess all and suffer the consequences, even though I had no guilt.

"I'm a table maid Ian, just a plain ordinary table maid. I work for Mrs. Fraser on High View Street. That lovely home is not mine, it is where I work. My father is a stonemason and he does build 'houses', and good ones too, but he builds them for a contractor, a Mr. Aikenhead of East Kilbride, and he doesn't have money, only a very modest home in East Kilbride where he lives with his third wife, as I told you. An older brother and sister are married and I have lost an older sister and brother by death."

By this time my face was flushed and tears streamed down my checks. I put my hands over my face and sobbed.

"Don't worry, I knew it was all a dream," I continued. "I knew it was a bubble that would burst. I knew something had to happen between us. It was all too wonderful, too thrilling to last. Now you know who I am, and I'm terribly sorry that I have caused all this trouble. Now please take me home. At least I'll have a wonderful memory."

Ian had been sitting fairly stunned for a while now, while I spoke. His mouth partly open in amazement, but now as I concluded my speech, his mouth gradually curled into a grin and he began to laugh.

"You're a maid, how funny, how utterly fantastic. You don't look like a maid, you don't talk like a maid, you don't act like a maid, but you *are* a maid. What a joke on me. I'd never have guessed it in a thousand years."

"You're laughing at me," I cried.

Coming to me now he placed his one arm around me as he turned my face up towards his.

"You're too beautiful to be a maid, and from now on you won't be a maid, you'll be Mrs. McDonald and that's that. I love you and it doesn't matter what you are or who you are, understand?" he kissed me firmly on the lips. "Now I've got to get you home."

The rest of the ride home was quiet with the obvious questions. What will your family think? What about your mother? Who will she talk to on Wednesday? She'll think I was trying to trick you into marriage.

"Never mind, I can handle her," he muttered, "and if I can't, Father can. Now stop your worrying."

"Will you tell her as soon as you get home, or will you leave that up to me on Wednesday?" I asked hesitatingly.

"Darling, Mother always takes things better from strangers. You tell her yourself and I'll tell Father so he knows when she gets home." He kissed me soundly at the door and said, "Now don't you worry about a thing, future Mrs. McDonald. I love you and that's all that matters."

Oh, how I wished I could feel the same way that he did. I should have been happy that Ian felt this way, but what about his mother? He was more than a wee bit afraid of her, otherwise he would have told her himself. At first when I had told him and he had laughed, I had felt he was laughing at me, but that wasn't the case. Probably I was worrying for nothing again as usual but I couldn't help it. My mind raced to Wednesday and I just knew I couldn't find the words to talk to his mother and make her understand. She was of strong aristocratic stock and the news just wouldn't please her at all. What would I do? What could I do?

Mrs. Fraser arrived home late Sunday night, and it seemed a relief just to have her quiet, unassuming personality around again. She had a serene way with her and she never got ruffled over anything. The only time she seemed to show any outward reaction was in her extreme concern for me. She still thought of me somewhat as a daughter. Oh, if only I had been her daughter, I thought, all my problems would never have arisen. The more I thought about the whole question the idea occurred to me to ask her to talk to Mrs. McDonald on Wednesday. Her calm, reassuring way might be able to calm Mrs. McDonald too. If anyone could do it, she could.

My next problem was what to say to Mrs. Fraser. I approached her at the breakfast table next morning. I began by asking about her trip and before long we were in a long conversation about her travels and experiences. Finally, after what seemed to me an endless amount of time, she asked the inevitable question.

"And how have you been while I've been away? Have you been traveling around with the girls this summer? Have you met any young man that takes your fancy yet?"

The door was wide open so I entered in with as condensed a description of my summer escapades as I dared, and yet still convey to her the facts. As I got to the part about my visit to Ian's home and gave his full name and address and described the home, she looked troubled.

"Oh dear, oh dear." she sighed, "You poor soul!"

"Why? Oh why did this have to happen? Why didn't you meet a nice, kind, loving boy of your own station in life? Why does life always have to be so cruel?" She got up from her chair and began wringing her hands. "Why can't things turn out like Cinderella just once in a while?"

I explained to her about the pending visit from Mrs. McDonald and hesitatingly asked if she would mind speaking to her on my behalf.

"Of course, of course, my child," she replied with no hesitation. "But, remember this: it is a very hard thing to accomplish, this breaking down of barriers between the rich and poor. I am not saying this to dishearten you, but it is a fact of life. We live in two separate worlds. There is no doubt in my mind, none whatsoever, that the love that you hold for one another could easily break this barrier and that you could live happily for the rest of your lives together, but that would be only if in-laws, relatives, and human nature was different than it is.

"The best this situation can offer you is the love of this man for a while. His mother, father, and sister are a haughty lot, for I have heard a great deal about them, and they would not take to this kindly. They would continually throw your background right in your face. You have nothing to be ashamed of, you are employed in good honest labor, but that is not the way they think. You might even find that after a few years, when you couldn't keep up with your husband educationally and socially, that he too would easily lose patience with you, and might even seek another. Not a happy prospect is it? However, I will do what I can on your behalf on Wednesday."

She was seated on the sofa now, and with tears streaming from my eyes, I bent and kissed her and thanked her for everything.

"Take the day off, my child. Have a good cry and begin to forget him for your own sake."

I took her advice. I cried myself out. I thought of Ian, of his family, his position in life and mine, and of Mrs. Fraser's summary of the situation, but I couldn't begin to forget him. I loved him.

By the time Wednesday rolled around I was quite a nervous wreck. Mrs. Fraser had told me to dress in my gray suit and greet Mrs. McDonald at the door and show her to the library. At the appropriate time, Mrs. Fraser would indicate that it was time for tea and I would serve it, although not in uniform.

My knees knocked and my blood ran cold as the hands of the grandfather clock in the hall slowly ticked away the minutes approaching three o'clock. My hands were like ice and my heart felt like lead. My head felt light and I drew a complete blank on the subject which was so important to me.

Suddenly the doorbell rang and I felt an uncanny shiver run through me as though I were about to die on the spot. Courage and obedience with years of practice helped me through. I slowly opened the door and greeted Mrs. McDonald with a cheery "hello" and would she please come in. I helped her off with her coat and hoped she'd had a good trip. She looked down her nose in her typical fashion and replied that she had had a most miserable day so far.

I invited her to follow me along the hall to the library, where Mrs. Fraser would be happy to speak with her on my behalf.

"And just who is this Mrs. Fraser?" she haughtily retorted.

"She's my employer," I matter-of-factly replied.

"She's your what?" she stammered in amazement.

"She's my employer," I repeated as I opened the library door and guided her over to Mrs. Fraser, who was sitting on the sofa near the bay window.

"I should like you to meet Mrs. Fraser, Mrs. McDonald." Then turning to "Mrs. McDonald, I introduced Mrs. Fraser.

"How, do you do?" Mrs. McDonald asked imperialistically, her eyes now examining Mrs. Fraser's face in the better light. "Haven't I seen you before?"

"Yes, I believe so," was Mrs. Fraser's calm reply. "It was at the Tomilties dinner-dance last year, but my husband had spoken about you often before that."

"At the: Tomilties? — Then is your husband the great financial tycoon — *that* Mr. Fraser?'"

"The same - -"

"I don't quite understand. I am indeed honored to be in your presence, but what connection do you have with Helen, with whom my son is considering marriage?"

"I employ Helen."

"As a personal secretary to your husband or yourself?"

"No, as a personal help to me - -"

"In what capacity?"

"As a table maid."

The hammer had fallen. My doom had been sealed. I could tell it by the look on Mrs. McDonald's face. She was flustered at first, taken aback, didn't know whether to take Mrs. Fraser seriously or not, but her calm imperialistic, haughty, stubborn self soon righted itself, and glaring from Mrs. Fraser to me and back to Mrs. Fraser she continued, "What is the meaning of this? Have you played some practical joke on me and my son? A maid, indeed! How did you dare to enter into *my* house as a maid?"

"You didn't ask me what I did for a living; you merely invited your son's fiancée into your home." I didn't have my red hair for nothing.

"It would be nice if you brought us some tea now, Nell," Mrs. Fraser quietly interrupted.

"Yes, of course," I replied, and was mighty glad of the opportunity of slipping out to the kitchen away from Mrs. McDonald's cold, contemptuous, and condemning stare.

In the kitchen, Kitty had the tea and pastries ready and it was merely a case of carrying them back, but I hesitated awhile, trying to get my courage back to face her again.

"How are things going, Nell?" Kitty questioned.

"Awful: so far. I think she's perfectly hateful. How can a perfectly wonderful young man like Ian have a mother like that?" I questioned. "He must take after his father."

"Don't be too sure about that, Nell, he'll have some of his mother in him too. Perhaps you've only seen him under the best of conditions and you've only seen his mother under the worst."

"That's true! Oh Kitty, I'm so nervous. I think I'm shaking too much to take this tea in to her."

"Oh no, you're not. Just get on with it and get it over."

Kitty helped me through the door, and I slowly walked along the corridor to the library door, which was open, but I hesitated before entering.

"Come on in, my dear," called out Mrs. Fraser.

Not a word was spoken as I placed the tray on the table and proceeded to serve it to the two ladies.

"Have a chair, my dear." Mrs. Fraser indicated the one opposite Mrs. McDonald. "We have been talking while you were away, and Mrs. McDonald does not find it possible to accept the fact that you are a table maid. She does not feel that you would make a suitable life companion for her son, and she wishes you to forget the entire idea of courtship or marriage."

"I most certainly do!" emphatically retorted the haughty Mrs. McDonald.

"But what about the fact — that we love each other?" I pleaded, looking from one to the other.

"You think you love him, and he thinks he loves you, however, this is nothing but another one of my son's ridiculously silly summer romances.

He's had them before you know and he'll have them again. However, I must say I never expected him to fall in love with 'a maid'. May I have the ring back, please?"

Slowly and reverently I slipped the ring off my finger, staring at it in disbelief as I handed it to her, and as she continued to discuss her son's romances my mind blanked out on her words. Tears filled my eyes and my bosom heaved with my contained sobs. My life felt empty, my dream of happiness once more had disappeared before my very eyes, through no fault of my own.

I was at the end of another road. Somehow, deep in my heart, I knew that Ian would side with his mother. Oh, not wholeheartedly at first, but as he gave it thought and realized the impact of the differences between us, he would slowly but surely change his mind about me. No prince charming really existed as in the Cinderella story. What King of England, for example, would marry a commoner from the countryside somewhere who had no wealth, let alone royal blood? Would he go to the colonies to find a bride? Never! Then why should I expect an aristocrat to marry a maid? Slowly I walked towards the door, aimlessly, forlorn, deep in thought.

"Nell, would you be so kind as to show Mrs. McDonald to the door, please?" called Mrs. Fraser.

Suddenly the fiery blood of the Scot came to the fore and I haughtily stated.

"Certainly not, she can find her own way out!"

Then I fled to my room and gave vent to my feelings as the tears flowed and drenched my pillow.

Just as I had feared, Ian took his mother's advice. How he really felt I never knew, for he didn't make the effort to come and see me. About three days after his mother's visit, I had a letter from him stating that taking all things into consideration he felt his mother's advice was right and he was sure that we would both get over it, and as time passed we would both come to feel it was the best way after all.

Chapter 14

Depression

I now found myself in another state of numbness, another period in my life such as I had experienced after Frank's death. Life didn't matter to me now. I seemed to have no purpose. It is true, I worked conscientiously enough each day and laughed at jokes with the other members of the staff, but it was all automatic, even artificial. My heart had been very deeply cut and I knew the wound wouldn't heal easily.

I talked with Mrs. Fraser the day following her encounter with Mrs. McDonald and thanked her for trying, but never again did I mention the incident. I asked her if I could borrow books from the library, and now I read almost every evening. On my days off I took the train into Glasgow and went shopping by myself. Elizabeth, my cousin, had a young man herself now who worked as an assistant in a grocery store. Dorothy had moved up north somewhere, and Janet had started working in the infirmary as a helper and her off hours hardly ever coincided with mine.

There was no use buying clothes now, for I had nowhere to go, and no one to see them if I did. Once Richard, the chauffeur, asked me out, but I declined and his comment was a bit pointed.

"Oh, I guess I'm not good enough for you. After all, you've had a taste of the other side of the tracks and you're still star gazing. Just don't stay in a daze too long, or you'll end up an *old maid* as well as a *table maid*."

It was all true. Ian had been so perfect in manners, language, and deportment that I didn't feel that I would ever find anyone like him, and I didn't feel like settling for less.

Could there be a man anywhere in the world that would have all of these qualities and yet not be rich, or have a wealthy intellectual background? Could anyone with all these qualities be honest and true to me?

Was I looking for the impossible in a mate? I didn't care. Next time I'd be more ready for him, I'd be well-read too, so into my books I plunged.

Peggy, the charwoman, asked me to go to church with her and meet some of the young people there, but I only laughed and said no thanks. I felt I had sized up the people in the church pretty well. They were no different from the rest of the world, often quite self-centered, trying to attain through church attendance the sanctification of God. No thanks.

I felt a little feeling deep within me that perhaps God didn't like me. After all, He had taken my mother from me when I was just eight years of age. He had seen fit to give me a lazy good-for-nothing stepmother and to send my sister and brother away. He had seen fit to destroy my chances to better myself by taking my stepmother away unexpectedly and leaving me to look after my father's house. He had made Father hardhearted regarding my continuing school studies. He had then laughingly replaced me at home by another stepmother, more domineering and hard to get along with than the first, causing my brother and me to leave home. He had allowed my brother's death in his prime of life, which in turn left me alone in the world except for aunts and uncles.

Now God had snatched away from me the chance of a lifetime of ease and perhaps happiness. If God had desired it, I reasoned, He could have softened Ian's heart and he would have married me in spite of his parents and we could have lived happily ever after. Surely God didn't like me.

My thoughts were wrong, of course, I knew they were wrong even as they formed in my mind, but I was depressed, and everything seems distorted when you're depressed. I knew God, the God my mother and Wee Frank had worshiped, just couldn't be like that. He was a God of love, He wouldn't wish for someone's unhappiness. He wanted my happiness. He wouldn't plan someone's downfall, but for the time being I couldn't think of it any other way.

One day Mrs. Fraser came to my room to see me. I was surprised by this unexpected act on her part. As she entered the room she crossed over to the window and drew back the drapes.

"You haven't gone anywhere or seen anyone for months now, Nell. You haven't even gone out on your days off. It just isn't healthy for a young girl like you to shut yourself off like you're doing. You should be out among young people of your own age."

I was abrupt and quite curt with my answer.

"As long as I'm doing my work satisfactorily for you, I don't believe it should concern you what I do with my own time."

She didn't wince with my shortness of temper, she didn't back off either. It seemed as though she almost expected it.

"You think life has dealt you a pretty hard blow, and it has," she wistfully looked at me and came over closer, "but it has done the same in other lives, too. The greatness in a person's life comes when one has the courage to get up and fight when hard blows come our way. You have done just that in the past, but this one has knocked the wind out of you, and the hope out of your heart. You must not allow it this great honor. The devil delights in watching us fall. Indeed, he plans it so. He wears us down little by little until our strength is low, and then he strikes again, usually with a very hard blow. His hope is that in our own weakness we will falter and fall and denounce God, while all the time our defense is the extra strength we receive from God, when we most need it, and we can so readily receive it, if we but ask."

Slowly she eased herself into the chair by my bed. "I have a story to tell you," she began. "I would like you to listen. Perhaps if you listen it will make my empty life worth living and put a bit of meaning into your own."

I wondered what she could possibly be talking about. Her life seemed so full, so lovely, so meaningful, so rich, and good. What could *I* possibly do for her? I sat on the edge of my bed in a comfortable position to listen.

"It all happened about ten years ago," she began, with her hands tightly clenched together. "My daughter, Elizabeth, had been dating a young Navy Officer. He was handsome, mannerly, beautifully spoken, and courteous. He loved her completely, you could see it in his eyes, but Elizabeth, although she dated him, only did so for her own convenience. The fact that he was of the same financial status also didn't attract her. She just couldn't and wouldn't see him as a sweetheart.

"One night, Art took Elizabeth to a naval dance, and as usual Elizabeth looked over Art's shoulder at the other men more than she enjoyed Art's attentions. Eventually a private from Blackpool stepped up to them and after introductions were made, asked Elizabeth to dance. He was tall, dark, and handsome and the English accent attracted her right away. She fell in love almost instantly. Words of affection dropped from his lips as quickly as butter melts on a hot griddle. His name was Tom, and he carried her off into ecstasy in the truly great navy man's fashion.

"He courted her with flowers, perfumes, and sweets. She thrilled to his voice, she thrilled to his touch. Unlike *your* story, they each knew the background of the other. Tom was just as poor as Elizabeth was rich. This didn't bother Elizabeth. It didn't bother her father or me, either, and it bothered Tom least of all.

"Easy come, easy go, he courted her with sheer abandon, free of all worries and cares and they never discussed their future. They lived one day at a time. Father and I thought often about it. We had it all figured out that with his temperament he wouldn't last too long in the navy, and before too many years we would likely have to keep them, but if Elizabeth was happy that was all we really cared about.

"Time passed, and Tom was on his next leave ashore. He was even more devoted to her than before. Together they went long walks, kissed in the garden, and held hands and kissed in the library. Gradually, everyone accepted the situation and left them alone to enjoy themselves. Father had to go on a business trip to Italy, and I did a rather foolish thing. I decided to go with him. It had been months since I'd had a break.

"We were gone about three months in all, and when we arrived home Elizabeth was acting unlike herself. She often went into moody spells when she felt lonely or left out, and Tom had gone back to sea, but this time she seemed extremely depressed. She wouldn't come out of her room for days and when she did she looked like a caged animal.

"I asked her over and over again if I could help but her answer was always negative. Then one day she did emerge from her room and without a word to anyone went out. I was just curious enough and fearful enough to follow her.

"She went to a doctor. Not our family doctor, but the office of a complete stranger. I waited in the shadows of a tall building, my heart pounding with fear. Eventually after about an hour's wait she emerged slowly into the sunlight from the darkness of the doorway. She descended the stairs slowly and pensively, head bent low, and then started the long walk home. I followed at a comfortable, unobserved distance. As she approached the front gate I quickly made my way into the maid's side entrance, and as quickly as I could ran on through to the front door and hung my coat up. I had just nicely turned and was fixing my hair in the hall mirror when she came in the front door.

"I asked her where she'd been. Her eyes were glassy and stared straight ahead. She told me, 'the doctor's' without hesitation. I asked why. 'Because I thought I was pregnant, and I am,' she stated matter-of-factly. Before I could answer her, before I could even fully accept the impact of her statement she collapsed right there in the hall.

"We put her to bed immediately and called the doctor she had visited. He came quickly and examined her and said it was her state of mind along with her condition - that of pregnancy.

"After she had had a good sleep I greeted her with her breakfast next morning. Her smile was cynical. 'Come to gloat over the fallen one?' she asked. I assured her that I hadn't. She laughed a hysterical sinister laugh. I can still hear it."

Mrs. Fraser got up slowly from the chair and walked towards the window, automatically putting her hands over her ears in a vain effort to block out the sound she could still hear in her mind.

"I tried, I tried; I really tried to convince her that we were not angry and that we forgave her and would look after the baby for her or find a good home for it, whichever she desired. I tried to reason with her that

God is not a God of hate, but a God of love, and that He too would forgive, as indeed He had already when He died on the cross for HER.

"Two weeks she stayed in bed and stared straight ahead and wouldn't talk. One day I went into the top drawer of the bureau in her room to get a special pair of gloves of mine that Elizabeth had borrowed, and there it was — a letter from Tom. I thought she hadn't heard from him. I took it out, my hand shaking madly as I did so. I held it up to her. She screamed and held her head. I went to put it back in the drawer but she motioned for me to read it forming the words 'read it' on her lips without sound.

"It read: 'Dear Elizabeth: I know you always wait anxiously for my letter, so I thought I should stop to write. I don't quite know where to begin. We had a truly wonderful time last leave, didn't we, and I know I'll never forget it, but when I stopped off at Halifax this time, something happened. I met a wonderful girl. No she's not nicer than you, but there is a difference. I love her, and she's not rich. After my trip to Montreal I saw her again on the return lap of my journey. Ann has agreed to become my wife and is coming to live in England next month.

"P.S. I do hope that this won't upset you too much. Ours was a good relationship, but without love, at least on my part. I think I was in love with your money and that would never have worked out."

"I stood staring at the letter for over ten minutes while I allowed the full impact to sink in. I was dumbfounded, insulted, disgusted, and appalled. Then I realized just how much more dreadful this would sound to Elizabeth. I turned to look at her and I didn't like the drawn, gray, blank countenance I saw.

"There'll be others," I began, "Just you wait."

"Then the silence broke and in a wounded, determined voice she proclaimed in bitterness, "Oh no there won't, NEVER!"

"Next day we found her in the stable. She was dead. She had crept out in the night and done away with herself.

Mrs. Fraser no longer looked the self-assured dignified aristocrat she usually did. The wrinkles seemed suddenly to appear on her drawn face, her hair seemed grayer than I had previously noticed. She covered her face with her hands and wept as if her heart would break, as if she had just relived it all over again. I walked over to her with outstretched arms and embraced her.

"I'm so sorry." There was no difference in status now, just love and concern for each other. Lady and maid wept together. Finally, I broke it off. "No need to fear about my doing that," I stated. "I have two good reasons and one bad one. Firstly, God made me and I haven't the right to take my life away from Him. Secondly, I love 'myself' too much to want to destroy such a beautiful creature." I primped and tilted my nose and smiled at her and she began to relax and smile through her tears. "Thirdly, I still go by my Uncle John's favorite statement, 'There's always more fish in the sea than ever came out of it.'" Then I sobered up a bit, and still looking at her sad tearful face added, "Of course, there is quite a difference between your daughter and me — I'm not pregnant."

In a stage whisper I heard her say, "Thank God."

Mrs. Fraser's story both sobered me and strengthened me. Inwardly I was now very grateful that I hadn't been taken on such an un-Godly ride as Elizabeth had. At least Ian had always been a perfect gentleman. I would be eternally grateful to him for the respect he had held for me. He had never forced his attentions on me; indeed he had gently prepared me for even the most casual of kisses. No, I had not been taken in by his small talk and forced to regret it for the rest of my life. Ian was a good man, although at the moment I could strangle him for being so easily persuaded by his mother, but then I figured it couldn't have been real love on his part, or he would have reacted differently.

Mrs. Fraser's words about the Devil also stuck in my mind.

The more I thought about it the more I could see the pattern. It was the Devil who had been trying to wear me down all these years with one disappointment after another, while my strength had always been found in my reliance on God. This time I had wavered under the blow, because it was such a bad one, and my failure to cope with the situation was simply because I was trying to do so in my own strength.

I hadn't gone to God this time. Wee Frank had pointed to God's strength in the scriptures when he had asked me to read mother's Bible. Uncle John had reminded me again, when I was spiritually starving after Wee Frank's death. Now, Mrs. Fraser was the instrument through which the Holy Spirit was working. For a while now a little voice within me had been telling me to read the Bible and I had resisted, but with Mrs. Fraser's statement ringing in my ears I went to the bottom bureau drawer and uncovered Mother's Bible, once more. Slowly but carefully I opened it and turned to my favorite book John and it was then that my attention was drawn to Chapter 15 verse 15.

"Henceforth I call you not servants; for the servant knoweth not what his lord doeth; but I have called you friends; for all things that I have heard of my Father I have made known unto you.

"Ye have not chosen me, but I have chosen you, and ordained you, that ye should go and bring forth fruit, and that your fruit should remain, that whatsoever ye shall ask of the Father in my name, He may give it you.

"These things I command you, that ye love one another."

There it was. I was not only a servant of God but His friend, just as I had felt the barrier drop between Mrs. Fraser and myself as she told her story. I was her friend. My greatest desire now was to serve my God, and

I knew I could do this by helping my friend, making her load lighter and proving to her that her friendship was valued very highly by me.

It all seemed clearer now. I wished to show in some way my love for God and to rediscover His love for me. How could I do this?

"Whatsoever ye shall ask of the Father in my name; He may give it you." There was my answer. Ask the Lord Jesus Christ to help me come out of this depression and show me the way to serve Him as a loving friend, and to ask Him to help Mrs. Fraser to overcome her self-guilt for having left Elizabeth alone.

Slowly, I did a thing I had not done since I was a child. I knelt down beside the bed and prayed to God in all sincerity and truth for help for Mrs. Fraser and myself, in the name of Jesus Christ. It seemed strange that I should hear no answer since I was sure I should have, but there came instead a sense of calmness over me that I hadn't known for weeks since my little romance. I felt that God had taken my problem and would help me solve it. I went to bed and slept like a baby.

Next morning, I approached Mrs. Fraser and before I realized what I was doing I pulled up a chair by her breakfast table and began to talk. It was strange because I had never before been so informal and never before had I been so unaware of what I intended to say but the words kept coming as though someone else was speaking through me. Finally I asked the question.

"What can I do to help?"

Her heart was prepared also for she answered, "You can forget your hardships of the past, including your romance, and make a new beginning. Look at your life squarely, discover what you want out of it, and go after it. Make a new beginning, starting now. Your success will be my happiness, because your success will help to calm the restless spirit within me that speaks to me of my failure to another in the past. Your future can be my future. Oh, I know you didn't know I had a restless spirit. I always seem so calm and appear to be enjoying myself, but this is my mask to the world. Even my husband hasn't realized what my daughter's death has done to me.

"Another thing you must do. You must forgive your Father. No doubt he was wrong, but you must conquer hate with love every time. You should go to him, and tell him you love him. As a parent myself, I know that he must love you dearly, no matter what he did, and he must be hurting very much right now."

I looked at her wistfully. I didn't know if I could carry out all of her wishes and expectations or not, but I must try. We now had a beautiful friendship, and she was like a mother to me. I now felt I had a mother again in Mrs. Fraser. I was a very lucky person indeed.

Now, I still carried out my table maid duties but I was accepted as a daughter. Often we had discussions on the important facts of life. Often we discussed passages from the Bible. Often she embraced me and kissed me as though I truly was her own.

As time passed, and after much thought and discussion, I decided I should really be attending church, so I spoke to Peggy and went with her the following Sunday, much to her amazement. I continued to go regularly and to seek God's guidance for my life.

I knew now that I had had things all wrong again. I had been blaming God for all my misfortune while it was the Devil who had caused them, and he had laughed from the wings of life's stage as he saw me floundering around in my own weakness. His hope was always that I wouldn't notice God in the 'other wing', with hand outstretched waiting for me to turn to Him for help. It was strange, but God was always anxious to help, long before I asked for it, if I continued to flounder and spin under the blow. The evil one was strong, but God was much stronger, and from now on I would put my faith in God, whether hypocrite, sinner, or saint sat beside me in church. After all I, too, had sinned and fallen short of the grace of God. Hadn't my thoughts been shamefully wrong against God - blaming Him for everything bad that had happened to me? What about everything good?

All these years when I had turned my back on God He had not forsaken me. He still loved me, although I denied Him and His church. He still loved me enough to keep me clothed and fed and warm and comfortable. He had given me friends to turn to, such as Uncle John and now Mrs. Fraser. He had given me happiness, but the Evil One had taken it away, hoping to destroy me, and he had almost succeeded. God had always been real in my mind, from the time of my childhood, but now, for the first time, I realized that the Devil too, was real, and a very strong power for evil in my life. I realized that I must not rely on my own strength, but upon God's strength, which is so much stronger than the Devil's. I realized for the first time also, that the Lord will not interfere in our lives. He stands at the door of our life and knocks, but he must be invited in. Until we ask Him in, and have faith in His strength for us, we flounder against the Evil One all on our own.

Life now took on a new look for me. I was now searching again for my life's guidance, but from God this time. It would be different than I had once imagined, but that didn't mean all was lost. Perhaps God had something more exciting waiting around the corner.

Chapter 15
Saying Good-bye to Father

The fall turned to winter and the winter to spring as I sought to find God's will for my life. God often takes His own time to answer prayer, and we must not become too impatient. I spent my days off' each week visiting Uncle John and my sister Jean, who had had another baby in late September. This time it was a boy and she had named him Archie. He was about nine months old now and was a dear little fellow with round cheeks and a cute grin. I hadn't visited Jean's home as often during my romantic experience and my depression period, and Jean had gotten it into her head that I didn't like wee Archie as well as wee Jean, which just wasn't true. I found it more difficult to buy things for a boy, but I loved him dearly. Wee Jean was a picture with her golden tresses hanging down her back, and I guess I naturally thought of her as being like myself when I was little. I seemed to have a strong desire to make her life happy and in some way protect her from the hurts that I had had. I often got cross at Jean for making her cry as she roughly brushed her hair, and Jean would laugh and say, "Mind the way I tugged at your hair, Nell, when I was taking care of the house for that little while?"

"Aye, right well I do," I'd answer, wincing at the very thought of it.

One day she ventured to ask, "Will ye no go over and visit Father, one of these days? He's wearying for a visit from you. There's never a visit here but that he inquires about you."

"He's wearying for me is he? Well he can just go on wearying. Do you ever go over and visit him, Jean?" I quietly answered with a sly but reasonable question.

"Indeed I do not!" was her reply. "I wouldn't go near that old woman of his with a ten foot pole. He asked for it, he can live with it and he knows where I am if he needs me."

It was on one of my visits to Jean's home, as I stood in the station, waiting for my train to East Kilbride, that I noticed a large signboard advertising the sailings to Canada and America. The word "CANADA" seemed to stand out in huge letters. My eyes skimmed along the wall to another sign, "Sail to Canada, Land of Opportunity." Something seemed to click in my mind like a call to adventure. As I boarded the train for East Kilbride I wondered what it would be like to board a boat for Australia, America, or Canada. What a perfectly wonderful adventure. What a thrilling experience. What excitement to see the world unravel before one's very eyes.

As I walked to Jean's house from the station it struck me that it just might be possible to do it. I had saved quite a bit of money over the past year, and with another year's savings I just might be able to afford it. Then the inevitable question of what I would do when I arrived. I'd have to work as a maid. A lump in my throat, and a tear in my eye, smashed my dreams for a moment, but I had no other trade, so I'd just have to work at it for a while and then change to another job later. After all, women and women's work was looked upon in a slightly different manner in the new world.

"My you look bright today," Jean remarked as she opened the door to greet me.

"Aye, I'm feeling great, Jean," was my reply as I kissed her and greeted her braw wee Jean and handsome wee son Archie.

When the time was right and we got settled in the kitchen over a cup of tea, I ventured to tell her about my new idea.

"Ah, you're daft, woman," was her quick reply. "What would you be doing in a strange country on your own with no money? Where would you live? Who would look after you when you were sick? Have you ever thought that if you really did go, chances are you'd never get back to see us again? What about that? They're all a mighty long way away from home, ye ken."

"Well I guess I haven't really given it much thought yet, but I'm going to."

Months passed and I thought about it often and saved my money. If I went to Australia I'd be so far away I just knew I'd never return home again, and somehow I felt I just might want to – after all there was Jean and her young family whom I was very fond of, and Uncle John, and even Father. America sounded very exciting and adventuresome, but *Canada* sounded the best of all. For one thing it was British, and because of this it would surely be a bit of home away from home. Canada that stretched from sea to sea seemed to be beckoning to me.

Mrs. Fraser walked into the library one evening as I was poring over the geography book, and upon seeing what I was so earnestly studying, she questioned, "Now why would a girl like you be so interested in geography, Nell? I always thought the subject rather dull myself."

I looked up from the page with a coy little grin, "Not if you're thinking of adopting a country, it isn't."

Her face took on a strange look of both pleasure and anguish simultaneously. "Do you mean to say, you're thinking of leaving Scotland?" She moved closer to the book and stared at the page that was lying open. "CANADA. Now that's a long way off."

"Not so far; really. The boat only takes about ten days and it sounds like a lovely country the way it's described here. Parts of it remind one of Scotland it says. The east coast is almost completely made up of Anglo-Saxon stock and the mountains in the west are higher than ours but somewhat similar to look upon. The climate is mild on the west coast. Then I could choose the prairies with their low-lying plains, and of course Quebec, where I'd probably settle if I was French. The part that seems to interest me the most is this part that dips down into America. It's called Southern Ontario, and it seems to be the most highly developed and probably the most likely place for me to find a job. At least that's what Mrs. MacKlintock at the Service Agency said."

"You've spoken to her already about this?"

"Oh, yes. She tells me that when I really make up my mind to take the step to contact her and she will give my name and references to a family in Canada in the area I wish to live in. If they agree to hire me, she will make all the necessary arrangements. She says girls are doing this all the time, and that there are some lovely homes applying for service help to come out from Britain."

"It sounds like quite an adventure, my dear. Are you quite sure you would want to leave your family and friends?"

"I have no family, as such," I reminded her. "My brother and sister are both married and have families of their own. I rarely see my brother, and while I would feel sad to say good-bye to my sister and especially to her little ones, I have no real reason for not going."

"What about your father?" she hesitatingly queried.

"My leaving would not upset him or his plans in the least. I haven't seen him for a couple of years now, and I'm sure he doesn't care what becomes of me."

"In that case, I guess it just leaves me. I'll certainly miss you. I do wish you'd reconsider. I know you haven't had things too exciting here, and if you feel you'd rather change your position you could go to another, more active household here in Glasgow, or even in Edinburgh, or in England for that matter."

"No, I think I've made up my mind. It's CANADA for me – Southern Ontario, somewhere around Toronto. If I don't like it I can always save my money and come back again, or head west to another position in Vancouver, and then it's only a hop across the Pacific to Australia and I'll feel more as though I've attempted something in life, even if it isn't that much. Canada's the place for me to start, though. I've made up my mind. I'll go to see Mrs. MacKlintock in the morning."

In the morning, Mrs. MacKlintock searched the map while holding some letters from different Canadian applicants requesting maid service.

"Here's one that looks interesting," she announced." It's from a doctor and his wife in a place called Brantford. Here it is, roughly about sixty miles south west of Toronto." We peered at the map for a while then she looked up Brantford in the index.

"It's in an agricultural belt and the biggest industry is agricultural implements. The weather is quite warm in the summer, hitting the 80 or 90 degree mark, and in winter there is lots of snow and temperatures range all the way down to zero, but rarely below." Looking up at me she asked, "Well, do you think that will suit you? It's a table maid and personal help she wants. Her only other help is a cook and a gardener. Are you interested?"

I stood for a moment in silence. This was a terribly important step I was taking. Would I be doing the right thing? Was this the right country? Was this the right home? My mind seemed to blank out at this point, I couldn't really answer any of my own questions, but I knew one thing. I was supposed to go. It was as though a little voice, an inner self, I can't explain it, but someone told me to go ahead and have my adventure. Could it be the spirit of God working inside of me helping me to decide?

"Yes, please make out my application for that position," I told Mrs. McKlintock.

About a month passed before I heard from her. My application had been accepted and they would expect me to start work on the first of June. My boat would sail on May 15th, and would take approximately ten days, Mrs. McKlintock told me. It would land in Montreal, where I would get a train straight through to Brantford.

With great excitement and rejoicing I went to see Jean on my day off.

"I'm going! I'm going! I'm sailing to CANADA next month!" I threw my arms around my sister in my excitement as soon as I entered her door. She was stunned, I could see, by this news and tears came to her eyes.

"Oh, I wish you were'na going," she cried. "I just hate to see you go that far away."

"I'm no' afraid," I replied confidently, reverting back to my old familiar dialect that we had always used at home, although taught the best of grammar in the school. "God will take care of me!"

"You'll go and see Father before you go, won't ye?"

"Well I hadn't thought about it yet. I — I'd — like to see him, but I don't really want to go over to the house to see him. It would bring back so many memories, and besides I don't want to run into *her*.

"You owe it to him nevertheless," Jean somberly stated. "You may never see him again, and after all he is your father."

"I know you're right, Jean. I'll just have to force myself for his sake. I hate good-byes. I'll be back, I know I will."

"Nevertheless, go to him. He needs to know you care that much for him, regardless."

"The week before I go I'll visit him," I resolved. "Then he won't be able to talk me out of it, after all I am twenty-two, almost twenty-three, surely I can take care of myself."

The weeks flew by quickly. So many things had to be done that I scarcely realized the passing of time and suddenly it was Wednesday, my day off and the day set aside to visit everyone in East Kilbride for the last time before my departure. The strain of meeting with my father loomed up in my mind as a terrible ordeal. I had dreamt the night before of seeing Father flying into a rage and demanding that I stay home and of my arguing with him over it.

I had visited Uncle John and Aunt Jane and said my good-byes. Uncle John, with tears in his eyes but a smile on his lips, told me he loved me as though I was his own, and with a kiss and a hug sent me on my way with all his blessings.

I then walked over to Jean's house. I could postpone my goodbyes here, as she and the family and my brother George were all going to see me off at the boat on Saturday. After a real good cup of tea and some delicious home-baked scones, Jean said the inevitable sentence. "Away you go, now. Say good-bye to your father. He has the day off and he'll likely be digging in the garden about now. If you catch him there you just might not have to go into the house."

"Have you told him, Jean?" I questioned, half hoping she had, so that my job would be easier.

"No, I haven't seen him since you made up your mind a month ago. It seems he was spending too much time here and *her royal highness* didn't like it. Mrs. Gillespie told me. Now off you go."

It was a lovely spring day as I set out down the street and turned up the old familiar lane towards the house of my childhood. The trees were swaying in the soft breeze. Here and there a wild flower peeked out of the underbrush at the side of the road. The birds sang in the trees and my mind raced over the years gone by. The carefree days I had skipped in the lane. The rainy day when Mother died and I looked through the windowpane down the lane anxiously as I waited for the doctor's arrival. The day I had Billy give me a ride on his bicycle, to get the doctor, and to take the news of Beatrice's death quickly to Father. I wondered what Billy was doing these days. I remembered the day when old Mr. Tom tried persuading Father to let me stay at school. I remembered the sadness in Wee Frank's eyes as we rode down the lane to take him to Uncle John's home to die. I remembered the day with cold pangs and loud heartbeat that I had walked out of that house forever, after Frank's death. Now I was walking towards it again. I loved it and hated it all at the same time.

My eyes were on the house and the little white picket fence as I approached, and I didn't notice for a moment the bent figure, half way down the garden, working away so diligently. It was Father, and for one awesome moment I hesitated. I wanted to run, to get away before he'd look up. I was afraid he'd spoil my chance for happiness again. My heart pounded and my head swayed a little as I clutched the fence. Then it was too late.

"Hello, Nell! So you've come tae see me at last. We'el now, isn't that nice of ye. I was just doing a wee bit-o-digging in the garden. I'm no' as young as I used tae be, ye ken, and it takes me a lot longer, the now, tae get my diggin' done." He came over to me and put his arm around me, a thing he had never done before. "Come on, my wee lass; over to the garden house where we can talk." He led me anxiously down the garden path, my mind paralyzed for the moment by his gestures. The setting was beautiful, the day was beautiful, and for the first time in a long, long while, I felt once again that my Father truly loved me.

"We'el now, what have ye been doing wi yourself? Have they been treatin' ye right in your place of employment? I heard you were goin' with a young man? — You're no goin' to tell me you're engaged tae be married are ye now? My, but its good tae see ye, but come now, I've been doin' all the talking. Now it's your turn." He got out his pipe and filled it full of tobacco and proceeded to light it and fold his arms comfortably across his stomach as he got ready to hear my answers.

He had grown a little stouter than I had remembered him, and his hair was now quite gray, but the beautiful twinkle of his eye had not changed, and as I sat there looking at him I could see why the ladies had fallen for and chased after him. The question I couldn't answer, even yet, was why *he*, such a wise, clever, intelligent man had been able to accept the ones that had chased him rather than doing the pursuing himself towards more likeable and loveable ladies for his partners in life.

He brought me out of my deep thoughts with a, "Come, come girl, tell me what you've been doing wi' yourself?"

"I've, I've come to say good-bye," I stuttered.

"What do you mean girl? Say good-bye. Why we're going to get to know each other, now, more than ever before. What do you mean good-bye?"

"I'm going to Canada, Father."

"You're what? Going to Canada? Oh, but you canna! I forbid it! I won't have it! You're too young to go away over there by yourself. What will become of you? Who will look after you? What will you do to earn a living?"

He was standing glaring down at me now, and then he broke the stare and walked a little back and forth, and suddenly for no reason at all I lost my fear of him. He now appeared as he really was: a desperate old man who was angry because life had crossed him up, even though he had asked for it. He no longer appeared as a threat to me, so I spoke out in a clear stern voice.

"I'm going to Canada, Father, and you can't stop me. I'm of age and I'm paying my own way. I sail on Saturday!"

After a slight pause, and a threatening glance at me, he continued pacing, but even faster. Every so often he would stop and lean against the trellis at the side of the garden house. I continued. "I will do house work in Canada the same as I have done here. That is all I am trained to do. I have a position waiting for me and as for someone taking care of me — I have not had that here — that is, no individual responsible for me. You must not worry, though, God will watch over me over there the same as he has done here. Of this I am certain."

Slowly he turned to me and sat down again.

"Then you haven't lost your faith, Nell?" I shook my head for a 'no' and he continued. "I've been praying that you would'na. Some told me that ye very nearly did when wee Frank died and you decided tae take off from home. Was that true, Nell? Did I let ye and Frank down so badly that ye lost your faith?

"No, Father, Frank never lost his faith. God is above all things that man can do, or not do, towards man. I must admit I've been a bit shaken from time to time though, and I've blamed God for my lot in life, but Frank always pulled me back to the truths in the Bible, so when he passed away, I just had to read it, for his sake, and in reading it I found myself again."

"I'm so glad to hear it, Nell. I've made quite a few mistakes in my lifetime, Nell, and I do hope you'll forgive me, even though I can't seem to forgive myself.

"After your mother died I felt as though the whole world had caved in on top of me. I wanted desperately to die too. My common sense told me I was wrong, that it was sinful to feel that way, but that didn't stop the feeling. I reasoned that I still had four children at home and that I must think of them and raise them the way Jean would have, but still my melancholy persisted.

"I didn't seem to realize that you children needed me more than ever. I didn't seem to have any interest in you at all, or anyone else for that matter. It was as though I walked in a false world and people were objects. I know now that I went around in a daze, ignoring all of you completely. I guess I was in a state of shock and that if I'd given myself time, I would have come out of it, but before I knew what was happening my wounded mind and body was receiving balm from a very sweet, wordy individual in the form of Beatrice.

"When I look back on it now, I realize that at first I didn't even hear Beatrice as she purred at my side and licked my wounds with her words of flattery, but as the time passed I began to feel better and attributed my whole improvement in spirit, to her.

"Mentally I was still thinking of your mother, and how she had always made me feel better when I was down about something. As time passed I began comparing Beatrice to her more and more. She was a woman, she had a slight look about her that reminded me of your mother, she made me feel good, even if the words were flattery and I knew it, but I seemed helpless to resist them.

"Another thing which affected me greatly was the physical attraction. She cuddled in towards me at every opportunity and it brought out the old animal instinct of sexual desire. Suddenly I felt hungry for the old intimacy I had had with your mother. I wanted her as my wife. I simply gave it no further thought. I wanted her and she wanted me, and as for you children having any rights, you just didn't, in my mind. I was downright furious when Jean disapproved of the marriage, and I was somewhat relieved and glad to see her leave home. I was glad to see the back of George also, as I figured I would have had trouble from him too, if he had remained at home. As for you and Frank, I thought of you as mere children, incapable of understanding my needs and desires and having no right to object on any account, anyway."

I interjected, "Father, you don't have to tell me all this now. It's all water under the bridge. It's all over and done with."

"That's where you're wrong, my wee lassie," he continued with tears swelling in his eyes. "That's where you're wrong. I've wanted to get this off my chest to someone for years. I've done some foolish things and I want you to know that I realize my stupidity, now that it's too late."

"Father, don't do this to yourself." I got up and went to him, and taking a hold of both shoulders I made him look at me. "You were all right back then. You had a right to remarry. You were a mature adult perfectly capable of making up your own mind, and we were just children."

"That's where you're wrong again, lass; wrong again. The very fact that I had children, wonderful children, four children I could well be proud of, should have been reason enough for me to think of your happiness first. You were part of Jean, after all, the girl I loved so very much for so many years. You should have been my first consideration."

He pulled away from my hold, and covering his face with his hands continued. "I knew this at the time, aye, I knew it. But I could'na do anything about it. Old Satan coaxed me with an evil lust, and along with my own egotism, lured me on in my blindness into the trap of the woman in question. Beatrice was never a home-loving body, never a child lover, never a home-builder, all she thought about was Beatrice, as Jean tried to tell me, and I soon rued the day I married her.

"I was not as blind as you thought during those years, you know. I remember the night that she slapped you and sent you back to bed after you had dreamt of your mother. I remember, too, that I didn't come to your rescue. I didn't want a scene. She was a jealous woman, ye ken. Jealous of your poor dead mother and jealous even of any love or affection that I might show to you and Frank.

"If I had been consulting my God, at that point in my life," he struck the corner post of the garden house as he spoke, "I would have waited until I had found a truly good woman, a homemaker, a loveable, selfless person that you too could have loved, but I wasn't consulting God, I was just thinking of myself. I just jumped at the chance of marriage and my own happiness, and when one thinks only of one's own happiness, one usually ends up with no happiness at all."

The words just kept pouring out of him, and I quietly sat down again as he continued to divulge his feeling to me.

"After I had married her and the truth began to dawn on me I couldn't expose my feelings. I had made my choice, and rightly or wrongly I had to carry on. How could I tell the world I had been a fool? Many a time, I too, was hurt badly by words or gestures, but there was also her leg to be considered. She was a cripple, and I did feel an inward need to take care of her and try to make her life happy and meaningful. Never having been married before, I felt that she had had a lonely and uneventful life and I tried to make up for this."

Several times I tried to speak, but Father, who had had all this bottled up for years, just had to get it off his chest.

"When Beatrice died, I didn't feel at all the same as I had about your mother's death. Of course I was sorry and upset for a while and readjustment had to take place, but I felt almost a relief which I, in turn, felt guilty for feeling. Why should I be happy at my wife's death? It was wrong. I hated myself for it, I shouldn't feel like that, and I felt I certainly didn't deserve another wife, so I put all thoughts of marriage out of my mind. I had to carry on the house for you and Frank though, so it seemed the most natural thing in the world to do, to demand that you stay home and keep house for us."

"I was deeply hurt and resentful about that, Father," I confessed, as he paused for breath. I had never seen my Father so talkative. I had never seen him so emotional. Beads of perspiration stood out on his brow and he reached for his handkerchief to wipe it off.

"I realized that, years after, but it took a long, long time. In my day, a girl never went on to more education; indeed she was very fortunate to finish her grade school. I just didn't give it a thought - that the times had changed sufficiently to encourage clever young women into the professions. I dubbed you a servant for the rest of your days by my actions, didn't I? I'm so sorry, Nell."

"Father, please, you weren't to know, I understand!"

"But I should have listened to Mr. Tom. He pointed out to me all the very valid reasons why you should have been allowed to continue your schooling but I was too selfish to listen, too selfish to try to see into your future. All I could see was my own immediate need. I needed a housekeeper, and I had a daughter old enough to take care of the home, so why pay someone else? I certainly didn't intend getting married again."

It was at this point that the front door of the cottage opened, and Maggie's stern and demanding head poked around it. Impatiently, she called out. "John, come now for your supper." She hesitated, squinting a little, trying to see who was sitting with her husband at the garden house. She gave up and closed the door. Later during Father's next few comments I saw the curtain being pulled back several times.

"I didn't think it was time for supper yet," he interjected, "but to get back to the subject, I just want you to know that I'm sorry I didn't keep you in school. Something could have been worked out. You could probably have gone to school and kept house too. It would have been hard, but you could have done it."

"I said supper was ready, John!" The voice from the front door sounded impatient.

"Well go in the house and eat it, woman!" he roared. "I'm talking to my daughter who's leaving for Canada on Saturday, and I'd like to visit with her in peace."

"Well of all the - - -" and she slammed the door behind her.

"You know you would think, in this world, that you'd live and learn, but I didn't," he continued. "I fell for the same flirting, the same flattery, the same desire to do my thing with *her*." He nodded towards the door that had just slammed. "She was different than Beatrice. Beatrice had been coy and smooth in operation, and I felt I was ready for that type of woman and could avoid her, but strangely enough I didn't recognize the same thing in another guise.

Maggie was so outspoken, so strong, so forceful in her every gesture and mannerism. She built me up, while allowing me to lean on her, which is something I had never experienced before. I seemed to be tired and ready for someone to take over and do my thinking for me, to take the initiative, and of course I was lonely again. I thought only of her ability to manage and nurse, and thought she would be good for Frank. Little did I dream that she would be so demanding and have so little heart. I was so sorry about wee Frank and you leaving home. I wanted to come and see you both and try to make up for it by explanation, if nothing else, but she insisted that that would show weakness on my part, and would have none of it, and I listened. I don't know why, but I listened.

"Well, I made my bed, and I'm lying in it, and it isn't very comfortable, but it was my mistake, so it's my problem."

Turning now towards me as I stood up, he put his arm around my shoulder. "Nell, I don't want you to go. I have a strange feeling I'll never see you again. Nell, please reconsider. Please forgive me and stay here in Scotland. I need you so very much. It is so wonderful talking to you. It's almost like having my Jean to talk to again. Will you please take a little more time to consider what you are doing?"

Now it was my turn to have tears in my eyes.

"No, Father, I'm sorry, but my mind is made up. I am going to Canada, but I understand how you feel, and it has been so good to talk to you. I now know that you really love me, and that means so very much to me. I'll write. I'll write often. I promise. We all make mistakes, and we all pay for them eventually, but Father, I want you to know that I love you in spite of everything, and I will try to get back to see you if it's at all possible."

He drew me near him in a warm embrace and we kissed and then we both cried a little. Turning towards the little white picket fence, he motioned to me to look up to the sky.

"See the moon coming up over there?"

"Yes."

"Well, you look at it from Canada and I'll look at it here in Scotland and we won't seem so far away from one another. It can be a sort of bond between us. As you said earlier, God can take care of you in Canada as well as in Scotland."

"Yes, Father," I answered in a whisper.

I clasped his hand tightly in mine for a moment before walking through the white picket gate, and with a smile and a kiss and tears running down his cheeks and mine, we parted.

I felt sorry for Father now. He had realized some of his wrongs and had wrestled with them inwardly for years. Why, oh, why — does a father and a child have to be so far apart for so long? If I hadn't been leaving for Canada he would never have opened up that way, and for years, maybe even into eternity, I would have thought of him as the hardheaded, opinionated, self-centered individual I had pictured in my mind for years now, instead of the warm, self-critical, guilt-ridden human being I had just talked to. Now I truly loved my father. Now I knew he had always truly loved me, in his own way, all along.

Chapter 16
Sailing to Canada

It was a beautiful Saturday in late May 1912, that I set sail for Canada. Mrs. Fraser took me to the dock and wished me well with much kissing and embracing and promising of letter writing. She said I had been like a second daughter to her, and she loved me very much. She made her departure before my family arrived, saying she'd rather not watch the boat leave, as it always seemed such a sad occasion.

I stood for a little while alone. People were everywhere, some saying good-bye, some weeping, some laughing, others checking baggage, and ascending the ramp to the boat and for a moment I felt a flood of fear surge over me. Was I doing the right thing, going so far away? As soon as I left this pier I'd be on my own for good.

What would Canada be like? Why did I have this pull to go there? What about the tragedy of the Titanic last month? She was supposed to have been unsinkable, and yet after striking an iceberg off the Grand Banks of Newfoundland on her maiden voyage, she had sunk with all hands on deck. What if my ship struck an iceberg? I mustn't think of it. Then a silent prayer to God, and with it, a calm feeling of reassurance came over me as had so often happened before in my life, as though God had spoken His word of approval on the whole idea, and that all would be well.

Turning, I saw George and his wife coming to meet me, and then Jean and Jim and beautiful bonnie wee Jean and bouncing, jolly, chubby, wee Archie and Mrs. Gillespie.

"I don't like good-byes, but I just had to come to wish you luck in the new land," Mrs. Gillespie said as she gave me a huge kiss and hug. In turn, I kissed them all and said good-bye, and the last one I kissed was wee Jean. I couldn't seem to let her go. She was the one I didn't want to leave behind.

I'd always remember her standing there on the dock waving her hands, dressed in her lovely green suit with hat to match and her beautiful long red ringlets curling down her back.

I waved until the people were mere specks in the distance, and then turned to look at the ocean. I had a lot of water to cross to get to my destination. I had a lot of thoughts to think. I had a lot of things to learn. I felt very much alone, almost panicky again, and then I remembered my friend and constant companion, my God. Why should I worry with Him at my side? Why should I worry with Him as my guide? He'll be with me in my Canadian home too, I reminded myself, and calmness came over me once more.

After the initial fussing around of getting my bags to the right cabin and learning the layout of the ship it was meal time, and I found myself standing in line with a rather nice-looking girl about my own age. Her name was Bella and we soon struck up an acquaintance that was to last a life time. Bella had met a young man in Scotland with whom she had fallen in love, and he had gone ahead of her to Canada, to the prairies where he was farming. He had now purchased a nice piece of land in Alberta, south of Calgary, at a place called Nanton and had sent for her to come. She was thrilled with the whole idea. She knew she would have hard working days ahead of her, but that didn't bother her as long as she had Bill for a husband. She also had a sister in Ontario and Bella was going to visit with her on her way out west.

I was glad I had met Bella because she wasn't interested in meeting a boyfriend on board and I certainly wasn't. I had had enough of meeting young men on boats, and falling in love with them only to discover that they had come from goodness knows where, and lived, thought, and ate differently than I did. No thanks! That isn't to say Bella and I didn't flirt a little with the sailors and the band members in the orchestra and had the odd meal during the week with a couple of lads from France who were going to Quebec City to live. We enjoyed dances and games, but the most memorable occasion was the entertainment held the night before we docked, when everyone took part, and even I sang a verse of a song and recited a favorite recitation and Bella danced with one of the kilties aboard.

The day we arrived in Montreal was overcast with drizzling rain. The pier was crowded with people from many countries, but French and English seemed to be the dominant languages spoken. We made our way through the crowds to a cabbie and had trouble making ourselves understood by the French driver. However, he knew the letters Y.W.C.A., and we were soon on our way. Both Bella and I felt that it would be the safest place for us to stay, as it came highly recommended by the agency, and of course was a Christian organization.

After settling into our room, we went out for supper and took a short walk around to see the city. It certainly was different from Glasgow or Edinborough, for there was a decidedly delightful French atmosphere, helped along by little cafes and large Catholic churches. The French provincial flavor was in much of the architecture and the interiors of the stores, and the decidedly French courtesy of the French gentlemen who winked as they opened doors for us or got a cabbie for us, or told us points of interest in the city, was thrilling indeed. We returned to our room, sorry that our visit to Montreal had to be so short.

The following morning found us at the railway station with our destination Toronto. We enjoyed a wonderful train trip. The trains were different in Canada. No compartments or side seats. More comfortable too, I felt – perhaps this was due to the great distances covered by trains in this huge country.

Beautiful farm land filled the landscape. Many farmers were on the land, and everywhere the fresh green look of spring abounded. It had a different appearance from Scotland altogether. Here was a land that could yield great agricultural crops, and a land bustling with enthusiasm for both work and play. The people looked happy as we passed them at cross roads and small village railroad stations. Life looked simple and good.

The huge big huffing and puffing iron monster that was pulling us along arrived at Union Station, Toronto, before we could believe it.

Toronto was different. Toronto had a stiff dignity about it that reminded one of Edinburgh, or what I had heard of London. People looked more serious, more drawn by worries and cares here. English seemed to be spoken everywhere so we had no trouble being understood, and again we made our way to the Y.W.C.A. for the night, as we couldn't make the right train connections that evening. The big-city atmosphere of Toronto appealed to me for its excitement, but deep down inside, I was glad I had chosen a smaller place to live.

The next morning again found us in Union Station, boarding a train for points west. Brantford was my destination and Bella was going to Windsor and then Sarnia, so I would be getting off first. After we left Hamilton the land seemed to flatten out and almost boast that here was gorgeous farm land, prosperous farms, pretty little hamlets, and friendly people.

My heart beat faster as we pulled into the red brick station at Brantford. There would be no one there to meet me, as I had been allowed plenty of time and I wasn't due at my new home until the next day. I said a fond good-bye to my friend Bella and wished her well, and of course we exchanged addresses and promised to write.

I stood on the platform and waved to Bella as the train pulled out of the station. She had been a new friend and a dear one, but now as I watched the train make its way westward and saw it take the last curve on the track before it disappeared from sight, I knew that I was indeed alone, thousands of miles from home, in a new country, without a soul to talk to. Then I shrugged my shoulders and pulled myself together, for I knew that I was never alone.

Slowly, I made my way to a horse and buggy that looked as if it was for hire. I gave my directions to go to the Y.W.C.A., and upon arrival changed and freshened up, and then made my way to a little restaurant for a lonely meal. Later, I went for a short stroll before returning to my room for the night.

As I made my way along the street the next morning, luggage and all, in another horse-drawn cab on my way to my new home, the sun was shining beautifully and tulips and daffodils added glorious color to every flower bed. Yellow forsythia bushes bloomed profusely and the freshness of the morning made me feel exuberant as we made our way along the fashionable tree-lined streets.

Finally we arrived at my new address. The house was not as impressive as Mrs. Fraser's had been, but it was quite large and lovely. It nestled close to the ground on a huge expanse of beautiful lawn, that dipped into a hill at the back of the property, giving a perfect setting for flower beds and rock gardens.

A huge iron fence surrounded the grounds and as the driver got down to open the gate he commented, "You the new girl for the Wilsons'?"

"Yes."

"Hope you like the place. They don't keep their help for very long. I don't know why, but they just don't seem to keep them."

"Well, thanks for the information," I gulped trying to keep my composure. "But I'll just give it a whirl anyway."

We turned into the driveway, and the cab driver helped me carry my bags to the side door. I paid him and he departed leaving me standing at the large doorway with my luggage by my side. Gingerly, I knocked twice. Soon a rather plumpish, pleasant young woman opened the door. She was dressed in a maid's uniform and she spoke with a broad English accent.

"Well, if it isn't our new maid from Scotland. Do come right in. The mistress is away shopping for the morning, but she'll be home for lunch."

She showed me to my room. It was a very plain room, with only the barest of essentials. The curtains and bedspread were faded and the rugs looked well-worn.

"After you've freshened up a bit, you'd better come down to the kitchen and I'll give you your instructions."

Katie told me my duties in a very nice way, as she gave me a general tour of the house.

"I hope you stay for a while?" she said with both a question and a sigh in her voice. "It's not the easiest place to work, you know. Mrs. Wilson is quite – ah – different!"

"In what way?" — I queried.

"You'll find out," was her only reply.

"Will I serve the noon day meal today?" I asked.

"Oh, no, Mrs. Wilson will have her lunch alone in the library, and you will eat with me in the kitchen today. I will serve her. You see, Mrs. Wilson won't allow you to serve her - yet - I mean - now - I mean not until —-!" she stuttered to a close without giving any information and then went on. "Oh, you'll find out."

I wasn't so sure that I liked the look on her face and I couldn't define it. Her look did indicate that the subject was closed though, so I left it closed too. For the rest of the morning she told me to just chat with her while she worked in the kitchen.

Katie served Mrs. Wilson in the library and we ate in the kitchen, as she had said we would. Coming from one of her trips into the library Katie nodded to me. "Mrs. Wilson will see you in your room now. You'd better use the back stairs."

Doing as I was instructed, I ascended the back stairs and made my way to my room. I went inside and left the door open slightly so that Mrs. Wilson could easily see inside. I sat on the bed waiting. There certainly was something strange about the whole thing. I had never met my employer in *my room* before. I wondered why, but I didn't have long to wait.

Suddenly the door was pushed open and I saw a small-built, thin, wiry woman standing before me. She had a pleasant but forced smile as she stood there holding the door knob, and I felt myself relax as I stood up and went forward to greet her with my hand outstretched.

In that instant I wondered why anyone wouldn't or couldn't get along with her but as Katie had said I'd soon find out.

"Don't come any further," she stated flatly as she motioned to me to keep my distance. "You're new and I don't know anything about you, so if you'll just strip off all your clothes and hang them on the line in the yard, and the clothes from your luggage as well, and leave all the rest of your things in the room, I'll have the room fumigated.

"You'll sleep in a spare room we have downstairs tonight and tomorrow night. I'll lend you some underclothes and give you your new uniform to wear after you've bathed and washed your hair." Then she made her exit.

I hadn't uttered a word, and I stood for a moment staring at the closed door, utterly flabbergasted, dumbfounded, and completely bewildered, almost in tears as she made her next entrance and practically threw the clothes at me, so that she wouldn't touch me.

What on earth had I gotten into? What did she think I was? Where did she think I had come from? I was as clean as she was. I had never had bed bugs or any other trouble in my home or anywhere I had worked.

Hastily, I gathered into a heap the clothes that had to be hung on the line. Then I made my way to the bathroom for a bath and to wash my hair.

I put my hair up in curlers and was making my way back to my room when I met the exterminator and Mrs. Wilson in the hall as he was coming to fumigate my room. He smiled in a friendly sympathetic way, but I was numb, too numb to respond.

"Now you just take your clothes outside and hang them up and then you can have the rest of the afternoon off to spend in the garden in the fresh air. Tomorrow you will commence your duties, but your room will be sealed for a day, so you will not be able to use it until the day after tomorrow."

Obediently, I gathered up my clothes and walked blindly down the back stairs, and asked Katie where to find the clothes pegs. She silently got them for me, and showed me out into the back garden to the clothes line. As soon as she left me, and while I was hanging up my clothes, I just couldn't hold back the tears any longer. Here I was, in a strange country without a friend, and treated like an animal – a dirty one at that.

The back green was terraced with steps down the middle with beautifully shaped flower beds, here and there. Under a tree and surrounded by a rock garden, I spied a bench, so I headed for it and sat down. At least I could dry my hair in the sun.

Already it seemed like a century since I left Scotland, and even a long time since that happy ride down the streets of Brantford in the morning. With my head in my hands I sat silently wondering why? Why had I even come to this country? Why couldn't things work out well for me, just once?

There was a rustle of tools behind me so I turned quickly around, for I had imagined I was alone, until then.

"You must be the new table maid?"

"Yes, I'm afraid so," I stuttered, drying my eyes. It was the gardener and from his accent he was English. He seemed to be a friendly person and he wore a typical English gentleman's moustache. He was average height and of a slight build and practically bald on top. He didn't resemble my father in the slightest but for some unknown reason put me in mind of him, probably because he was a gardener. My face was still red from crying, and I know it grew even redder as he approached me.

"Now don't you be upset, my dearie," he reassured me as he patted me on the shoulder and then circled the bench and sat down beside me. "She does this to everyone who comes to work here. She never has any visitors. She never invites anyone, afraid they might be carrying germs or bugs I suppose. Everything has to be double checked that goes in or out of the house. She's germ crazy, you know. It's a proper shame, it is, as her husband is a right nice gentleman and a very good doctor, too, I understand. Can you imagine having a woman like that as a wife? Poor man! The blessings aren't all with the rich.

"Now, tell me, where are you from, lass?"

"Scotland sir, I just arrived today."

"And you had to land into this, poor thing. Oh well, after you get this over with, it won't be too bad. She isn't that hard to live with really, it's just this obsession with cleanliness, mainly. By the way Miss – what's your name? Mine is Daniel Hands, and I'm from England, as you can tell from my accent. We came out about five years ago."

"I'm Nell Sweenie," I replied. "I'm so glad to meet a friendly person to talk to. Do you like it here? In Canada, I mean? Are you glad you came? Did you say you had your family here?"

I asked many questions and he seemed to enjoy telling me about himself.

He had been a gardener in England on several different estates, so decided to do the same thing in Canada. His son had encouraged him to come out to this country, and had actually paid his father, mother, and sister's passage.

We had a wonderful talk, and I felt like a different person as Katie came to the door to call me for supper, and I made my way up the garden steps to the back door.

"Cheerio," he called as he waved good-bye, "and remember, don't let it get you down."

The weeks passed rather slowly, but they were better than I had dared to hope that first day. Mrs. Wilson was a compulsive talker, and as I looked after her personal boudoir, she never stopped talking. She told me many things about her finances, her jewelry, her stocks and bonds, and many other things. In fact, I began to feel uneasy about the many confidences she was revealing to me.

She also told me many bits of tasty gossip about neighbors and other people who lived in Brantford, most of them in the moneyed class, which I would rather have not known. She loved to look at herself in the mirror as she talked, and as a result there were at least two or three mirrors in every room in the house, so that she would have a mirror to talk into wherever she went. She would primp and fuss with her dress or hair and smile at her reflection approvingly as she talked to the mirror.

Apart from her fear of germs, and her obsession for talking to herself in mirrors, she appeared quite normal and I figured I could live with it for a while at least, even though every so often she would get another strange idea about germs and would demand that this or that room be fumigated immediately, and the whole house was set askew for a while.

I often went shopping with Katie and I met her friend Dorothy, who attended the Presbyterian Church that was nearby. I started going to church with Dorothy and met many new people there. Life seemed brighter now, and I could hardly believe that I had been living in this new country for a whole year.

One day, as Katie and I were walking along Brant Avenue towards downtown, a strikingly handsome man in a reserve army uniform passed us and saluted a hello to Katie. I caught myself in time from turning to stare after him but summoned up enough courage to ask Katie who he was.

"You'll never guess, so I'll tell you," she teased. "He's the gardener's son, and a right handsome gentleman, I might say. I wish he'd give me a tumble, but there isn't a chance. Seems he had a disappointment in love in the old country and now he won't bother with girls."

I thought of this handsome fellow several times after that, as I often had a chat with his father in the garden. We had become quite chummy, really, because he was so friendly and understanding and he reminded me of my father as he went about his work.

"I wish you'd come down to see us sometime, Nell," he would suggest. "I know my wife would love to meet you and visit with you, especially when you're not long out from the old country."

Of course I never took him up on it, even though I felt a little more inclined now that I had seen his son. Then it happened. It was a beautiful day in May, and I had finished my morning's work and was in the kitchen helping Katie prepare lunch, when much to both Katie and my horror, Mrs. Wilson burst into the kitchen, screaming at the top of her voice and waving her finger at the both of us.

"One of you stole my diamond brooch. Come now, confess. It won't do you any good to deny it, for I'll catch you with it. No one is to leave this house, I'm warning you, or I'll call the police."

I was very grateful to God that day that her husband returned home for lunch. I'll never know why, but he walked into the kitchen about that time and begged her to calm down, as he was afraid she might take a heart attack or something, and the brooch wasn't worth that much anyway.

"Oh yes, it is," she argued. "I want both of these girls to come up stairs while I search their belongings to see if they have it."

We were marched up stairs, and stood dumbfounded and staring at one another, as she pulled each of our dresser-drawers apart, throwing article after article upon the floor as she went. She searched the cupboards, under the beds, and even stripped the beds before our eyes, but she didn't find the brooch. She turned our purses upside-down on the dressing tables and examined each item. Almost in tears, and in a rage that appeared to me to be on the verge of insanity, she lunged at Katie. Katie side stepped her and she fell over the bedding that she had left lying on the floor. Her husband lifted her up and again tried to calm her.

"Perhaps it's in your own room somewhere dear," he suggested.

"Never, never," she protested. "You always take the servant's part."

"Now, now, my dear, let's just have a look," he led her slowly down the hall and motioned to us to follow. "Now where do you generally keep the brooch?"

"In the jewelry box, of course, and it isn't there."

"Let's just have a look," he said, turning it upside down and spilling the contents on the bed before our eyes.

"Are you going to allow these thieves to stand and look at all my valuable jewelry?" she screamed, but he patiently looked at each item that had been in the box, and carefully put it back.

"It's not there dear, you're quite right, but where could it be, now think."

She began moving items on her dressing table, looking here and there, and I couldn't help noticing that she didn't touch a small ring jewel box with tiny legs that sat on her dressing table, but I said nothing. She then searched her husband's dressing table, the sewing table, the night table and then turned on Katie and me again. "Where is it? You know where it is! Tell me! Tell me!" she shouted.

Still wondering about the ring box on the dressing table, I blurted out the suggestion for her to look into it. As she lifted the box up off the dressing table, there lay the gleaming brooch under it. She lifted it up, fondled it for a few moments and then turning on me with a weird and wild eye, accused, "You knew where it was all along. You had it all the time and when you were afraid of being caught you put it back and asked me to look there so that it would appear that I had misplaced it. You're the thief!"

Her husband knew she had misplaced it and tried to calm her down and sent us to our rooms. It was good to get away from her, but I knew that she thought I was a thief, and I felt dreadful.

That night, as soon as I got my chores done, I went to bed. I lay for a long time just thinking about the long chain of events that had happened to make me want to come to this country. Here I was, in a strange country without a soul to really call my own, living in a house where a woman was on the verge of insanity and had already accused me of theft. What if something else, more valuable should go amiss? Would she blame me again? There wasn't any doubt in my mind that the answer was in the affirmative. If such an accusation took me to the courts of this new country, I, as a maid, wouldn't have a chance against a well-to-do local dignitary. I didn't have any alternative. I'd have to look for employment elsewhere.

I reached for my well-worn Bible, my comforter, and opened it with a prayer on my lips that God might direct me to a meaningful passage. I wanted to cry, but I couldn't. "Please, help me God, I'm all alone."

"Fear not, for lo, I am with you always, even unto the ends of the earth."

The words answered my prayer and relieved my soul, allowing a flood of tears to roll down my cheeks as I felt contentment come into my very being. God was with me in Canada. He would show me what to do.

The next day was my day off, so I went down town by myself, wandering aimlessly from store to store seeing nothing and buying nothing. It was a lovely day, so I decided to take a detour on the way home. The detour would take me past the gardener's house, as I had secretly wondered what the house was like that he lived in and talked so much about. "It's the first house we've ever owned. My wife is tickled pink with it. You must come and see it," he had said it so often. I knew he had a beautiful garden at the front of his home, and he had told me why. It seems that there had been a garbage dump where his backyard now was, so nothing would grow and a gardener just has to have a garden, so he went back to the old English custom and had his garden at the front and sowed grass seed at the back.

As I walked along the street he lived on, I soon spotted the house. It was the only one with a beautiful garden at the front. It stood almost alone on the north side of the street, back to back with Lorne Crescent, where some of the largest homes in Brantford stood. Actually, Mr. Hands' home had been the gardener's or coachman's house for one of the homes on the Crescent at one time, but now most of the homes were severed from the Crescent properties and new houses were being built along this street as a new development.

There was a lane beside Mr. Hands' home that still connected one of the Crescent homes, and as I got to the lane, a coachman was driving a coach out of the lane across the sidewalk, so I had to wait for him to pass by. I was later glad for this delay, for it was at this precise moment that Mr. Hands saw me standing there as he came around to the front of the house.

"Well, Nell, you've come to see us at last. Come on in and we'll have a cup of tea with the wife." I thanked him graciously and went in to meet Mrs. Hands. She was a slender, sweet lady, very anxious to please, and a bit timid to talk to me, a stranger.

"Now, tell me, how is everything going with you at your work these days?" Mr. Hands finally asked as he prepared to smoke his pipe after our tea.

"Just dreadful," I sighed. "Now she thinks I'm a 'thief'." I poured out my whole story to them, as I was so pleased to have concerned and sympathetic ears.

After I had told all, Mr. Hands simply waved his arms in disdain. "Don't let it bother you, my dearie, the woman is mad. It's not the first time she has accused the hired help of stealing. She thought the last girl had stolen some of the silver flatware, and the girl before that, the silver candlesticks. I didn't mention these traits in her before to you, as I was afraid of your reaction."

"I'm thinking seriously of leaving," I confessed, "but I don't know where to go or how I would get a reference, now."

"Maybe its coincidence and maybe it's the hand of God, but the Dunbars are looking for a table maid and a girl to be a nursemaid to their two children. If you're interested, you could apply. They have one of the nicest homes in Brantford up on Dufferin Avenue, and I'm sure you'd like it there."

"Do you mean Henry Dunbar the owner of the Dunbar Implement Company?" Everyone knew Henry Dunbar. Much of the reason for Brantford being considered the agricultural manufacturing center of Ontario was due to the big Dunbar Farm Implement Plant.

"Yes, that's the one. I'm their gardener too. I take care of four different estate homes. The estates are not as large as they were in England."

"It sounds great, but I'll never get a good recommendation from Mrs. Wilson now, I know I won't."

"You'll hardly need one. Just the fact that you've stuck it out with Mrs. Wilson for a year will be recommendation enough. Everyone knows her, but to be safe I'd ask Dr. Wilson for one. He is a wonderful man and he will understand, and I am sure he will give you one, and may even talk to the Dunbars himself on your behalf if you ask him."

Just then someone came in the front door, and before I knew it, that handsome young man I had thought about so often after seeing him on the street was being introduced to me.

"This is my son, George, Nell," and turning, "and I'd like you to meet Nell Sweenie from Scotland, George."

Shyly he responded to the introduction, and just as quickly made his retreat to the kitchen and out of sight.

"I must be going," I hurriedly ventured and thanked them for all their help. Mr. Hands showed me to the door and then out to the front gate, talking garden all the way. He was certainly a wonderful man and a great worker.

That night when I heard the doctor arrive home about nine o'clock, I slipped down the back stairs and through to the front hall.

"Could I get you a cup of coffee or something?" I asked, trying to be helpful while getting an opening.

"Yes, I'd enjoy that very much," he answered in appreciation. "Where is my wife now?"

"She decided to go to bed early, said she felt drowsy."

"That's understandable, because I have her on sedatives."

I brought the coffee, gave it to him and stood hesitating for a minute.

"Did you wish to say something?" he asked.

"Yes sir, could I speak with you for a moment?"

"Most certainly, come and sit down."

"No, I prefer to stand, thank you, sir. I just wanted to tell you I am planning to leave your service here, and I wondered if you would be so kind as to give me a recommendation?"

"Certainly, I will be only too glad to do so, and a good one too. I suppose you are leaving because of the incident with my wife?"

"Yes sir."

"Well I can't say I blame you, she can become trying at times. Her spells of bad behavior seem to come more often now. I don't quite know just how much longer I can take it. She is slowly losing her mind, and here I sit, a doctor, with my hands tied. I simply don't know what to do for her. She seemed to like you and talked with you a great deal, and yet when she gets an idea about a person, it seems to play on her mind, and she has the idea now that you are a thief. It certainly would be better for all concerned if you left, although you mustn't take this personally. The truth is I hate to lose you. Where do you plan to go?"

"I would like to apply to the Dunbar's as their table maid and nurse-maid to the children."

"Splendid, I'll speak to Henry tomorrow morning, and you needn't worry, you practically have the job now."

I thanked him most sincerely and made my exit.

Life wasn't so bad after all. My friend the gardener had helped me, and God had opened the way. Sometimes God takes a long, long time to answer prayers, but other times he answers them almost before we can believe it.

Chapter 17
I Love You So Very Much

I applied to the Dunbar's and soon heard back from them accepting me on Dr. Wilson's recommendation, so I left the Wilsons' and went to work for the Dunbars' almost immediately.

The Dunbar girls, Sheila and Mary, were darling children to work with and I enjoyed them immensely. My job was to keep them well-fed, well-clothed, bathed, and happy. I often frolicked and played with them in the large garden that extended down the hill behind the house, and we often went for walks together and generally had a wonderful time.

My only regular duties were serving the table, dusting, and cleaning. The girls waited anxiously each day for me to finish my duties and get back to them. At night, I had the regular routine of baths, snacks, and bedtime stories. I compromised and alternated one of their stories with Bible stories every second night. They became very interested in the Bible this way. Life was good, life was full. I loved the girls and they in turn loved me, even though I was the hired help.

One day, I walked with the girls to the Blind Institute Grounds, not far from the Dunbar home, where a lovely winding path made its way through the pine trees, leading to the main building. The sun, streaming down through the branches of the trees, made a beautiful lacy pattern on the fresh green grass and a bench at the side of the path beckoned to us to sit down and rest.

It was Sheila who drew my attention to a young man, a fair distance from us, feeding nuts to a squirrel from his hand. We watched him from our bench for a while, then the girl's curiosity got the better of them, and they begged me to go closer. As we approached, the squirrel scampered up a tree, so I motioned to the girls to keep back, and as they backed up, the squirrel descended the tree again, and went right up to the man. As quick as a wink, that tiny furry animal darted forward, took the nut out of the man's hand, and leaving a safe distance between himself and the man, sat up on his haunches and proceeded to eat the nut, turning it around and around as he ate, thoroughly enjoying himself.

The girls crept closer and closer, quietly, as they thought, but soon the squirrel ran up the tall pine tree out of sight again. The man turned to see what had frightened the squirrel, and it was none other than Mr. Hands' son George, that handsome man I'd seen only twice before on very brief encounters.

"Hello!" I ventured, "I'm so sorry that we frightened your squirrel away. That is quite an art you have there. I understand it takes great patience to train a squirrel to eat out of one's hand. Do you come here often?"

"Yes, I do. I enjoy walking and it makes a nice walk from our house up through these grounds and around via Ava Road to Lovers Lane and back home. I don't recall seeing you here before, though. You work for the Dunbars, don't you? Is your name Nell?"

"Yes, it is." I was thrilled that he had remembered me and my name.

"I met you at our house once, didn't I? Father often talks about you."

"All good: I hope."

"Absolutely, but he does wish you'd come to see Mother again sometime. She seems to get lonely with no one to talk to from the homeland."

Secretly, at that moment I was wishing that he would come to visit me, never mind my visiting his mother.

"Will you teach us how to train a squirrel?" Mary piped up from behind his elbow.

"Certainly, I'd be glad to," he replied as he gave me a shy grin. "But it could take a long time. You must have a great deal of patience. Do you think that you have that kind of patience?" By this time he was down on his haunches, talking quite seriously to the two little girls.

"I have *lots* of patience," broke in Sheila, then pointing an accusing finger at Mary she continued, "She's too noisy, she'd start to giggle and frighten him off, but I'm older, I wouldn't."

"Well, let's see now. Here's a nut for each of you." Standing up now, he handed each of the children a nut and then turning to me asked, "Would you like to learn too?" His eyes were a deep dark brown and they twinkled ever so slightly as he handed me a nut. As his hand touched mine, I felt a decided thrill pass through me which I couldn't explain and didn't want to. All I knew was that I enjoyed it. I wondered if he had felt it too, as he was now blushing.

The lesson began, "You must stay absolutely still, and show the squirrel your nut, like this." He demonstrated. "Then, you must place your nut over near the bottom of the tree trunk, and step well back, to give him lots of room to come down the tree and retrieve the nut in safety."

"Do you mean he doesn't come near you at all at first?" Sheila asked.

"That's exactly what I mean. You have to win his confidence. He's afraid of us, and timid, so you start slowly to win his friendship. Let's put the nuts under the tree now and step back."

We all obeyed his instructions to the letter, and with exchange of gestures and eyes only, made our way back to the bench and sat, stock still, waiting for the squirrel to make the next move. Slowly but surely, the brown squirrel made his way down the trunk and very hesitatingly went from one nut to the other, as smiles of satisfaction were exchanged between us.

"There now, that's your first lesson. Now all you have to do is come here regularly and place nuts closer and closer to you, until one day you hold them in your hand, and by that time the squirrel trusts you, and will dare to come right up and take it from your hand."

"Can we come again tomorrow, Nell? Can we? Oh please, say yes. Please?" The young man had caught their imagination, and they were eager to try this new experiment.

"I don't know about tomorrow, but we'll come as often as we can."

I was surprised by George's reaction then, for he said, "I'll be around again on Sunday about this time. If you could come back at that time, I'd be glad to help." He was speaking to the children but his eyes seemed to turn with a smile to me, or was I mistaken, reading too much into things?

"We can, can't we Nell? Can't we?" urged Mary.

"We'll try very hard to come on Sunday, of course, dear, but it depends on what your parents have planned."

"Are you walking home now?" George asked.

"Yes, we are," I answered somewhat surprised.

"May I walk along with you?"

When I spoke to Katie later that week she exclaimed, "What a breakthrough that was. As far as I know he hasn't spoken more than two words to any girl I know of. I thought he must be a woman hater, and what a waste that would be. Of course you're going to go, aren't you?"

"Well, I will if the Dunbars aren't taking the children out."

"If that happens, go yourself. You're crazy if you don't. Of course, I could always go in your place," she laughed. "He tipped his hat to me one day, remember."

"Sorry, he's mine," I quipped.

"Now wait a minute, I knew him first." We laughed and kidded, but deep down I had made up my mind to be there on Sunday come rain or come shine. There was something very good and upright about this young man that I admired greatly, and I wanted to get to know him better.

Sunday was a handpicked day, and as the Dunbars had company they were glad to have the children occupied for a while, so we headed straight for the Blind Institute Grounds with our wee brown bag of nuts. I believe

I was more disappointed than the children when I couldn't see our friend anywhere.

"Never mind," I tried to cheer them up. "We'll feed the squirrels anyway. Now, put your nuts under the tree and let's sit down over on the bench and watch for the squirrel. Maybe he isn't around today, either," I mused.

We had attracted a squirrel and were placing our second nuts just a wee bit closer when a voice came from behind our bench.

"You've learned your lesson well, I see. Sorry I'm late. I went for a ride in the country on my bicycle and it took longer than I thought it would. You should just see the country today, Nell. It's beautiful this time of the year. Everything looks so fresh and new. Do you have a bicycle?"

"No, I don't, and I miss it very much. I used to ride quite a bit in Scotland."

"You should get yourself one and maybe we could go riding together."

The look of surprise on my face must have shown for he soon interjected, "Oh we wouldn't go very far, the roads are too rough in many places. Not like the roads back home. I was in a cycle club in England and we went out every weekend. I traveled a fair bit around the English countryside with that club. Wonderful fun! They don't seem to have cycle clubs here. The road conditions are not so good and the distances are so great, I guess that is why."

George was talking freely, intently, and seemed to be enjoying every minute of it, I could tell. His shyness seemed gone. The children had to remind him to put out nuts for the squirrels every now and then, as he rambled on and on about cycling, the country, gardening, and many other subjects.

After a few similar Sundays and the odd early evening meetings in the park, always with the children playing with the squirrels while we talked, he finally ventured to ask me for a date, of a sort. A bicycle race was being held and he was interested.

It turned out to be an exciting race, because George knew some of the competitors and just being with him alone made it a most enjoyable experience for me. He teased me about my big floppy hat that almost took off in the breeze and offered his coat to me when it started to spit rain on our way home.

After the bicycle race, I gained courage enough to invite him to our Garden Party and Bazaar at the church. This brought forth a whole flood of discussion about religion. He had been brought up in the Anglican Church, quite strictly too, and had attended an Anglican grammar school, but lately had fallen away from the church. He seemed to enjoy the fun and fellowship we had at the bazaar though, and after that day we went for walks, mostly on my days or evenings off and on the weekends.

George was employed by the Toronto, Hamilton, and Buffalo Railway, which was a subsidiary of the Canadian Pacific Railroad. When he first came to Canada, he had worked for a couple of years at farming on a farm north of Toronto. He had agreed to do this when he immigrated to Canada in order to qualify for a reduction in the boat fare. Canada was in great need of workers for the land, and this plan insured her of workers and also insured the immigrant of a job, for a while at least. The hope was that the young men would stay on the farms and make farming their career.

George, while a gardener and farmer at heart, could see after a few years that he could never earn enough money to buy a farm that way and would always be a farm hand, so he decided to try the big city again, and went to work at the Toronto Stock Exchange.

He soon discovered that his hearing wasn't up-to-par and he couldn't hear the Morse code properly, so left it for a desk job at the railway station in Brantford. His father about that time answered garden advertisements for southern Ontario, and had gone straight to the gardening jobs in Brantford, while his mother took in boarders and his sister Liz went out to service.

In England he had been born near Warwick and lived in the gardener's house of a large estate. The more I got to know him, the more I could see an intense dislike for the upper class. I often thought of his early childhood as a gardener's son, living in the gardener's house, and it was easy to picture him having no one to play with but his sister and the rich man's son, who would no doubt look down on him. I could well imagine that the other boy would not be encouraged to play with George too much, and I could understand how this could hurt a young boy, and make him lonely and angry, giving him a desire to fight the world and its systems all on his own.

I then reasoned that he should have come out of this hostile feeling in later years because his father gave up gardening for a while and moved to London when George was around ten years of age. As I got to know George better, however, he began to tell me more about his family and what they were like as indeed I told him about mine.

'I think a great deal of your Father," I said one day.

"I'm very glad you do, Nell, but Father was not always as likeable as he is now, you know. He has changed very much for the better since coming to this country. He got very discouraged in London, and after a few years began to form the habit of drowning his disappointments in liquor. Often Mother would send me to pull him out of the pub after payday when we needed the money desperately to meet our debts. Mother would cry and get very upset, and then I would have to go and tell him he had to come home. It wasn't easy for a young man of fifteen to go into a place like that and try, to persuade his father that he'd had enough and that he should come home now. I often look back on it and think of all the temptation that was around me then."

"But you didn't give in?"

"No, just watching Father and his friends lose their senses and money was enough for me. Alcohol just doesn't solve problems. When you go on a binge you wake up the next morning with less money than you had before, you have a splitting headache, and your family is mad at you. You hate yourself for being a fool, you hate your wife even more for thinking you're one, and you hate the world at large for encouraging you to be so foolish. It just isn't the answer to life's problems. If anything, it makes more."

"Did you stay at school long?"

"Only through grade school, I'm sorry to say, and I was through it at eleven years of age, but I couldn't legally leave school before I was fourteen. My parents didn't have the money to send me on to a secondary education, so I put in two years as an assistant teacher or instructor. Believe you me, I knew Shakespeare by the time I was finished, as I went over many of the plays many times. After that, I worked in a grocery store for a couple of years, and then decided I needed to earn more money so that I could help Mother meet the family budget. I managed to get a job with a good salary, but I didn't like it as it was serving liquor and wine in a rich man's drinking club in the center of London. I used to travel to and from work into the center of the city on my bicycle, which wasn't exactly easy, even then."

"Do you mean to say you served liquors and wines but didn't taste them? That's a bit hard to believe."

"I know," he answered. "But it's true nevertheless. The first day I was employed I was told to taste the wines so that I would learn the different kinds, but I memorized the labels and the location of the different vintages in the wine cellar and listened to people's comments on the different kinds. I didn't take them up on their offer to taste. I was afraid I might get a liking for the stuff and I didn't want to lead a life filled with an aching desire for it."

"I've often wondered what a place like that would be like."

"Amazing, is the best word I can use to express my own feelings. The place was extremely plain on the outside so that no one would suspect what it was, but it was very gorgeous indeed on the inside, taking on an air of elegance very hard to believe. Plush chairs, carpeted floors, satin-brocaded drapes and beautiful chandeliers made up the decor. Men would arrive in elegant suits and in stylish coaches or new motor cars and they looked terrific, but by the time they left they were in a crumpled, disgusting, debauched state."

"Tell me, is this why you have such a dim view of the well-to-do?"

"It's all part of it."

One time I ventured to ask the question why George himself had decided to leave England and come to Canada.

"Land of opportunity, I guess," he laughed. "I decided while working at that club to save up my money and leave England to see the world. I began reading about the huge exodus being made to America and Canada and became interested in the new countries. The more I thought about it the more I wanted to come to Canada and start a new life for myself and my family. I'm so happy that we did come. Father is like a new person here – he's back on the land, doing the job he loves to do and he has left the liquor alone completely. Mother has a home of her very own, a thing she never dreamt she would have. You should have seen her face when she first saw the house she's in now. Her smile was radiant, and then she began to cry for happiness. My sister is getting along nicely, too."

"God has been good to you, George."

"Yes, I guess you could say that, although most of the changes for the better have been brought about by my own sweat and determination."

I sensed a deep bitterness that was turning George away from God, but I couldn't seem to find its base, and I didn't want to probe too deeply. It was sort of like the game with the squirrels, you had to go slowly so as not to frighten him away, gradually gaining his confidence until he could trust you enough to tell you what his deep-seated trouble was.

He surprised me on my birthday with a lovely gold bracelet, beautifully engraved, George Simpson Hands to Helen Laird Sweenie, June 25th, 1914. I was thrilled. I knew he must like me a great deal to give me such a thoughtful gift, and while I hadn't known him long, I knew my love for him was growing stronger day by day. I could feel it every time I got close to him, every time he flashed his deep brown eyes at me and every time I saw him dressed in his Sunday best, walking around the gardens or coming up the side walk to the house. He carried himself with dignity and poise, and yet he still had a shy way with him.

Katie left the Wilson's in early October, and like me, managed to get a job with the Dunbars. It was like old times again, only much better, for Katie was more relaxed and a real ball of fun. There was a group of us going to the church now, and we had many happy times. I missed George's company on these occasions, however, so kept talking to him about it until I persuaded him to come, too.

At first he felt strange in the Presbyterian Church, after his experiences in the Anglican, but soon he was comfortable and enjoying the fellowship of our friends as much as I did. On occasion we would attend the First Baptist Church's evening services because, they had a terrific program for youth at that time. I felt that George took to most of it in a beautiful way, and we were both happy together.

"When are you two going to make something out of this romance?" questioned Katie one day.

"I wish I knew," was my reply.

I didn't inform Katie further, but I searched my own heart a great deal for the next few days. Why was George so hesitant and nervous when kissing me? He acted as though he was afraid of me, and yet he wanted to get close to me and talk with me. One night in March, after a very good night at church and a lovely walk home, I invited him in. Katie was there making herself some tea, so we joined her. After tea, Katie retired to bed and we had a good chance to talk, except for the occasional interruption by Dick, the butler, who was serving company that night.

As we stood near the door saying our good-byes, George reached towards my waist and drew me to him. He placed a firm and beautiful kiss upon my lips as I held my breath in sheer enjoyment, loving every minute of it. Then, I realized, as I had many times before that, suddenly the kiss slipped from my lips. His arm fell from my waist and he was ready to say good night. It was as if a cold chill fell over him every time he kissed me or got near me, and words just didn't materialize.

This particular night it suddenly made me angry and for the first time I lashed out at him. "What, in the name of goodness, is wrong with you? Or is it ME? Every time we get close to one another, you turn cold. What is it? You owe me an explanation at least, and then you can go, and we'll not bother to see one another again, but please tell me. Do I have bad breath? Does my perfume repulse you? What is it?" I was almost in tears, as I gestured for him to sit down across from me at the table again.

"Yes, you're right; I do owe you an apology. It hasn't been fair to you. Please forgive me?" he stammered.

"Never mind the apologies, just tell me what's wrong? Now! I want to know! I have the right to know!"

I thought for a moment he was going to cry. His eyes got red and as he sat down at the table he covered his face with his hands.

"I love you, Nell. You must know that, above all things. I love everything about you. Your face, your hair, your build, everything, but most of all I love YOU your inner self. It's beautiful. You love people. You help people. You comfort people and enjoy children. You love God with a very strong faith, and for all these reasons, I love you."

"Are you trying to tell me that while you love me for all these qualities, you couldn't think of marriage? You had another love affair in England didn't you, your father told me that, and you were disappointed in love, and determined never to love again. I see it all now!" I jumped to conclusions. "You're still in love with her! You can't love me because you still love her! Well my advice to you is to go back to her and the sooner the better." I stood up and walked to the door and was just reaching for the handle to show him out when he caught hold of my hand and led me back to the table.

"Please let me explain. I am NOT still in love with her. As a matter of fact, I *hate* her, with an intense hatred I don't even like to admit to myself."

"Did she jilt you, then?" I ventured.

"No. It's a long story, but I can see now that you must know it and believe it before we, as a couple, can have any happiness."

There was a long pause and then he continued, as the perspiration began to stand out on his brow.

"It was my first cousin, and we were seeing a great deal of each other and felt fond of one another. I guess I figured I was in love, and asked for her hand in marriage. She accepted, and we both told our families. My mother and my aunt were very happy with the arrangement, as were both families. I have always been a saver by nature, so I started putting as much money aside as I could, towards our future marriage.

One fortnight when I had a bicycle trip scheduled with my cycle club, she went out to the country to visit an uncle who worked on a large estate much the way my father had done before moving to London. The long and the short of it is that she came back pregnant. She met the lord of the manor's son by a chance meeting, and he made a play for her immediately. Sort of swept her off her feet, she said."

"But you —-"

"Let me finish," he pleaded as he rubbed his hands over his face and got more and more fidgety. "The worst is yet to come. She told *me* what had actually happened, and all about this rich fellow, but she informed her parents that *I* was the father. Naturally they believed her, because they knew nothing about the lord's son. They didn't even know he existed."

"Oh, no: George! What a horrible situation! How could she do such a thing?"

"She could, and she did. I guess she took me for a proper fool. She said that I was good and dependable and the right kind to marry. When I refused to marry her, she still wouldn't tell her parents the truth, so they thought I was a cad and a liar, deserting her and my own child. Guess I'm not the first man to be blamed for a sin he didn't commit, but my love for her turned to hate at that moment. If she had really loved me, she wouldn't have gone out with the other fellow in the first place. She had betrayed me, and I couldn't bring myself to think of marriage, let alone looking after a child that wasn't mine for the rest of my life."

"Didn't the rich fellow ever know what he had done, or have the opportunity to provide for the child? Perhaps he would have married her."

"I wondered about that too, and asked her if she had told him. She said that just as soon as she knew her condition she had gone for a second fortnight to her uncle's place expressly for this purpose, but the lord's son only mocked her, and said it was just her hard luck. He explained that he couldn't marry her, as he was married already. I asked her if he had forced himself on her and could she charge him with rape, but she said, no, that she had just been carried away by his handsome face and suave manner, and of course his beautiful automobile.

"The whole thing made me so furious that all I could think about was revenge. I threatened to seek him out and kill him. I knew his name, Ian MacDonald, and his address. Apparently his folks were very wealthy and lived in Scotland, but they also had an estate near London, and after he married he came to live on it. He was just one of those idle rich, who thought he could do anything, to anybody and get away with it. I wanted revenge. My mother and father reasoned with me that it wouldn't solve anything, and would only make matters worse. They said, 'If you are telling the truth, you must keep yourself free of all of this.'

"It made me angry that they too, had doubts in their minds. It was very uncomfortable at home for a while, with my parents not knowing whether to believe me or not. My aunt accused me outright and demanded that I marry my cousin. My cousin kept begging me to marry her and give her child a name, but I couldn't Nell, I couldn't. I didn't love her anymore. My reaction to it all was to swear off girls forever, and I guess I have until now. I'm all mixed up inside, Nell. I've even blamed God for my unhappiness. It all seemed so unfair."

"Did you say his name was Ian?" I questioned. "Ian McDonald?" A cold shiver ran down my back.

"Yes, that was his name. I have heard since, that he has always been a problem to his parents, and that they thought, when he got married that perhaps he would settle down. Not much chance. That kind never change, can you imagine being HIS wife?

"You look so white, Nell! I'm afraid this has been a terrible shock to you, I'd better go. I knew that telling you the story would be the end for us. You couldn't possibly love me now. You suspect me too, just as they did, and I wouldn't blame you for one moment."

"No, please don't go!" I said as I stood up and went over to him, placing my hands on his beautiful square shoulders and running my hands through his hair. It thrilled me just to touch him and comfort him. I knew now, without a doubt, that I loved him.

Slowly he stood up, and I slipped my arms around him and cradled my head against his chest, allowing myself the pleasure of the closeness of his body. As I rested there, my mind tried to grasp the significance of the news I had just received. Ian —- my Ian —-married to one woman and having an affair with another —- just as Mrs. Fraser had predicted he would. I couldn't believe it, and yet I could. No doubt he had been bored with his wife and wanted a thrill, not counting the cost to another. In a flash, I thought how I might have been this wife, deserted for the first pretty face or interesting stranger to come along. Once again, I realized that God had led me away from danger, even though the process had meant much heartache.

Then, remembering George's statement about blaming God for his un-happiness, I backed off a little, looking up into his face and trying to comfort him with my words. "George! You mustn't blame God for this bad turn of events in your life. Blame the Devil maybe, but not God. When evil steps into the heart of a loved one like that, and causes them to do evil, it is not God, but Satan at work. You can't blame God, when a person's acts are wrong. God doesn't have us on a string. He doesn't *make* us do things. We are free agents to decide our destiny: God's way, the narrow way, or the Devil's way, the wide open road. Your friend chose the wide easy route with the Devil urging her on, but don't blame God. Rather thank him for letting you find out what she was, before making the mistake of marrying her, and having a broken heart for the rest of your life."

"I hadn't really thought of it that way before, Nell. Please promise to forgive me for acting so strangely with you. I just don't trust anyone anymore. I know it is wrong to feel this way, but there it is. Every time I take you in my arms I wonder if you have, or will, betray me, too." He folded his arms around me and pulled me closer to him hugging me to his chest.

He was suffering from a combination of bitter disappointment in love, betrayal, condemnation in the eyes of his relations and friends, fear of another heartache should he give his love to another, and worst of all, he had turned away from God, whom he had always loved dearly.

George seemed to wish to spread everything in his troubled mind before me, so continued. "What I have told you about my desires to come out to Canada were true, but the rumor that she spread about me was the deciding factor in my move to Canada. I planned to come on my own at first, and make a new life for myself. I guess I thought of myself as an adventurer, seeking my fortune in the vast new land, unhindered by a woman or family. However, as I watched my mother straining under the situation, and listened to my father complaining about the conditions in England at the time, and talking about the huge number of people who were sailing to the colonies to get away from it all, I decided to call my parent's bluff. One day I told them I'd pay all the family's fares to Canada if they wished to come with me. I had the money and I didn't need it for marriage, now. They surprised me by saying they'd love to go. We came, and you know the rest."

He rose to go, gathering his coat up in his arm, with his head still low, and then looking at me with a beautiful wistful smile, he continued, "Oh, how I love you, Nell, and now I have probably lost you. If you never want to see me again, I don't blame you."

I placed a kiss on his cheek and gave him a big hug. "Oh, George, I love you so very much, and I know you are telling the truth. I almost married the same Ian McDonald you speak of, and but for the grace of God, I would have been his betrayed wife. God saved me from that marriage because I was a table maid, but now look what he has done. He has led me to you.

"God is wonderful, he guides us and protects us, and leads us all the way through life, if we will only trust Him and allow Him to lead."

"You believe me, then?" George questioned with astonishment and delight.

"Of course I believe you, my darling, and you can trust me that I will never betray you in any way. I love you too much.

"Will you marry me, Nell?"

"Yes, George, I will."

From that time on, he was like a different person. Released, from his burdensome load, and at peace with God, he enjoyed life again. His smile was radiant and he stood straight and tall, but more relaxed than before. He took a new interest in the church, and his life took on a new zeal, as he was assured of God's forgiveness for the sin of guilt, which he had felt for so long, because he had not married his cousin. In his new reconciliation with God, he found the happiness he had always been seeking, and I found my true love.

Chapter 18
Marriage, Home and Family

We became engaged almost immediately, and decided to build our own home, as George had been saving his pennies for some time now. We chose a three bedroom cottage plan and contracted a builder to build it. The builder, Mr. Harold Bowie, was one of the young men from the church, and he and his new bride were living in a similar cottage that he had built for her. I had fallen in love with it when we visited them one day.

Spring Street was now being subdivided all down both sides for residences, so we quickly bought the land next door to George's father and mother's home. Mr. Bowie started building just as soon as he could that May, and George started cultivating part of the yard for a garden. He was in his glory to be on the land again. The house wouldn't be ready for occupation until January the next year but we were both enjoying ourselves so much watching the house being built.

On January 18th, 1916, I walked up the aisle in St. Andrews Presbyterian Church to the strains of 'Lohengrin' in a navy blue serge suit, and a beautiful large-brimmed navy hat with a white flower right in the center. It was a simple, but lovely wedding, with all our friends present, and Mr. Bowie took my Father's place and gave me away.

We went to Niagara Falls for a weekend and then returned to our new home. It was wonderful to own a home of our very own. It was fun to choose furniture for the different rooms. It was fun to get back to doing some cooking again, and George was just thrilled with his garden.

We planted a small apple tree, seeded grass under it, and put a flower bed around three sides of it. George said, "In a few years from now, when the tree has grown up, we'll put a bench on that little spot and enjoy the shade." He made a path down the center of the yard and couldn't wait to plant some flowers down each side of it and vegetables behind the flowers.

That summer, we walked back up around the Blind Institute Grounds to reminisce, and illegally dug up a tiny, tiny evergreen. I wrapped the roots up lovingly in my handkerchief and when we got home we planted it at the back, near the corner of the house. The house was red brick, so we decided to trim it in green and white, and George planted shrubs along the foundation at the front. He was in his glory working out the garden plans, and it made me feel good to have a gardener in the family again.

Not only were we growing beautiful flowers, shrubs, vegetables, and trees, but I soon discovered that I was pregnant. I was thrilled with the prospect of having a baby. I had enjoyed Jean's wee ones so very much, and now I was having my very own. With my mother-in- law living right beside me, it was great, because I could always count on her to help me.

Two days before our first wedding anniversary, God gave us a beautiful baby boy, and we called him George after his father. He weighed in around twelve pounds, and had reddish-colored hair and hazel eyes. I enjoyed being a mother so very much. I now felt completely fulfilled, more than ever before.

Two years later, I became a mother again. This time God gave us a gorgeous baby girl. I called her Elizabeth after her grandmother Hands. She was beautiful, with the same coloring as George, red hair, and hazel eyes. By this time, George's hair had turned to a blond, but Elizabeth's hair was a darker red, so I thought that eventually she would become auburn.

I now had the family and home I had so often dreamed of, and I was ever so happy. I wrote to my father often, and he wrote back to me. As letter followed letter, I got to know him better and better and grew to love him more and more.

George was a wonderful provider, and he loved his children very much and seemed quite contented to work in the railway station office all day and in his garden at night. He took an active part in the church as well, becoming the church treasurer. Life was good, life was full, and my cup did run over, just as God promises that it will if we will just follow Him and trust in His promises.

It was wonderful to watch the children grow day by day, and as the years passed, contentment seemed my portion for a while, but then slowly and unmistakably a longing began to grow within me to see my homeland again. I believe the name of the disease is 'homesickness.'

Chapter 19
Homesickness - Life's Surprises

There is only one cure for 'homesickness,' and that is to go home. Nothing else will suffice, you just have to see your old home again and get it out of your system. I had to see my loved ones in Scotland, especially Father. I couldn't get him off my mind. I thought of him day and night. I pictured him in the garden that last day saying, "Nell, I don't want you to go. I have a strange feeling I'll never see you again."

Finally, I gathered up enough courage to speak to George about my strong longing. George felt that I should plan to go back the following summer. My daughter, Elizabeth, was eight years old now and reminded me a great deal of wee Jean, even to the long red ringlets. Should I take her and George with me? Could I bear to leave them behind?

I kept thinking of wee Jean constantly too. It was more than the fact that Elizabeth looked like her. I had received a letter from my sister Jean telling me that wee Jean had shown some signs of tuberculosis lately, and was being treated for it. How I prayed that she would get better real soon. I knew that she would get tender care from Jean, so I was sure she would recover from it. All I could think of was wee Jean and my Elizabeth meeting each other. I felt I must take Elizabeth with me, but for some reason that I couldn't explain, I was reluctant to take George, my son, along. I think in the back of my mind I had a fear of icebergs, and if anything ever happened to him I'd never forgive myself. I knew that women and children were put into the lifeboats first, and I was afraid that George, now eleven, just might be left behind with the men if anything happened. George Sr. had no desire to return home, and besides, we didn't have enough money for all of us to go; in fact it was going to be a struggle to find the money for Elizabeth and me.

Finally, the day came when, having made all arrangements, I sat down to write a letter to Father telling him of our proposed visit. I was thrilled at the thought of seeing him again after fifteen years, and I wished that I didn't have to wait until August. I could picture him opening this letter. He'd smile, a big tear would run down his cheek and he'd say, "Aye, my wee lass is comin hame tae see me."

I mailed the letter and continued with my happy planning, but we are not always granted our fondest wishes, however, and I received a telegram two days later saying my father had suddenly taken a heart attack and passed away. He would never receive my letter.

I was dreadfully upset. I wept off and on for days and all I could think of was how he had poured out his heart to me in the garden that day. Now it had come to pass, we would never again see each other in this world. I was devastated, but life must go on.

As the days passed, I realized that my desire to go home was just as strong as before, and I reasoned with myself that Jean and George's children were growing up, and I mustn't wait. The next few months seemed forever, but eventually the day for our departure came and Elizabeth and I said our good-byes as we boarded the train at the red brick CNR Station in Brantford for Montreal, where our steamship ocean liner, 'The S.S. Montcalm' awaited us.

It was July 1, 1927, and finally safely on board, I forgot my fears of the Atlantic and began to enjoy the trip immensely. Elizabeth soon became friends with several other little girls aboard, and I struck up friendships with some of their mothers. The food was delicious, and just the pure luxury of having all my meals prepared and set before me was wonderful indeed. The musical entertainment at night thrilled Elizabeth no end, and we were both having a marvelous time.

Then it happened, —- in mid Atlantic. There was a terrifying bang, and the ship jolted to a stop and sent everybody flying in every direction. I fell to the floor and as I desperately tried to get up I heard someone scream, "An iceberg! We've hit an iceberg!"

My thoughts were racing now. "I must get back to Elizabeth." I had left her in our cabin for a moment, playing with one of her chums.

Becoming panicky now, I tore down the stairway pushing past all the people as they rushed up to the upper deck. As I ran I prayed, "Oh, please God, let me find her! Please don't let her be alone at a time like this! Please help us! Please save us! Oh, why did I bring her? Please, God! Please!"

As I approached my cabin, I saw the door was ajar and as I ran in I could see no one. I now screamed, "Elizabeth, Elizabeth, where are you?" Tears began to come to my eyes and for a moment I was numb with fear. Fear of losing my daughter. Fear of drowning. Fear of death itself. Closing my eyes and in total anguish I screamed out, "God, please hear me! Please! Please, let me find her!"

Just as I looked up, Elizabeth appeared in the doorway, crying and running to me, "Mommy, Mommy, I went looking for you and Peggy's mother when we hit the iceberg. I was so scared, Mommy. It threw us across the cabin. Why are you crying Mommy, were you afraid, too?" I sat down on the bed for a moment and gathered her up in my arms, kissing her and hugging her, as I silently prayed. "Oh, God, thank you, thank you for bringing her to me, and please, please save this ship and all the people."

Now I became conscious of survival rules, and I reached for our life preservers and fastened one on each of us. I had seen no signs of water, but we must hurry or we might not get on a life boat. Rushing up stairs we met people that seemed unusually calm for a time like this. I couldn't understand. I had expected chaos but everyone was so very calm.

"What's happening? What's happening? Why aren't we getting on the life boats?" I asked a man who was standing very still but looked very frightened.

"Well, we didn't really hit the iceberg, we slid onto a hidden underwater ledge of ice, and we are sitting on that ledge right now. The ship has been damaged but they say they can keep that under control, but we are just sitting here like a little toy ship on a shelf.

"Have you seen the iceberg? It is gigantic! It towers above us for miles, with icy mountain-like peeks faintly showing in the misty haze. They don't want us in the life boats. They sent for help on the wireless, but how could a ship come and rescue us from this ledge? They couldn't. We are prisoners here in the grip of an ice giant. We are drifting south along with the berg, and when it melts enough it will dump us out like so many sardines."

Slowly we made our way up to the top deck. There through the mist we could barely make out the outline of the ice peeks against the skyline on one side of the ship, and the mighty Atlantic on the other. "Oh, my God," I prayed, "please save us." The cold coming from the berg made us shiver, although it was a summer day.

"What can we do now?" I asked a passing officer.

"We just have to wait, and pray, I guess. There is really nothing we can do but wait until the berg releases us, and only God knows what will happen when it does. We have sent for help and some ships will be standing by to rescue us."

We waited all day, a long night, another day, and still we drifted along helplessly on this shelf. It was a long, cold wait and I had much time to think. I despairingly wished I had not brought my daughter to a watery grave, and I was exceedingly glad that my husband and son were safe at home.

There was great tension as everyone aboard ship waited, but people went through the motions of ordinary living. We ate our meals as usual and tried to carry on normal conversations, but the longer we waited the more the tension grew, and the cold temperature was a constant reminder of this giant iceberg that held us in its grip.

Many people tried to keep calm by going on deck and looking the foreboding "berg" in the eye. Some even tried to take pictures of the monster, but I felt best when my daughter and I knelt together in our cabin, privately talking to God.

God is love, and I felt His love bringing the same calmness that I had felt on other occasions. I couldn't explain why, but somehow I knew that all would be well and we would get out of this alive.

In the afternoon on the second day, just after we had been praying in our cabin, the ship gave a terrible lurch and we both fell and slid across the floor. After a few frightening seconds of quietness, we looked towards each other and then scrambled to a standing position.

Our next move was to head out into the corridor, with the hope of making it to the lifeboats. Then, to our surprise and utter amazement, we heard the engines of the ship going again and everyone began shouting, "We're safe, we're off the berg!" People were kissing and hugging each other and laughing and singing. IT WAS A MIRACLE! The ship had slipped off the icy ledge and cleared the iceberg, as neat as you please, without anyone being hurt. The engines were going full-steam ahead again, taking us farther and farther away from the iceberg and closer and closer to Scotland.

I heard a woman passenger praising the captain for our safety. The captain's replied, "My dear woman, it was not my doing. Only by the grace of God were we saved this day."

I later found out that back home in Brantford my husband had been notified of our great peril, and as it was Sunday morning he had requested the church to pray for us. After the prayer, the congregation had joined in the singing of this great hymn:

"Eternal Father, strong to save,
Whose arm hath bound the restless wave,
Who bid's the mighty ocean deep
Its own appointed limits keep:
O hear us when we cry to Thee
For those in peril on the sea."

The ship slipped off the ledge at approximately four-thirty on the Sunday afternoon, and taking into account the time difference, it would certainly seem that God had answered their prayers.

Chapter 20
Home Again

When I arrived in Scotland I was greeted at the dock by Uncle John, who was crying. Was he crying for joy at seeing me again and meeting Elizabeth? We were naturally late arriving, so he would have heard of our narrow escape at sea, but we were safe, so why was he crying? He looked much older now. His wife had passed away a couple of years ago, but why was he crying so now?

As soon as we got a little way out of the crowd and were waiting for our luggage, he threw his arms around me, and with tears streaming down his face, greeted me. "My dearest Nell. It's sae gid tae hae ye hame again. It's almost like old times. I am indeed sorry you missed your father, by only a few months. I hate tae be the bearer of bad news again, Nell, but someone has tae tell ye. Wee Jean died yesterday, with tuberculosis, like your brother, Frank. She was just nineteen. The funeral is tomorrow."

We stood and cried together while wee Elizabeth stood with a worried expression. She wasn't sure she liked this new country with all the sadness it seemed to be giving her mother. Wee Jean dead! The words could hardly penetrate. Wee Jean, the wee four-year-old with the long red ringlets, whom I just couldn't seem to leave fifteen years ago, was dead. It was as though I could still see her waving to me from the dock. I looked down at my own wee daughter with her red hair. I gave her hand a squeeze and gave a little prayer that my children wouldn't contract that dread disease.

Soon we were on our way to Uncle John's house, where we stayed, but I rushed over to see sister Jean. What a sad meeting, I could hardly bear it. I just wanted to cry and cry. Not only had I come home too late to see Father, but now wee Jean as well. It was good to be able to put my arms around my sister again and to see young Archie, although I wouldn't have known him. He was seventeen now, and quite the young man.

I was glad to be near Jean in her time of sorrow and not on the other side of the ocean, but it was a sad, sad homecoming. It was wonderful to see my brother again, and he drove us around in a Rolls Royce, and although these cars were easier to come by now, it still spoke out that he had been successful in his life's work. He also had a very happy marriage to the girl he had gone with so long ago, and they had four boys to be proud of.

Right after wee Jean's burial, I went over to my father's grave site, and later on that day asked brother George to drive me past Whitemoss. I didn't really want to visit my stepmother, but I felt I should, somehow. George stayed in the car with Elizabeth, as he had no desire to see Maggie.

As I opened the white picket gate into the yard and made my way towards the front door, I felt a chill run through me. I thought again of Father as I glanced towards his garden, neglected for the first time in years. Over in the corner stood the garden house where we had had our long chat. Oh, how I wished I had come home sooner. Oh, how I wanted to rush into his arms once more as I had done fifteen years ago.

Finally, I reached the door and knocked. After a few minutes, there was a rustling behind the door and it was opened a crack as Maggie peered out to see who her visitor was. She glared at me as surprise of recognition dawn on her face. Hesitating for a moment, she finally asked me in, and nodded towards the living room. As we entered this familiar room, memories flooded across my mind. The day Mother died and I waited there alone until Father and Jean told me the sad news. The sight of Father and Beatrice standing embracing and kissing while silhouetted against the light from the fire in the fire place, that day I crept along the hall and peeked, so many years ago. I pictured wee Frank sitting beside the fire trying to read, but being interrupted continually by his irritating cough, just months before his death. Oh, how I loved and hated this room.

Maggie walked over to the window and opened the curtains wide, letting the sunlight invade this dark gloomy room. In this bright light I could see the hard lines that marked her face after years of hardness of heart and lack of love. I asked about my father's death and she curtly replied, "He had a heart attack and died the next night, that's all there is to tell."

"Was he in pain?"

"A little, I guess."

Needless to say our visit was very short, as our conversation was going nowhere. She was not interested in my life in Canada, my husband or my children, so after a few more awkward attempts to converse, I departed.

From there, I visited the new neighbors who lived across the road from Whitemoss. Their name was McKinnon, and Father had often spoken of them in his letters. It seems that they had been very friendly with Father after Mrs. Gillespie's death, five years ago.

The McKinnons welcomed me into their home with open arms. They wanted to know all about my home in Canada and my husband and family. After a while the conversation got around to the night Father died. They told me that Maggie came over banging on their door asking for some whiskey or tod-y to help John's pain. Mr. McKinnon had given her some and then decided to get dressed and go to see if he could be of any help to Father. Upon entering the cottage he had gone straight in to see John and found him in excruciating pain.

"Did the tod-y, no help, John?" Mr. McKinnon tried to sympathize.

"What tod-y?" Father asked. "I had no tod-y, I wish I could have some it might ease this terrible pain."

When Mr. McKinnon went out into the kitchen he saw the empty whiskey bottle sitting beside an empty glass held by Maggie.

"Did you give the tod-y to John?"

"No, I did not," was the tart reply. "I needed it far more than he did. He's almost gone, but I'm the one who will have to stand his passin'."

She hadn't changed over the years! She was still the hard-hearted woman who wouldn't give water or whiskey to a dying man.

A few days later when we were walking down the street in East Kilbride, I saw my stepmother on the other side of the street. She was dressed all in black, and now had quite a bend to her shoulders. I pointed her out to Elizabeth, and the child's reaction was, "She looks like *a witch.*"

During the last week of my vacation, Elizabeth and I took a train into Glasgow with the sole purpose of visiting Mrs. Fraser. Ever since I had left Scotland fifteen years before, Mrs. Fraser had corresponded with me. She had known all my heartaches and all my happy times, and had reacted accordingly like a mother might have done.

As the taxi cab drew up at the door of the large house, Elizabeth voiced her thoughts, "These people must be rich!" Immediately, my mind flashed back to Ian and how he had come to the same conclusion. I smiled to myself. It is strange how things work themselves out. I knew now that it had all worked out for the best in my life, and I was grateful to God for His never ending guidance, and to Mrs. Fraser for helping me in such a real and true way during my romantic crisis.

The maid answered the door, and when I gave my name she smiled and said to come right in, as Mrs. Fraser was anxiously waiting for my visit.

As I entered the library, I saw Mrs. Fraser sitting by the window. She tried to get up to greet us, but even though she used her cane it was difficult. "Do come in, my child," she said in the warmest welcome ever.

We had a long talk, and got caught up on the latest family news and my visit to Scotland. Mr. Fraser had passed away two years before, and she was now a very old and lonely lady. "I knew you'd find happiness someday," she said as she looked at Elizabeth, and we talked about my home in Canada, my husband, and children. "Enjoy life while you're young," she advised. "Enjoy your family and your husband. Life is very short. Make the most of it." We embraced and cried a little, and she lavished Elizabeth with love, kisses, and candy. Then we departed.

Chapter 21
Now, I Could Settle Down

I was actually glad when it was time to return home to Canada. I would always love the heather, the hills, the moors, and streams of Scotland. It is a picturesque country, and it would always hold a great and loving fascination for me, as well as a countless number of memories, but CANADA was my home now, and I was anxious to return to her.

CANADA – 'the quiet giant stretching from sea to sea' — with her offer of shelter to the wayfaring stranger. Her sense of loyalty to her Motherland, and yet a wonderful bustling spirit of youth as she strained to show her independence. CANADA, with her beautiful lakes and mountains! Nowhere in the world is there such a magnificent string of lakes to rave about, or such majestic peaks. Even one of the Seven Wonders of the World is found on her border, the Great Niagara Falls, but never mind these wonders, it is the people that count. The people are a wonderful throng of determined individualists, working to carve a new nation from a unique pattern they have designed, and continue to design for themselves. Now I was a part of that dream.

Now I knew I could settle down. Now I knew I could enjoy my new found life in Canada, where my husband and son faithfully waited for me to return to them. CANADA! Oh, how I had grown to love her. The land where there would be opportunity for my children. I now wanted desperately to get on the boat and go home. I, who had been so desperate to get back to Scotland, realized at last, that CANADA was indeed home to me now.

I thanked God for the wonderful care He had given me through my various experiences in life, and the knowledge that His love would be always with me for the rest of my life and through eternity. Oh, how wonderful God truly is, if we will but put our hand in His, and let Him lead us through life's devious and tricky paths.

We had a delightful sail back, and Elizabeth enjoyed every minute of it. Having docked at Montreal again, I couldn't help remembering my earlier visit to this city with Bella, but now, much as I loved the French atmosphere, I couldn't wait to board the train to Toronto, Hamilton, and finally to Brantford, and my husband and home.

As the train pulled into that familiar red brick station again, I looked out the window, and searched the platform for two familiar figures.

"There's Daddy and George! See, Mom? See? Right over there!"

Elizabeth squealed with excitement, her hands waving anxiously as the train finally came to a stop. We quickly made our way to the closest exit and descended the steps, with the help of the porter. My husband was soon at my side, picking Elizabeth up and giving her a big bear hug and kiss, and then, gently allowing her to slip down to the platform to greet her brother, he turned lovingly to me. There were tears in his eyes, and as he embraced me tenderly but passionately, whispered to me, "Oh, Nell, I'm so glad you're home! Thank God you're safe, I've missed you terribly. I love you so very much!"

• • • • •

Nell's youngest child, Helen (the author) was born the following June and she would like you to remember Uncle John's words —

"You are never alone.
God is always near ye.
God knows your problems.
He loves ye, and will always stand by ye
No matter what happens
Just believe and trust in Him."

Dorrance Publishing Co
701 Smithfield Street
Pittsburgh, PA 15222
Visit our website at www.dorrancebookstore.com

ISBN: 978-1-4809-0985-4
eISBN: 978-1-4809-0869-7

C46044306$

DORRANCE
PUBLISHING CO
EST. 1920
PITTSBURGH, PENNSYLVANIA 15222

1
Approach

Every approach needs to presume upon its reception. And, so, in beginning we never fear that we shall be wholly misunderstood; we trust that our hesitancy, our stumbling talk, and our choice of words are not a search in the dark. To begin is confidently part of the work of building and sharing an understanding. It is ideally the institution of making sense together within a common life and a common world.

Any approach asks for an understanding. In this sense our approach is never just a casual opening, any more than the opening of a Platonic dialogue or the break of dawn is irrelevant to the experiences that are to follow. An opening is never just a beginning except in retrospect. We begin in the midst of things, that is to say, when it is already late and we are caught irrevocably in the web of understandings, borrowed back and forth against the time we have spent together—in thought, in work, in play, in love or in hate.

Our approach is self-consciously a presentation: the presence of others and of ourselves to them. Thus it is **we** who are latently the resource and circumstance that permits us to

1

choose our ground, to start here rather than there, to abide and concede, to question and answer. And we would never get under way were it not for a certain surrender to the tide of presence, the invitation of a look, or of a word that launches us on a voyage of meaning and truth in which each will have different tasks and different dreams, yet all come safely to the shore. For such a voyage the irresistible call is that of truth to which we must fit our talk and all it involves; just as we fit out our ships, not knowing everything they will encounter but trusting everything men have learned from the sea to build into themselves and into their ships in order to sail. In this enterprise we can be confident of ourselves only in the chain of work. We have not to start from the posture of loneliness, nor amidst any babel of tongues. This does not mean that we may not in search of truth keep lonely watch or fall upon exotic islands and strange sights. Yet all these things can be told in our tales, which are somehow suited to bringing back and keeping memory for the telling of things unseen and deeds unheard.

Nor can we set out until we are ready; and thus our voyage begins at home in the world of familiar objects, among friends and everyday scenes. We cannot take our leave without a word or a smile; without checking the ropes, our trusty knife, the matches, the salt, the back door, the tickets, and the passports. Whether we leave for the Orient, the cottage, or the moon, we do not expect to encounter a totally alien scheme of things. We take along toothpaste, a clean shirt, and everyone's best wishes for our new life, whether in marriage or in Canada. We remember all we have been told by friends, novelists, poets, wise men, and even science-fiction writers. We never go alone; we are always ambassadors, representatives of the people, missionaries, or anthropologists.

And something of the sort must be true. Or else by what right do we leave home and friends? By what right do we exchange day and night and wander into regions where our own language and customs become self-conscious, strained, and perhaps unusable? What is it that drives us to know more, or to know anything else than what those around us know, those who have always known us and loved us and never thought we would leave or want anything else than what we had between us? For this is a difference at the heart of things, greater than all the variations of man and woman, of childhood and maturity, of race or class or history. Once we no longer believe that all knowings and misunderstandings and all loves or hates lie within the same flesh and fold of humanity, we do not simply invite the philosopher's loneliness, we suffer the agony and ridicule of solipsism. This is not just to think bravely on one's own, as it might seem to be, but a betrayal of the bond between us and man that, for all it has cost him, God himself has never wholly broken. We shall have to deal with the temptations of solipsism, but not as a beginning. First we must make our preparations for leaving. For then the bustle of getting ready pushes loneliness into a sentiment of things to come, an adventure within our journey rather than the ground from which we start.

To begin is to approach our work; to be alone is to be at work. Yet we must remember the variety and seasons of work to understand its common load. We must remember the terraced vineyards, the railroads, and the docks; we must not forget the insides of factories, mines, and ships; we must be able to hear the roar of trucks, the screech of sawmills. We must feel the fisherman's cold, the weight of things, how they tear and waste those who work them. But if we wish to start right, it is not enough to remember these things in a casual glance, the way we might thumb through an atlas. We must think of the joys of labor as well as its pains, its celebration in things as well as its struggle with them. We must know what it is people do in their work, how they feel, what they see, what they hear, what they need from steel, or marble, or bread; and how all this is metamorphosed into everyday life and in the simplest exchange between us, in friendship, in families, in love, in fear, in anxiety, and in cruelty, in strikes and reconciliations.

In approaching our own task of making sense together, we naturally reach backward and forward, and in this we heighten our sense of commitment to the commonplaces of meaning, habit, and community to which we have been accustomed. For years now I have read and talked and studied. I have written books and critical papers. I have attended conferences and discussions, quarreled over methodologies and relevances, and taken sides. I have been persuaded as well as persuasive. I have learned how to lecture, to give a talk, to chat, to amuse and cajole, to criticize and anger. On every occasion I needed an audience as much as I was needed by them. And yet this exchange hides all that went into the years in which I learned to make an audience what it wanted to be and to find in the audience what I could not find in myself. I needed them because of a simple conviction that the sense of things is not alien and that knowledge and truth have only messengers and no experts. Truth has a face: it is the work of man and earns his bread. Thus in the work of knowledge we intend only to open paths that others can follow. Messengers, of course, carry news that they do not know will be well received in the community. But at first they are made welcome, brought in from the cold and rain, given food and drink and a place to rest from their journey. And it is the same when we get our news from the morning paper over a cup of coffee. We think of the truth as part of the well-being of our community; we receive it as sustenance, or as a friend or guest. That is why the truth is painful when it reveals that things are not well in the land, in our lives, or in our community.

To begin a work is to solicit an encounter between ourselves and others present to us here and now, or through their work and its legacy. Such a beginning is of the order of intimacy and revelation in which we discover a primitive sense of closeness. Yet our approach would be unbearable if it were not like the meeting of eyes in which there can be no primacy of the self or of the other but only a kind of alternating life. Our approach is rather an invitation to friendship and love, unsure yet certain. It is a warm embrace in which we are caught up in that overlap in which we spend our lives together and which invites comparison and understanding as much as fear or uncertainty. This is the ground for starting with one another. The encounter with someone or something new to us awakens in us a sense of openness, the sharing of need, that provides the horizon to our own vocation and is prior to all motivations of love, anonymity, creativity, or destruction. In this sense the encounter with beginnings, or first times, is not a radical break with everyday life. It is like a breath we draw more deeply at first and then let go, just as the fullness of life may rush in upon us and then recede, returning us to the ordinary absorption of living. This encounter of first things is both a nostalgia and an ideal to which we compare our everyday experience without willfully courting either terror or ennui, yet not without longing and yearning.

> We are talking now of summer evenings in Knoxville, Tennessee, in the time that I lived there so successfully disguised to myself as a child. . . .
> . . . All my people are larger bodies than mine, quiet, with voices gentle and meaningless like the voices of sleeping birds. One is an artist, he is living at home. One is a musician, she is living at home. One is my mother who is good to me. One is my father who is good to me. By some chance, here they are, all on this earth; and who shall even tell the sorrow of being on this earth, lying, on quilts, on the grass, on a summer evening, among the sounds of night. May God bless my people, my uncle, my aunt, my mother, my good father, oh, remember them kindly in their time of trouble; and in the hour of their taking away.
> After a little I am taken in and put to bed. Sleep, soft smiling, draws me unto her: and those receive me, who quietly treat me

as one familiar and well beloved in that home: but will not, oh, will not, not now, not ever; but will not ever tell me who I am.[1]

There is a kind of sufficiency to things in which they realize themselves, neither falling short nor exceeding their limits. Here we have begun the enterprise of exploring our need of one another, thereby making thematic something we always assumed. We are engaged in an exercise that will involve us in mentioning what might never need to have been said and in falling short, or rather falling back into that embrace that surpasses all reason. Our task then is one of memory, of the care of first and last things, and in this the world and those around us are our support. We wish to understand and love one another, to be understood by others and by ourselves. We look about for certainties and find the memory of a summer evening on the grass among our family invading us with the presence that comes in the weight and lift of our bodies, in the sight and sound of our brother and sister and the goodness of our mother and father. And we borrow our own presence from theirs who in all the comings and goings of their own lives are here with us this evening and dwell in our heart by a marvelous chance of warmth and love. These are arrangements that are lasting like a family that lasts against its own troubles and dyings, as summer evenings last all the while that they, too, are dying. It is certain that we are not deceived in these familiar memories and do belong to them. Yet in the slip of time we do not hold and so become a question to ourselves, even while those around us still care and treat us as one so well loved and known to them, but who will not now or ever tell us who we are. And who can ever forget the places of memory?

We need to understand what moves us, what it is in the way a table is set, a garden cared for, or the way a mother dresses

1. James Agee, **A Death in the Family** (New York: Bantam Books, 1969), pp. 11, 14.

her child, that holds us and makes us either cry or sing somehow to tell about it—to hold it against time, against profusion, against our own indifferences or the times we are not watchful. In part this is what we can mean by simplicity, that is to say, a way of allowing ourselves to be the occasion of the fullness of things, of the world, of man. For the rest, it is the transcendence or transfiguration of things through us that is love's union of the mind and heart in love's thought **(amor intellectualis)**.[2] What I have in mind here is the "world-building" character of love that makes its objects absolutely necessary, sometimes in themselves but also altogether, so that we feel we shall burst with the world inside us. Not everyone knows this feeling; or rather, it is rarely a beginning. For many, the world is in pieces; analysis is their soul or else a methodology of indifference that separates and reduces the world so pitifully that a man can empty the world.

It is sometimes thought that the thinker is a man without passions, a homeless figure. But this is false to the passionate understanding that is the very circumstance of things; it is false to the world that the thinker beholds and moreover shares in principle, though for want of company he may appear to hoard his love.[3]

Since Descartes we have been persuaded that a solitary and sedentary thinker could achieve certain and public knowledge of the world. The price of such subjective certainty, namely, the split between mind and nature, including the thinker's own embodiment, has been considered "proper" to thinking. Indeed, insofar as embodiment enters thinking or the effort to think, it

2. M. C. D'Arcy, S.J., **The Mind and Heart of Love: Lion and Unicorn: A Study in Eros and Agape** (Cleveland and New York: The World Publishing Company, Meridian Books, 1956).
3. Soren Kierkegaard, **Concluding Unscientific Postscript**, trans. David F. Swenson and Walter Lowrie (Princeton, N.J.: Princeton University Press, 1941), bk. 2, chap. 3, sec. 4, "The Subjective Thinker: His Task, His Form, His Style."

has been only as something to be put out of play. The techniques of disembodied thinking have varied from closing one's eyes in order to shut out the fleeting world of the senses, or raising one's eyes toward heaven in thought or prayer, in order at least to be in the right way of what is noble and abiding, not to mention the practice of more ascetic spiritual disciplines of the body and soul. These gestural and postural choreographies of thought, to which must be added a number of other seclusive devices, such as the study cell lined only with the silent voices of the past, or the habit of working at night when the world shuts down and the senses in particular are handicapped, run deeper than the behavioral quirks of philosophers. For all kinds of work result in a certain physiognomy, in the peasant's bent back, the waitress's varicose veins, the heavy shoulders of the truck driver. Indeed, certain kinds of work, such as surgery, piano playing, tightrope and high wire walking, are essentially body work and as such demand a regime that can no more be reduced to a technique than can thinking in the true philosopher. The activities of the body, whether proper to such work as that of the acrobat, or apparently circumstantial, as in the work of the philosopher, cannot be reduced to a lower order, except as a metaphysical posture—as the determination to redeem nature, or to dominate it by means of an ascesis.

Once we understand the world-building nature of love, we can make sociological thinking a daily practice that does not isolate us before things or them before us—which is the favorite mode of contemplation—but is instead beholden to the scenes in which we live, in streets, in gatherings, in labors, in ways and customs. In other words, we shall understand love's thought as a mode of everyday care. In addition, we can see that it is ordinarily improper to separate knowledge and morals. For we do not look upon things indifferently but rather for the goodness that is in them; and we measure our own maturity by what it is we can appreciate in this life. In this sense, then, the simplest heart is the most learned; for it knows how to take account of the ways of things and of people in their ways.

What is the direction of such thinking? To some it will be quite beside the concern with the accumulation of sociological knowledge and the domination of the world. To others it will seem to ignore the hierarchy of being and concern that has been the essence of philosophical thought. Well, this thinking, like love itself, does not move out of the plenitude in which it finds itself; it dwells in a concern with the things and people around us. Such thought does not treat its circumstances as a background for its own act; it does not abstract from its circumstances, rising above them. I do not mean, however, that we cannot learn to think heroically, forever leaving the land of circumstance and the place of everyday cares. But then the hero dies young, for there is nothing to age him, nor anyone whose ways borrow from his life so that he and they grow older together. Today, more than ever, we need to cultivate what is near to us, to make of thought a garden rather than a bypass or a perishable collection that can only land us on the moon. Such a retreat would not weaken the universality of sociological thought. "We must try to find for our circumstance, such as it is, and precisely in its very limitation and peculiarity, its appropriate place in the immense perspective of the world. We must not stop in perpetual ecstasy before hieratic values, but conquer the right place among them for our individual life. In short, the reabsorption of circumstance is the concrete destiny of man."[4]

We make our lives from what is around us, from our family, our house, street, playmates, school, teachers, friends, books, comics, and church. But we forget this. Our projects take us away from home; they sweep everything behind us as a past we

4. José Ortega y Gasset, **Meditations on Quixote**, trans. Evelyn Rugg and Diego Marín (New York: W. W. Norton & Co, 1961), p. 45.

hardly remember. We move on, looking for wider perspectives, new experiences, unseen things. Our thoughts destine us for utopia and in this we are for a time heroic figures, resisting the inertia of things, giving them our own extraordinary accent. But things beckon us back—the weight of things, their touch, their smell; the time of things, their seasons; the way of things, their uses—all these offer us a chance of salvation, a redemption rooted in things, often comically, but in an ultimate wisdom. For the truth of the life-world is that the way of things is the way of ourselves with them, like the friendship of a man and his dog —a bond of faith, a mutual need, each unthinkable apart from the other, even in argument and anger.

To think sociologically is to dwell upon a question we have answered long ago: How it is that men belong to one another despite all differences? This is the task of a **wild sociology,** namely, to dwell upon the platitudes of convention, prejudice, place, and love; to make of them a history of the world's labor and to root sociology in the care of the circumstance and particulars that shape the divine predicaments of ordinary men.[5] The work of sociology, then, is to confront the passionless world of science with the epiphany of family, of habit, and of human folly, outside of which there is no remedy. This is not to deny scientific sociology. It is simply to treat it as a possibility that has yet to convince the world. Wild sociology is mindful of the poverty of sociology, of its ambitions and its easy alliances. It sees no other way than to remain in the world it needs for its own vocation and for the particulars of its reasoning. It has no unprecedented claims, and its meditations draw ever deeply

5. "The essential is to describe the vertical or wild Being as that pre-Spiritual milieu without which nothing is thinkable, not even the spirit, and by which we pass into one another, and ourselves into ourselves in order to have **our own** time." Maurice Merleau-Ponty, **The Visible and the Invisible,** ed. Claude Lefort, trans. Alphonso Lingis (Evanston, Ill.: Northwestern University Press, 1968), p. 204.

10   Making Sense Together

from the very ground they seem to make strange. Wild sociology exhibits without end its appeal to the ancestral orders of our everyday conventions. Yet this does not mean that sociological thinking lacks any election. It simply means that the vocation of sociology is never in hand as a hard and fast beginning but is to be found over its way and through its concerns. It is therefore never reducible to a matrix of procedural rules. The success of wild sociology lies in the integrity of its concerns and not in the division of its labor.

Our approach to sociology cannot be hasty with the imperatives of science if we are ever to know its worth. What is the necessity of sociology, in what need do we stand of its particular concern? This is a question of fulfillment, like asking someone we love what it is they are doing so as to bring their labor closer to us than our very eyes because we want to take it in and hold it to our heart. Wild sociology cannot be self-serving. Nor should it borrow from others mindlessly. Either way, we accumulate with nothing to call our own. We need to start conscious of others, willing to learn, to be overwhelmed, to struggle, to fight back, and to stand. But this is a time of waiting even when it hides itself as worldly success. True growth needs origins, a return to first things, to place, time, and pattern. Intellectual order is not simply an instrument of domination; it involves just as much a capacity for reliving our thoughts. It is perhaps more like housecleaning, a rearrangement that in welcoming others leaves more room for ourselves. In such welcome there is a yield of being that is achieved in the arrangement of simple things to do honor to one like ourselves. The integrity of our beginnings is the source of our welcome. It also strengthens our speech and the commitment of our interests and thereby reminds us of our freedom. For in thinking and speaking we choose paths much as in life we choose careers and marriages, that is, as ways of resolving the history and geography of our lives.

The language and history of sociology may seem far removed from all this. It is, indeed, if we think of our approach to sociology as an initiation into a logic of generalization and precision to which we have no native claim. But it is just this way into sociology of which I do not want to take advantage; I do not want to settle before I begin the question of the relation of scientific languages to everyday speech and talk. I have begun by trying to show a concern for how it is we manage any departure together, how we approach understanding building upon the great platitudes of our experience as embodied beings, with our speech set in local needs and circumstances. To say that we are sociologists is only to remark on the materials at hand, upon the necessity of working on this rather than that. We must first raise the question of what it is that is presupposed by the field we have chosen to work. The practice of sociology, like any other discipline, is precarious. It soon leaves us unable to remember our first motives for doing it at all. The aim of method, as I understand it, is to test in us that strange distance between our work and those for whom we intend it. Sociologists are particularly attached to methods for the sake of their claim to scientific status; I am concerned with the poetic claims of method. I think these two belong together in our working lives. Method plays the music in what is of interest to us; it shapes our sensibilities, determines our passions, and defines our world. Method is our practical idealism; it is the opening in things and of ourselves toward them. This is possible because we are able to convert our private enthusiasms into objective enterprises that, in turn, are never accomplished once and for all and so require of us a constant response according to our own need.

Finally, in what follows, I have adopted the commonplace method, as I understand it. The notes and texts upon which I have relied, whether shown for themselves or through my own reflection, are intended as places of embellishment. Their work is to celebrate the world's own appeal rather than to defend the authority of science. They are copied as holy works seeking the redemptions of correct spelling in the salvation of divine and human reading.[6]

6. Cassiodorus Senator, **An Introduction to Divine and Human Readings,** trans. Leslie Webber Jones (New York: Octagon Books, 1966), p. 133.

2
The Conversation of Mankind

So much of language was poetry before it became prose, and still today not much of "ordinary language" is prose however different it is, and it is not much different from poetry.[1] Indeed, in the everyday language of children and adults, for they are often to be found together, poetry continues to be a power not only over words and thoughts but also over things and behavior. Therefore, like Vico we believe poetry is essential to our living and is not to be overlooked by wild sociologists. Or, at least, poetry cannot be overlooked by sociologists once we do not begin with the assumption that our speech is governed by language in its literal, or scientific, form. It is time for sociology to consider how it means to connect language and reason once it sheds the outworn conception of science and poetry as two hostile knowings. We are aware, of course, that societies vary

1. Maurice Merleau-Ponty, **The Prose of the World,** ed. Claude Lefort, trans. John O'Neill (Evanston, Ill.: Northwestern University Press, 1973); **The New Science of Giambattista Vico,** trans. from the 3d ed. (1744) by Thomas Goddard Bergin and Max Harold Fisch, revised and abridged (Ithaca, N.Y., and London: Cornell University Press, 1970).

in the respect they accord to the works of knowledge and imagination. What we know of this makes it conventional for sociology to aspire to the status of scientific knowledge and thus to shun the fall into poetry as a failure of power and control. Because we know this we need to find out that, all along, this organization of knowledge and language has been a conventional arrangement and that other visions have gathered around it, if not inside.[2]

We should not overlook the attractive power and pride of science, its ability to keep ranks and well-ordered speech. In comparison, other knowledge is a poor thing and common sense sounds like the babble of children and elders or of the scrambled wits of the careerless. Yet we know very well that language is not all of a piece. We know this because we know that ordinary men are neither obsessed nor privileged with a single vision. Language is not outside the variety of human conditions. The generalities men care for are more like the hills and valleys they see around them, more like the fates of their children, their animals, and homes, than the high-sounding generalizations of science and mathematics—more like prayer and poetry. But then sociology ought to exercise care in its own speech, since it cannot presume upon its scientific allegiances to hold it in faith with its proper place in men's lives.

The sociologist's speech is not separable from his manner of speaking, for sociology accumulates no determinate body of

2. Elizabeth Sewell, **The Orphic Voice: Poetry and Natural History** (New Haven, Conn.: Yale University Press, 1960); Michael Polyani, **Personal Knowledge: Towards a Post-Critical Philosophy** (Chicago: University of Chicago Press, 1958); **Intellect and Hope: Essays in the Thought of Michael Polyani**, ed. Thomas A. Langford and William H. Poteat (Durham, N.C.: Duke University Press, 1968); Hans Jonas, **The Phenomenon of Life: Toward a Philosophical Biology** (New York: Dell Publishing Co., 1966); Erwin Strauss, **The Primary World of the Senses: A Vindication of Sensory Experience**, trans. Jacob Needleman (New York: The Free Press of Glencoe, 1963); Maurice Merleau-Ponty, **Phenomenology of Perception**, trans. Colin Smith (London: Routledge and Kegan Paul; New York: Humanities Press, 1962).

knowledge outside the need of society to be persuaded of its use. To the extent that the sociologist is forgetful of this dependence, he speaks to himself only. But this is the source of his pride. Such pride may comfort the sociologist in his distance from the daily conversation of mankind. This attitude is more likely due to the sociologist's loss of ability to handle the tension between what is urgent and what is easy in everyday life. Yet to live with this tension is the mark of ordinary maturity. Fortunately, nothing preserves sociological speech from foolishness and banality once its content is known. Nothing is more vain than a sociology whose content cannot be found except as the promise of science. Yet the sociologist cannot wholly avoid these dangers if he is to respect common sense while nevertheless urging its improvement.

The sociologist is in danger of speaking as though only scientific utterances were true to the practical bearing of life. Rather, sociology fosters the practicality of life in order to make of itself a scientific exemplar. Yet because of the necessity of making himself heard among the other voices of science, history, and economics, the sociologist seeks to persuade common sense that the spirit of science lies in the voice of inquiry and discussion, thereby allowing for the possibility of his own place in the conversation of mankind. This is an insidious argument. For once it is admitted, it easily serves the usurpation of genuinely different modes of discussion by the high-sounding voice of expertise. Yet sociology, more than any other voice, should be concerned with the preservation of that meeting place of mankind for which Michael Oakeshott has so marvelously furnished us with the image of conversation rather than of inquiry or argument.

> This, I believe, is the appropriate image of human intercourse —appropriate because it recognizes the qualities, the diversities, and the proper relationships of human utterances. As civilized human beings, we are the inheritors, neither of an inquiry

about ourselves and the world, nor of an accumulating body of information, but of a conversation, begun in the primeval forests and extended and made more articulate in the course of centuries. It is a conversation which goes on both in public and within each of ourselves. Of course there is argument and inquiry and information, but wherever these are profitable they are to be recognized as passages in this conversation, and perhaps they are not the most captivating of the passages. It is the ability to participate in this conversation, and not the ability to reason cogently, to make discoveries about the world, or to contrive a better world, which distinguishes the human being from the animal and the civilized man from the barbarian. Indeed, it seems not improbable that it was the engagement in this conversation (where talk is without a conclusion) that gave us our present appearance, man being descended from a race of apes who sat in talk so long and so late that they wore out their tails. Education, properly speaking, is an initiation into the skill and partnership of this conversation in which we learn to recognize the voices, to distinguish the proper occasions of utterance, and in which we acquire the intellectual and moral habits appropriate to conversation. And it is this conversation which, in the end, gives place and character to every human activity and utterance. I say, "in the end," because, of course, the immediate field of moral activity is the world of practical enterprise, and intellectual achievement appears, in the first place, within each of the various universes of discourse; but good behaviour is what it is with us because practical enterprise is recognized not as an isolated activity but as a partner in a conversation, and the final measure of intellectual achievements is in terms of its contribution to the conversation in which all universes of discourse meet.[3]

Science, common sense, and poetry are varieties of language rather than declensions of controlled communication. Man does not always seek things poetically. He may equally seek to dominate things, to subject them to his will and control, to construct them. In this case, the presence of things recedes in favor of their analytic composition, which together with their

3. Michael Oakeshott, "The Voice of Poetry in the Conversation of Mankind," in his **Rationalism in Politics and Other Essays** (London: Methuen & Co., 1962), p. 199.

laws of combination permits man's assembly of the world. Or else things are subject to traditional use and need, and concern us only insofar as they serve our purposes. Language is anchored upon ourselves, our relations to others, to God and nature, and in the history and stories that accumulate in our communities. Our care for language shapes our responsibility to ourselves and others; it is the mark of our faithfulness to the nature of things, to their shape and drift. Our use of language is not ruled by the scandals of philosophy and science. Yet its patient task of shaping common sense into good sense is often hurried by the claims of logic and method to inaugurate a republic of knowledge. Language suffers in all this because clarity is the enemy of ornament and epiphany, and throws out poetry in favor of public knowledge, health, and security.

Method is hostile to the gratuities of poetry and myth. Thus science seeks to conscript sociology to its ideals of well-ordered speech. Sociology in turn is tempted to regard the efficiency of speech as the workings of an external order of progressive revelation moving from magic and myth to science and plain sense. Moreover, sociology is enamored with mastery and technique. But these are equally the responses of speech in addressing nature, language, and society as the others of dialogue.

The acquisition of sociological speech does not begin with the postulate of social facts. In Durkheim and Weber the birth of sociology owes as much to prayer—society is God, society is spirit—as to the method of its fathers. In this, sociology is tied to singing itself as much as the world it furnishes. Where would sociology find any other path to knowledge than science, and how would this shape its speech? It is not even possible to raise this question so long as sociology clings to the skirts of science without any knowledge of the place of science itself in the conversation of mankind. Rather, sociology must learn, as King Lear learned, that it is in ourselves that we encounter the division of reason working irresistibly against the kingdom of love, mutilating the power of language in its prayers, its names, and its truth-telling. Sociology must learn that in the end it is we who gather the world and are its true metamorphosis. For even in our asylums God's spies gather up the heavens against the day when they will prevent the Machiavellians and charlatans who twist the grain of our humanity.

> No, no, no, no! Come, let's away to prison;
> We two alone will sing like birds i'th'cage:
> When thou dost ask me blessing, I'll kneel down,
> And ask of thee forgiveness: so we'll live,
> And pray, and sing, and tell old tales, and laugh
> At gilded butterflies, and hear poor rogues
> Talk of court news; and we'll talk with them too,
> Who loses and who wins; who's in, who's out;
> And take upon's the mystery of things,
> As if we were God's spies: and we'll wear out,
> In a wall'd prison, packs and sects of great ones
> That ebb and flow by the moon.[4]

King Lear's lesson is the lesson of wild sociology. For what he has to learn against the demands of Hobbesian will and utility is the regeneration of the bonds of service and family, of the generics of natural society. Lear's tragedy is the tragedy of relation to which we are born, on which we depend for love, friendship, truth, and service. In youth we challenge relation; in old age we depend upon it for our peace. In all else we define it, defend it, resist it even to honor or destroy it. Relation is the metaphysics of our humanity; it is our alliance with the world's fools.

Sociological knowledge is a knowledge of metamorphosis. For it is we who are the substance and form of social life whose structure is in turn commentary upon its methodology and matter. "One cannot come back too often to the question what is

4. **King Lear,** Act V, Scene III.

knowledge and to the answer knowledge is what one knows."[5] It is in this sense that Harold Garfinkel has revealed to us the poetics of sociological knowledge in the everyday metamorphosis and method of its narrative. It is from this fundamental principle that wild sociology, or what Garfinkel calls "ethnomethodology," invokes a version of sociological knowledge that is neither narcissistic nor alien with regard to the intrinsic generosity of the platitudes of commonsense values and knowledge of the social world. "For Kant the moral order 'within' was an awesome mystery; for sociologists the moral order 'without' is a technical mystery. From the point of view of sociological theory the moral order consists of the rule-governed activities of everyday life. A society's members encounter and know the moral order as perceivedly normal courses of action—familiar scenes of everyday affairs, the world of daily life known in common with others and with others taken for granted."[6]

The conversable attitude of daily life is grounded in the monumental achievements of commonsense perception, knowledge, and values. These are the work of everyone and no one, furnishing the considerations and relevances of our living that lie upon us a daily and sacred part of the mind. For the most part rationalism in science and philosophy consists in the demand that things and action be conformable to the standards of rationality. Properly speaking, however, theory is only rational when it abides by the troublesome contingency of things and human conduct. The rationality of wild sociology, unlike scientific rationalism, refrains from imposing reason upon reality: it seeks rather to make sociological theory rational in the acceptance of the contingent modes of social reality. What Garfinkel calls the indexical or occasioned features of everyday talk and

5. Gertrude Stein, **Lectures in America** (Boston: Beacon Press, 1957), p. 11.
6. Harold Garfinkel, **Studies in Ethnomethodology** (Englewood Cliffs, N.J.: Prentice-Hall, 1967), p. 35.

conduct, namely, the very features of self-reference that scandalize the generality and abstraction of science, are precisely the scattering of our divinity in the mundane particulars of everyday living and its umbilical ties to the here-and-now practices of commonsense knowledge and values. All this keeps our talk to itself in the small gatherings of our lives, between families and among friends, in kitchens as in high places, protected only by the warmth of our own people and remembered kindly despite its pain and injuries.

And thus, too, these families, not otherwise than with every family in the earth, how each, apart, how inconceivably lonely, sorrowful, and remote! Not one other on earth, nor in any dream, that can care so much what comes to them, so that even as they sit at the lamp and eat their supper, the joke they are laughing at could not be so funny to anyone else; and the littlest child who stands on the bench solemnly, with food glittering all over his cheeks in the lamplight, this littlest child I speak of is not there, he is of another family, and it is a different woman who wipes the food from his cheeks and takes his weight upon her thighs and against her body and who feeds him, and lets his weight slacken against her in his heavying sleep; and the man who puts another soaked cloth to the skin cancer on his shoulder; it is his wife who is looking on, and his child who lies sunken along the floor with his soft mouth broad open and his nakedness up like a rolling dog, asleep; and the people next up the road cannot care in the same way, not for any of it: for they are absorbed upon themselves: and the negroes down beyond the spring have drawn their shutters tight, the lamplight pulses like wounded honey through the seams into the soft night, and there is laughter: but nobody else cares. All over the whole round earth and in the settlements, the towns, and the great iron stones of cities, people are drawn inward within their little shells of rooms, and are to be seen in their wondrous and pitiful actions through the surfaces of their lighted windows by thousands, by millions, little golden aquariums, in chairs, reading, setting tables, sewing, playing cards, not talking, talking, laughing inaudibly, mixing drinks, at radio dials, eating, in shirt-sleeves, carefully dressed, courting, teasing, loving, seducing, undressing, leaving the room empty in its empty light, alone and writing a letter urgently, in couples married, in separate chairs, in family parties, in gay parties, preparing for bed, preparing for sleep: and none can care, beyond that room; and none can be cared for, by any beyond that room: and it is small wonder they are drawn together so cowardly close, and small wonder in what dry agony of despair a mother may fasten her talons and her vampire mouth upon the soul of her struggling son and drain him empty, light as a locust shell: and wonder only that an age that has borne its children and must lose and has lost them, and lost life, can bear further living; but so it is.[7]

Self is circumstantial through and through and is utterly lost if it does not learn to save circumstance in the expression of its needs and knowing. Wild sociology cannot trick the relation between self and circumstance by making of self or of circumstance a thing, an organization, or a contract. The corporeal composition of self and circumstance involves us in a daily metaphysics of contingency, relation, caprice, and corruption in which culture is not an abstract and universal organ but a concrete and circumstantial practice without any other resort than the great natural orders of our daily living.[8] Wild sociology embraces the common dilemma of making sense together that it must share with all other lay practitioners of the art. It exercises a limited reflexivity[9] that attaches us to the conversable particulars of use, limit, and value, which engender the immense perspectives of the world, of family, class, gender, truth, and rationality. Wild sociology refrains from the ecstasy of conventional sociology in the presence of hieratic values rather to celebrate the integrity of everyday conduct and its own artful accomplishment of concrete destinies. It is to be expected that such a sociology of everyday life will involve a certain outrage

7. James Agee and Walker Evans, **Let Us Now Praise Famous Men** (New York: Ballantine Books, 1966), pp. 51–52.

8. John O'Neill, "On Simmel's 'Sociological Apriorities,' " in **Phenomenological Sociology: Issues and Applications**, ed. George Psathas (New York: John Wiley & Sons, 1973), pp. 91–106.

9. John O'Neill, "Can Phenomenology be Critical?" **Philosophy of the Social Sciences** 2, no. 1 (March 1972): 1–13.

as well as systematic misunderstanding when viewed from the perspective of establishment sociology. There is a certain irony in the terms of this antagonism, for it is precisely wild sociology that is a sociology of convention and establishment because of its patient apprenticeship to the anonymous labor of social institution and of the great natural orders of our communal life.

In practice wild sociology achieves a return to things that is the direction of poetry. All of modern thought addresses nature's body, bringing reason to its sense through the recollection of the primacy of perceptual knowledge. In speaking of the poetics of everyday thought and emotion, I have in mind the connections between the seemingly hopeless condition of circumstance—the condition of no one in particular and yet of everyone—and the massive presumptions and uses of order in our sentimental and political lives. Moreover, this poetry is in keeping with the viewpoint of modern science, provided that in both cases we properly understand that the very notion of viewpoint in no way involves a fall into subjectivism and relativism. This needs to be said for the sake not only of critics but also of many who believe they are the new poets of relativity.

We deal in knowledge, perception, and values that are neither the universal acquisition of a disembodied and unsituated ego nor merely a local and willful imposition of sensory limits. Rather, the fact that the world has a different face for a fifth-century Athenian and a twentieth-century Torontonian, so far from making objective knowledge impossible, is the very organizing element of truth and its historical acquisition. Truth is never the achievement of once and for all agreements, any more than it is merely a temporary pact. These simple alternatives leave out of account the strength and appeal of local arrangements whose fame spreads upon the stream of generations, linking neighbors and posterity in the general labor of culture. "Culture for the dark-eyed men who meditate, argue, sing, preach, and dream in Ionia, Attica, Sicily, and Magna Graecia, means what is firm as opposed to what is unstable, what is fixed as opposed to what is fleeting, what is clear as opposed to what is obscure. Culture is not the whole of life, but only the moment of security, of certainty, of clarity. And the Greeks invent the concept as an instrument, not for replacing the spontaneity of life, but for making it secure."[10]

Today, of course, we are not much given to the patience of circumstance. We are sophisticated relativists, anthropologists, vulgar Freudians and Marxists, forever seeing through the candor of primitive use, weighing motive in the scales of class injustice, invoking that universal truth that is the trick of university, newspaper, and tourist culture. Modern culture assumes relativism so strongly that it will seem prescientific to deny it. We may grant this relativism and yet still reject its conclusion. For the relativity of science is a conclusion of classical mechanics rather than the sense of Einstein's relativity theory. Galileo and Newton regarded our empirical judgments of time, space, and motion as relative because they themselves postulated observer's absolute space, time, and movement. Einstein's mechanics rejects the absolutism of Euclidean space with the result that the relativity of space-time observations no longer yields mere appearances but a relative reality that is absolute because it is all we can know. The new relativity differs in its absolutism from that of the rationalist mechanics of Galileo and Newton inasmuch as it treats perspective as a constituent feature of reality. Thus viewpoint is an absolute ingredient of modern science and not at all a prescientific provincialism.

Yet in the social sciences we continue to treat knowledge as the conclusion of an absolute observer who confounds subjective experience in the relativity of appearance and perspective. In this way, the social sciences alienate the daily labor of each

10. José Ortega y Gasset, **Meditations on Quixote**, trans. Evelyn Rugg and Diego Marin (New York: W. W. Norton & Co., 1961), p. 96.

one of us in bringing to bear our viewpoints, beliefs, attitudes, needs, and desires into the great stock and exchange of human culture and its shaping sensibility. **We are ourselves and our circumstances:** this is the natural light of a wild sociology that has genuinely absorbed the convergence of science and poetry in the modern world.[11] It is from our circumstance that things and others have the ancestral shape of need, of friend and family, of instrument and advice. It is from circumstance that we have our moods like the changing light of day, our resignation, our hope, and our brooding memory. We and our circumstances are the material of metaphor and relevance as well as of plain talk, vice, and unfulfilled virtue. And we are these things day in and day out, and what we are in the midst of these things, small towns, trades, and landscapes, is their very light and our own reflection, their own offering and our own gift. The panorama of our beliefs, needs, and values is not given to the unsituated perspective of science; it is an everyday reality forged from the conversable uses and sufficiencies of our daily living.

> . . . Are we perhaps here only to say: house,
> bridge, brook, gate, jug, olive tree, window,—
> at best: pillar, tower . . . but to **say** them, understand me,
> **so** to say them as the things within themselves never
> thought to be. Is not the hidden craft
> of this secretive earth when she urges two lovers on,
> that in their feelings each and everything should be
>   transported?
> Threshold: what is it for two

11. "I am myself plus my circumstance, and if I do not save it, I cannot save myself. **Benefac loco illi quo natus es,** as we read in the Bible. And in the Platonic school the task of all culture is given as 'to save the appearances,' the phenomena, that is to say, to look for the meaning of what surrounds us" (Ortega y Gasset, **Meditations on Quixote**, pp. 45–46). Cf. Julian Marias, **José Ortega y Gasset: Circumstance and Vocation**, trans. Frances M. Lòpez-Morillas (Norman, University of Oklahoma Press, 1970); and Owen Barfield, **Saving the Appearances: A Study in Idolatry** (New York: Harcourt, Brace & World, Harbinger Books, 1965).

lovers that they wear down a little
the older threshold of their own door. They too, after
the many before them, and before all those to come . . . ,
    lightly.

Here is the time for what can be **told**, here its home.
Speak and confess. More than ever
do the things we live with fall away, and
what displaces them is an act without image.
An act under crusts it will rip as soon
as its strength outgrows them and seeks new limits.
Between the hammer strokes
our heart endures, as does
the tongue between the teeth, which still
is able to praise.

Praise to the Angel our world, not the untellable:
you can't impress **him** with grand emotion. In the cosmos
where he so powerfully feels, you're only a newcomer.
Then show him some simple thing, grown up through
    generations
till it became ours, and lives near our hands and in our eyes.
Tell him of things and he'll stand astonished, as you stood
beside the rope-maker in Rome, or with the Nile potter.
Show him how joyful a thing can be, how innocent and ours,
how even lamenting sorrow can take purely its own form,
serve as a thing, or die in a thing—and in ecstasy
escape beyond the violin. And these things,
that live only in passing, understand that you praise them;
fugitive, they look to us, the most fugitive, for rescue.
They want us entirely to transform them in our invisible
    hearts
into—oh, infinitely—into us! Whoever we finally are.[12]

Wild sociology is a species of intellectual love. For sociology
cannot turn away from the consenting goods of human need
and natural circumstance that bind us to the perfection of
things as our own accomplishment and as the salvation of our
souls. Sociology truly seeks a radical comprehension of human
circumstance. But it has vulgarized its vocation in an impatient

12. Rainer Maria Rilke, **The Duino Elegies**, trans. Stephen Garmey and Jay
Wilson (New York: Harper & Row, 1972), The Ninth Elegy, pp. 66–67.

reduction of circumstance to environment, organization, class, and ethnicity. Sociology has reduced circumstance through its mathematical collection of motive as self, thing, and environment to nothing else than sociology's own possibilities of world-making.[13] To the extent that it is successful in this enterprise, sociology is an alien science and a hostile medium rather than the beneficent shell of human circumstance and need.

In its attachment to circumstance, wild sociology saves the appearances of communal life from the normative ironies of the scientific attitude that abstracts from the horizonal truths and inscapes of daily living. Circumstance is not the instrument of reason, nor is it its bare material waiting upon the inspiration of science for its furnishing and interpretation. Circumstance is the inscape of sense and reason. It is the self's surround, the open sublation of inside and outside, of self and thing, of self and other. Circumstance is the reminiscence of sensibility and reason folding back upon the world's embrace of our daily living. Human circumstance is never a bare instrument but rather a loving care and inscription of those fantastic universals that are the poetry of time's body and Vico's first conception of wild sociology.

13. I intend to treat the mathematical and nonmathematical collection of thought, self, thing, and speech in my forthcoming On the Way to Sociology, first presented as lectures to the Department of Psychology, Duquesne University, Pittsburgh; the Department of Sociology and the Program in Modern Thought and Literature, Stanford University; and the School of Social Science, University of California at Irvine, in January and February, 1973. Here and in this later work I am happy to acknowledge the thoughts of my colleague Alan Blum, in Theorizing (London: Heinemann Educational Books, 1974). I want also to thank Hans Mohr, Kurt Wolff, Hans Bremer, and Ken Morrison for helping me to improve my first attempts at this work.

The Conversation of Mankind 27

3
Time's Body

Ours is an age in which everything is said clearly and concisely. What is not clear and concise only points to the need to keep up with this age. The clarity of our age is not an easy acquisition, though its style and uses are to be presumed upon among enlightened men held responsible to the larger circle of those who place their faith in clarity as the fruit and sustenance of the republic of science and democracy.

Clarity in language and thought naturally allies itself with frank and open conduct. Thus we are unwilling to allow privacy to our public men; and since no one wishes to be accused of private ways, every man seeks to conduct as much of his life in public as society can conveniently cater. If obscenity and pornography are issues in our age, as indeed they are, it is only because we wish everything to be seen in the light of day, without benefit of difference, without magic, and without any

I am grateful to Dr. Giorgio Tagliacozzo for the original invitation to consider Vico's philology in an essay for his **Giambattista Vico's Science of Humanity** (Baltimore: Johns Hopkins University Press, forthcoming), in which this chapter will also appear.

appeal to poetry. Thus we are as much concerned to exhibit corruption in the body politic as we are fixed upon celebrating the conquest of body odors. For cleanliness is next to clarity.

Our age reckons that language is the instrument of thought and that we have nothing to find in language that we have not ourselves put into it. Thus the well-formed languages of logic and science are calculated to separate language from the history of man's speech about himself in order to make of the future a thing of rule. Language itself encourages our ambition to rule the world as a thing. For in its ordinary use language never obtrudes between us and the world, its virtue as the vehicle of thought and action being to efface itself. Thus it appears that we owe nothing to language except its proper use, which is ruled by the world's connections and not by anything our own life lends to language.[1] Clarity is therefore the only embellishment of scientific language that cultivates simplicity and precision in order to make of itself a universal prose.

The modern world holds time in its hand. We consider that we have broken with the past and that we are headed toward the future launched upon nothing else than our present abilities. This is a story that is related to us by our historians and social scientists in the unvarnished prose that is the emblem of their extroverted character. For we mean to make an open book of society and nature. It is essential to the success of this enterprise that we rid man and society of any universals other than those of science. Thus science is forgetful of the roots of its own practice and possibility and has no desire to be reminded of the sources of inspiration and madness that have brought history to the self-made arts of science, technology, and democracy.

It is a paradox of the age of prose that men are learning again

1. Maurice Merleau-Ponty, **The Prose of the World,** ed. Claude Lefort, trans. John O'Neill (Evanston, Ill.: Northwestern University Press, 1973).

to see and to hear, to read and to write, are learning to talk and to listen. This is especially disturbing in a society that has made an industry of knowledge and so presumes upon its expansion that communication hardly means more than the speed with which the republic of science and commerce consumes its own self-image. For communication is the soul of extroversion; it feeds off the dead body of language and the extinction of style. Yet amidst the ruins of language and the collapse of history and character, men begin to turn over words in search of oracles, of the myths and metaphors that restore the human family and the fantastic universals of time's body.[2]

Science means to set men free from the idols of everyday language and from the mysteries of arcane speech. To achieve its purposes scientific enlightenment must teach men to speak of history as progress and to conceive of society as the engine of character and motive. It is essential to this view that social facts are what they are only by means of clear and distinct rules of analysis and combination and that social facts are not in any way beholden to their profound interior or to their generic bonds. Thus sociological knowledge accumulates at the same time as men lose their collective memory. In this situation time's body fractures into the elements of individualism, contract, guilt, and violence. These are the material of history's progress and the daytime efforts of reason to reduce itself to an instrument without a body—a thinking calculus.

Enlightenment declares mankind to be a task of reason separated from passion and its own origins. Liberal history schedules reason in favor of the late born, unshackled by myth, family, and the body's dreams. Liberal enlightenment rules the world by making children out of three quarters of mankind; the other quarter learns to repress its origins in order to make civilization the engine of its discontent. Thus reason's war against

2. Norman O. Brown, **Closing Time** (New York: Random House, 1973).

oracles joins in the war against the body's orifices, which are the way in and the way out of the world's round.[3]

The modern world retains its youth while all else dies young or comes to unwanted old age. Science, technology, and democracy are unseasonable work inspired by change and progress wrought upon language, reason, and the passions in order to make a thing of mankind without any regard for the great body of human time. Socrates turned from the study of science in order to live among men, to dwell upon the life that is gathered in men's language and with a chance of wisdom risked in irony, to prepare for death. For Socrates understood, just as Vico was to argue later, that science is a passion of youth but quite unable to make men.

> And to his cost he learned that that study [geometry] proper to minute wits is not easy for minds already made universal by metaphysics. So he gave up this study as one which chained and confined his mind, now accustomed through long study of metaphysics to move freely in the infinite of genera; and in the constant reading of orators, historians and poets his intellect took increasing delight in observing between remotest matters ties that bound them together in some common relation. It is these ties that are the beautiful ornaments of eloquence which make subtleties delightful.[4]

Science makes the world over in the name of men unconcerned with self-ignorance; it hopes to measure wisdom by what a man knows about the world outside and beyond his own life. Thus science is always defeated by death, or rather, science ignores death because it presumes upon the future to accomplish its task. But Socrates understood that knowledge is redeemed only by death and community and in the gathering of men according to their own manner of speaking and living.

3. Norman O. Brown, **Love's Body** (New York: Random House, Vintage Books, 1968).

4. **The Autobiography of Giambattista Vico**, trans. Max Harold Fisch and Thomas Goddard Bergin (Ithaca, N.Y.: Great Seal Books, 1963), p.123.

Thus Socratic ignorance anchors upon time's body and the human family whose conventions are the ground of man's nature. Socrates founds the tradition of vulgar metaphysics from which Vico later creates his wild sociology.

Kinship is the substance of wild sociology because Vico, like Socrates, understood that the good of knowledge lies in the world between men; in other words, in human institutions and not in the world outside of men, or in nature, except as science itself is a human institution. Philology is the method of Vico's new sociology because the acquistion of language is the same thing as our humanity, the same in our childhood as among other men whose ways we learn by understanding their language. For we are just as strange to ourselves as other men in other times are to us unless we learn the history of our language. Vico's wild sociology is therefore grounded in the love of language and kinship, in a poetry of the archetypes and fantastic universals that have shaped time's body into the natural institutions of human intellect and imagination.

> This was the order of human institutions: first the forts, after that the huts, then the villages, next the cities, and finally the academies.
> This axiom is a great principle of etymology, for this sequence of human institutions sets the pattern for the histories of words in the various native languages. Thus we observe in the Latin language that almost the whole corpus of its words had sylvan or rustic origins. For example, **lex**. First it must have meant a collection of acorns. Thence we believe is derived **ilex**, as it were **illex**, the oak (as certainly **aquilex** means collector of waters); for the oak produces the acorns by which the swine are drawn together. **Lex** was next a collection of vegetables, from which the latter were called **legumina**. Later on, at a time when vulgar letters had not yet been invented for writing down the laws, **lex** by a necessity of civil nature must have meant a collection of citizens, or the public parliament; so that the presence of the people was the **lex**, or "law," that solemnized the wills that were made **calatis comitiis**, in the presence of the assem-

bled **comitia**. Finally, collecting letters, and making, as it were, a sheaf of them for each word, was called **legere**, reading.[5]

The cycle of language is the cycle of our great family history. But enlightenment seeks to dissolve the human family into a political contract grounded in fraternal guilt. In this way imagination is cut off from its universal roots. Men are forced to abandon poetry in favor of that prose that is suited to speak about what men see who no longer see into themselves. The language of imagination is therefore pushed into dreams, myths, and poetry, which store up man's common nature as a treasure to be discovered only by those who still love words, language, and song. But Vico's wild sociologists are **philologists,** that is to say, men whose love of language loves mankind from its birth.

> It [the New Science] must begin where its subject matter began, as we said in the Axioms. We must therefore go back with the philologians and fetch it from the stones of Deucalion and Pyrrha, from the rocks of Amphion, from the men who sprang from the furrows of Cadmus or the hard oak of Vergil. With the philosophers we must fetch it from the frogs of Epicurus, from the cicadas of Hobbes, from the simpletons of Grotius; from the men cast into this world without care or aid of God, of whom Pufendorf speaks, as clumsy and wild as the giants called "Big Feet," who are said to be found near the Strait of Magellan; which is as much to say from the cyclopes of Homer, in whom Plato recognizes the first fathers in the state of the families.[6]

Modern man lives as unsure of birth, marriage, and death as he does of the past and the future. This is strange because modernity is essentially a historical consciousness, obsessed with the stages of its own development. But liberal individual-

5. **The New Science of Giambattista Vico**, trans. from the 3d ed. (1744) by Thomas Goddard Bergin and Max Harold Fisch, revised and abridged (Ithaca, N.Y., and London: Cornell University Press, 1970), p. 36.
   6. Ibid., p. 57.

ism cannot achieve more than a guilty love of the past, for the past is beholden to its family gods who rule the beginning and end of human life, determining its fruits and sorrows. Modern man aspires to live outside of the family; his need is to make of birth and death mere null points in order to destroy time's body. Thus modern society submits equally the womb and the grave to its cosmetic denials. The present, then, is only the dream place of beautiful losers.

Language fractures in the modern world because our speech is no longer the reflection of anything that is ordered either inside or outside of us. Every historical order ultimately collapses the literary, artistic, and philosophical languages that for a time allowed an age to speak of itself and to gather its particular goods and evils. It is an axiom of Vico's wild sociology that if history is at all saved it is saved by language. For it is in the history of our language that we recover our humanity. It is in language that we discover the gradual making of the institutions that have made us human.

But then the wild sociologist is required against the spirit of the times to love the human family and to make a method out of remembrance and imagination. The wild sociologist will therefore need to avoid telling mankind's story according to the pattern of progress, as though man had a future quite beyond himself or unweighted by his past. Yet to reject this story requires more strength than was needed by the early heroes, for it requires looking back into the face of the family and to our first awkward steps toward humanity. Thus it is easier to reject the gods than to reject man but harder still to accept man. Such is the piety of wild sociology.

Vico's conception of wild sociology is patient with its own origins and thus it does not speak solely through the mouths of gods and heroes. By the same token, it is not anxious about ends and so it does not hasten man's speech with logic and science. The pillars of the poetic commonwealth are religion, marriage, and burial, which found our humanity upon what men everywhere owe to themselves and not to priests, philosophers, or scientists. For human law is nothing but the bonds men place upon themselves to clothe their nudity in the civil beauty of family, community, and speech.

Man is nothing else than the way he talks about himself. Wild sociology holds together the fractured speech of modernity because it rejoins time to its body, to its seasons and cycles of human fortune.[7] It is an axiom of wild sociology that science never leaves man behind; science itself is one more faith of mankind, another version of family and deliverance. This is a necessary axiom, since we should otherwise have no call to read Vico himself anymore than he had to read others before him. The call that is answered in Vico is the same call that language makes upon us today. It is the call for the renewal of the springs of language dried out in an age of precision and clarity.

> But the nature of our civilized minds is so detached from the senses, even in the vulgar, by abstractions corresponding to all the abstract terms our languages abound in, and so refined by the art of writing, and as it were spiritualized by the use of numbers, because even the vulgar know how to count and reckon, that it is naturally beyond our power to form the vast image of this mistress called "Sympathetic Nature." Men shape the phrase with their lips but have nothing in their minds; for what they have in mind is falsehood, which is nothing; and their imagination no longer avails to form a vast false image. It is equally beyond our power to enter into the vast imagination of those first men, whose minds were not in the least abstract, refined, or spiritualized, because they were entirely immersed in the senses, buffeted by the passions, buried in the body. That is why we said above that we can scarcely understand, still less imagine, how those first men thought who founded gentile humanity.[8]

7. Stuart Hampshire, "Joyce and Vico: The Middle Way," **The New York Review of Books** 20, no. 16 (October 18, 1973).
8. **The New Science of Giambattista Vico**, p. 76.

We read Vico today because our task is to renew the names of things together with the edges of their special silence. Vico recalls that benign nominalism that brought men out of the forests into the light of language. At first men were the children of time's body; they sang out the names of things in bodily play, in pleasure and love. They built up language through metaphor, that is, by playing upon words. And because they were not ashamed of their bodies they named things after the body and gave to nature the body's own moods and sensual speech.

> The human mind is naturally inclined by the senses to see itself extremely in the body, and only with great difficulty does it come to understand itself by means of reflection.
> This axiom gives us the universal principle of etymology in all languages: words are carried over from bodies and from the properties of bodies to signify the institutions of the mind and spirit.[9]

Today we recall our ancestral condition not because we mean to be ruled by it but because we cannot be sure of our future without trying to hold together how man began. Vico's wild sociology saves reason by anchoring it to time's body and its civil beauty. For reason is not the zero point of passion but rather an involvement in the needs of our time acquired through a language that inhabits us and through which we in turn make our lives. The life of reason is therefore inseparable from its beginnings in poetry, myth, religion, and vulgar metaphysics. Reason is human when it is not forgetful of these origins but rather remembers them kindly for the sake of its own birth.

> The most sublime labor of poetry is to give sense and passion to insensate things; and it is characteristic of children to take

9. Ibid., p. 36.

inanimate things in their hands and talk to them in play as if they were living persons.

    This philologico-philosophical axiom proves to us that in the world's childhood men were by nature sublime poets.[10]

Vico inspires us with our own language just as he renewed in himself Latin eloquence. Thus etymology is the music of Vico's wild sociology inviting us to hear our beginnings in the birth of language. Therefore, thinking is not ahead of speaking and speaking is not ahead of our bodies, so that thinking is not ahead of time's body, which is the time our senses need to become human, to speak, and to think. In any man whose thinking listens to his speaking there is founded the soul's city, hearkening to the principles, nature, and laws of mankind. But to listen to principle and nature is to begin again, to remake sense and sensuousness, to make of time's body a renaissance of reason and its divine pleasure. This is a communal birth, and history is its only midwife, for the soul's deliverance is nowhere else than into this beautiful world.

    Finally, beginning with the idea by which every slight slope was called **mundus** (whence the phrases **in mundo est, in proclivi est,** for "it is easy"; and later everything for the embellishment of a woman came to be called **mundus muliebris**), when they came to understand that the earth and the sky were spherical in form, and that from every point of the circumference there is a slope toward every other, and that the ocean bathes the land on every shore, and that the whole of things is adorned with countless varied and diverse sensible forms, the poets called this universe **mundus** as being that with which, by a beautifully sublime metaphor, nature adorns herself.[11]

Like birth itself the human world comes about only in a given time and place marked by our weakness as much as by our strength, by pain as much as joy, by ugliness as much as beauty.

10. Ibid. p. 29.
11. Ibid., p. 226.

But at no time is human nature, whether bestial or savage, heroic or divine, anything less than man's nature. This nature is not wholly passionate, for otherwise we should not have established any public grounds of truth nor any of the fixed institutions of society. Yet we ought not to attribute to men more of reason and calculation than governs the present age. For then we should make of society a preposterous contract, or else a noble lie, instead of a family that has gathered despite what it has reasoned for itself, despite its lusts and its powers.

Vico's wild sociology is a science of reason renewed. Although it is born in the age of men, wild sociology gathers its own beginnings poetically from the temples of the sky from which all human institutions and sciences are handed down. Vico's wild sociology collects its own rough origins, recalling what it owes to our domestic labors in gathering acorns and animals, binding men and letters in law and parliament.

Vico's wild sociology is ultimately a life science. He who undertakes its work must penetrate the veil of time that separates his thinking life from the brooding body that is the place of reason and sense and their sole monument. For man is a work of his own hands and eyes, of his own lips and ears, a drama of his own passion and his own reason. Thus the eloquence of science and the civil beauty of law and religion are the true embellishments of humanity.

4
Wild Sociology

Science always obliges us to forget what we know. In this way we learn much though we may still lack wisdom. In the case of the natural world, our power over things is compensation enough for the separations of knowledge. But in the social world we cannot start with any certain distance between what we know ordinarily and the reports of sociology. For the social world does not wait upon the constructions of scientific reasoning. It makes sense from the first day until the last in the all-day and everyday surroundings of others whose life we share. Nothing lies outside of this circumstance, neither its ignorance nor its fears, neither its joys nor its injuries. The mystery of this circumstance measures the poverty of sociology.

Wild sociology seeks to establish how it comes about that without any explicit appeal to rule or benefit of science, what we ordinarily know and value, and in the variety of ways that we come to know it, has the massive feature of being "known in common with others"—how, in other words, commonsense knowledge and values achieve the status of fact or, rather, **moral fact**. It is here that we adopt Garfinkel's recommendation that we treat the presuppositions of the natural attitude of daily life as maxims of everyday conduct through which we derive our average sense of competence and moral membership with the institutions and values that are our daily circumstance. In other words, wild sociology treats the natural attitude as an **ethnomethodology** in which, for example, questions and answers, time and place, work, self-revelation, and advice, are the ways we have of deciding the sensible and warrantable status of events or actions by referring to their particulars as occasional evidence of our institutions of family, home, school, manhood, sincerity, and true love. These are in turn the reasonable grounds of our talk and commitments and could never be wholly the work or accomplishment of the social sciences.

We ordinarily experience the everyday social world as something that has preceded us and now faces us as an orderly scheme of things whose interpretation is handed on to us by parents, teachers, and almost anyone with whom we live and learn. On the basis of the general legacy of language and knowledge into which we are born, we use and enjoy the world in typical ways; we sit in the shade of trees, avoid barking dogs, drink milk, eat the right things, and run to mother for protection. The way in which we speak and act in the world and among others is shaped by our immediate purposes and conventions, which furnish a schema of relevances regarding what features of the world are to be selected for generalization, rule of thumb, reminiscence, use, and avoidance. We commonly assume that things will continue to be as we have known them and that we can go about our business in a routine way . . . and so on . . . and so forth . . . so as to minimize doubt and decision. Or, when something goes wrong, we expect to be able to regularize it, to fix it without having to take apart the whole scheme of things on which we have relied so far.

In the natural attitude of our daily lives the world has for us certain and constant features. We assume that the objects, persons, and regions of the world with which we are familiar will continue to be as they are; similarly, we assume that the experiences and emotions we have relied upon hitherto will continue to work for us as before. We assume that the world is amenable to our purposes and needs and that we shall be able to realize our interests through action in and upon the world. Of course, each of these expectancies may fail to be realized, producing practical and emotional as well as theoretical problems. When this happens we do not entertain open and permanent doubts about our knowledge in general but only insofar as this enables us to restore what is questionable in our working knowledge, belief, and values.[1]

The world as we know it presents itself to us in a massive face, the faces of family and friends, of street and neighborhood, with receding contours of familiarity and reach that we expect to be able to penetrate without becoming entirely lost and without meeting others with totally incommunicable ways. Each of us has a certain amount of "expert knowledge" for his particular needs, or else available upon thorough inquiry and application. But the greater part of this knowledge will be merely what it is necessary to know for all practical purposes, as tricks of the trade, rules of thumb, proverbial and folk wisdom. Where our general knowledge suffices for the definition of our task and situation, that is to say, where it enables us to discover its theme and its elaboration in and by particulars of the situation so as to engage its normal values, likelihoods, and causal texture, then we are able to treat what is required of us as a routine matter. We may, of course, be frustrated in our expectations and activities. But any stoppage in our conduct is

1. Alfred Schutz, **Collected Papers**, vol. 3, **Studies in Phenomenological Philosophy**, ed. Ilse Schutz (The Hague: Martinus Nijhoff, 1966); Alfred Schutz, **Reflections on the Problems of Relevance**, ed. Richard M. Zaner (New Haven, Conn.: Yale University Press, 1970); José Ortega y Gasset, **Man and People**, trans. Willard R. Trask (New York: W. W. Norton & Co., 1957).

perceived in the frame of its overall temporal course, which allows for others to see what has gone wrong, give help where needed, and so get us on our way.

These commonsense presumptions of conduct are the basis, then, for our being open to the influence of others, to their advice and aid. It enables others to see what we are up to and where we are, and thus to sustain a common schema of here-and-now, here-and-there relevances, that is to say, to locate the **occasional** or **indexical** properties[2] of the other person's action or talk and thus to generalize its sense. Thus in the common-sense attitude our own presence in the world is regarded as directly relevant to our understanding of the world and others and in turn their understanding of us. For example, what I am saying now depends very much on how I have approached this work, on how I try to breathe into it the sense to be made of it by us together once you share in it as a reader and as one who can be called upon to have some general sense of the allusions, the references, and the overall question that I am addressing. I am aware, of course, that you will not see things exactly as I do, reading rather more or rather less into what I am saying than what I have in mind to say. By the same token, there is a chance that I am thinking along the very same lines as some of my readers, or that they are even ahead of me. But whatever the background differences among us, we assume as a matter of course, though not without art, that we can share viewpoints, sentiments, and beliefs without elaborate recourse to the disci-plines of logic and science. This reasoning, however, is not established without general discussion, through which we al-ways seek the resource of agreement.

2. Harold Garfinkel, **Studies in Ethnomethodology** (Englewood Cliffs, N.J.: Prentice-Hall, 1967), chap. 1, "What is Ethnomethodology?" pp.1–34; and Edmund Husserl, **The Crisis of European Sciences and Transcendental Phenomenology: An Introduction to Phenomenological Philosophy**, trans. David Carr, (Evanston, Ill.: Northwestern University Press, 1970), p. 122.

In exactly the way that persons are members to organized affairs, they are engaged in serious and practical work of detecting, demonstrating, persuading through displays in the ordinary occasions of their interactions the appearances of consistent, coherent, clear, chosen, planful arrangements. In exactly the ways in which a setting is organized, it **consists** of methods whereby its members are provided with accounts of the setting as countable, storyable, proverbial, comparable, picturable, representable—i.e., accountable events.[3]

The commonsense attitude of everyday life is not just a given. It is something that is evinced in our social conduct as part of our claim to a grasp of how things are, as our ability to handle our social surroundings, relevant others, and our own face. The attitude of everyday life is thus not simply a cognitive attitude but also an expressive or ethical attitude, which Garfinkel refers to under the concept of **trust,** or "a person's compliance with the expectancies of the attitude of daily life as a morality."[4] It is a feature of everyday life that it supports our self-conceptions much of the time so that it is only when for some reason it leads us on to a disappointment or failure that we become aware of our self-investment in the way we see things. To withdraw such investments and to find new outlets for old selves can be painful indeed; it requires the presence of others, even of the very persons who may have led us on, as they may later confess.

We are naturally surprised and shocked when things do not conform to our commonsense expectations of them. Every question of fact raises questions of moral identity as well as cognitive competence. We assume there is a world held in common that has certain constitutive features of sharedness which we manage in a self-patterned way, working back and forth, glossing meaning, taking particulars as evidence of an

3. Garfinkel, **Studies in Ethnomethodology,** p. 34.
4. Harold Garfinkel, "A Concept of, and Experiment with 'Trust' as a Condition of Stable Concerted Actions," in **Motivation and Social Interaction,** ed. J. O. Harvey (New York: The Ronald Press Company, 1963), pp. 187–238.

order of events yet to be established and, in turn, using this emerging order of events as "evidence" of the sense of its particulars. We regard the working of this scheme of things not just as an essay in knowledge but rather the same thing as a moral claim to our grasp of reality, of our competence and responsibility in the working of an order of events to which we are partner, so that commonsense knowledge of social structures is for us the same thing as moral knowledge.

The scientist, it is said, breaks with the daily world of the natural attitude. He lays aside the common fabric of belief, habit, and custom in the service of a systematic doubt and his subscription to rationally constructed knowledge. In the pursuit of doubt the scientist aims at the overthrow of conventional knowledge, the destruction of routine, and the emancipation of choice and decision. To achieve this the scientist must disengage himself from the world of pragmatic interest and relevances and thereby reinterpret the world solely in keeping with his own scientific purposes, namely, to achieve the solution of a problem for its own sake.[5] Even with regard to his solution, the scientist is prepared to see it defeated, improved upon, or made more rigorous and free of contradiction. The scientist also suspends the spatiotemporal relevances motivated by his own presence in the world. He adopts a timeless and objective stance in which space-time coordinates function solely to state the conditions for repeating an experiment. Because the scientist has no "here" within the world and is immune to the reciprocity of viewpoint, with its horizons of intimacy and generality, he is obliged to construct a **model actor** to whom he

5. Max Weber, "Science as a Vocation," in **From Max Weber: Essays in Sociology**, trans. and ed., Hans Gerth and C. Wright Mills (New York: Oxford University Press, 1958) pp. 129–156. Cf. Herminio Martins, "The Kuhnian 'Revolution' and Its Implications for Sociology," in **Imagination and Precision in the Social Sciences**, ed. T. J. Nossiter, A. H. Hanson, and Stein Rokkan (London: Faber and Faber, 1972) pp. 13–58; Robert W. Friedrichs, **A Sociology of Sociology** (New York: The Free Press, 1970).

imputes a **rational consciousness** interacting with others des-
tined similarly to act like any-rational-man.

> The homunculus is invested with a system of relevances origi-
> nating in the scientific problem of his constructor and not in the
> particular biographically determined situation.of an actor within
> the world. It is the scientist who defines what is to his puppet
> a Here and a There, what is within his reach, what is to him a
> We and a You or a They. The scientist determines the stock of
> knowledge his model has supposedly at hand. This stock of
> knowledge is not socially derived and, unless especially de-
> signed to be so, without reference to social approval. The rele-
> vance system pertinent to the scientific problem under scrutiny
> alone determines its intrinsic structure, namely, the elements
> "about" which the homunculus is supposed to have knowledge,
> those of which he has a mere knowledge of acquaintance and
> those others he just takes for granted. With this is determined
> what is supposed to be familiar and what anonymous to him and
> on what level the typification of the experiences of the world
> imputed to him takes place.[6]

Sociological accounts are beset by the pervasive problem of
the encounter between the everyday world of the commonsense natural attitude and the problem-specific interests of
scientific inquiry and explanation. There are a variety of ways
to express this difficulty. The particular approach that I should
like to develop starts from the problem of the **mutual account-
ability** of the commonsense and scientific attitudes. It is possible, for example, out of evolutionary and rationalist fervor, to
dismiss the articulation of commonsense knowledge as an idol
of the marketplace from which science delivers us. Such an
attitude has the support of the philosophical tradition and
serves to qualify the superior social status that men of knowledge claim for themselves by appealing to the asceticism of
rational thought in its struggle with license and foolishness. But
this tradition belies itself inasmuch as it also appeals to the

6. Alfred Schutz, **Collected Papers**, vol. 1, **The Problem of Social Reality**,
ed. Maurice Natanson (The Hague: Martinus Nijhoff, 1964), pp. 41–42.

sobriety of common sense to rescue us from the intoxications of speculative thought. For what is reasonable in human affairs is often found to be closer to common sense than is flattering for the scientists of conduct. Men are ordinarily aware that they are born much like any other men into a world whose ways and wisdom precedes them. So far from inspiring subjectivity and disorder, common sense allies itself with that proper human folly that men find it necessary to acquire to live with themselves. True folly is alien to the corrosive fantasy of perfectly rational character and community.

It is in the interest of scientific sociology to destroy custom and to deride convention in order to make of human assembly a rule of reason. In this unseasonable aspiration sociology strives to be immune to the exigencies of conviviality and collective sentiment. If this were at all a possibility, then sociology would truly be a science of difference, that is, of egoism, interest, and violence collected in the division of labor, in contract, and in the republic of method. But it is precisely this aspiration that limits scientific sociology to the rule of appearances. This rule in turn saves the rational management of social life by hiding its antisocial foundations. It is in this fashion that Erving Goffman reveals to us the folly of descriptive social science. That is to say, his labor shows that there is nothing behind the surfaces of sociological description once sociology itself is no longer beholden to the grounds of collective life.[7] In such a situation sociological description merely glosses the practices of vanity, equal hope, and the fear of death. Once scientific sociology engages in the unseasonable folly of breaking with communal sense, its own appeal becomes problematic, or

7. Erving Goffman, **The Presentation of the Self in Everday Life** (Garden City, N.Y.: Doubleday & Co., Anchor Books, 1959); **Relations in Public: Microstudies of the Public Order** (New York: Harper & Row, Harper Colophon Books, 1973); Daniel C. Foss, "Self and the Revolt against Method", **Philosophy of the Social Sciences** 2, no. 4 (December 1972): 291–307.

rather, it is reduced to an uncertain voice crying against an uncommon society. For the assembly of society and sociology is not a power of science.

> But suppose, right here, some wise man who has dropped down from the sky should suddenly confront me and cry out that the person whom the world has accepted as a god and a master is not even a man, because he is driven sheeplike by his passions; that he is the lowest slave, because he willingly serves so many and such base masters. Or again, suppose the visitor should command some one mourning his father's death to laugh, because now his father has really begun to live—for in a sense our earthly life is but a kind of death. Suppose him to address another who is glorying in his ancestry, and to call him low and base-born because he is so far from virtue, the only true fount of nobility. Suppose him to speak of others in like vein. I ask you, what would he get by it, except to be considered by everyone as insane and raving? As nothing is more imprudent than unseasonable prudence. And he is unseasonable who does not accommodate himself to things as they are, who is "unwilling to follow the market," who does not keep in mind at least that rule of conviviality, "Either drink or get out"; who demands, in short, that the play should no longer be a play. The part of a truly prudent man, on the contrary, is (since we are mortal) not to aspire to wisdom beyond his station, and either, along with the rest of the crowd, pretend not to notice anything, or affably and companionably be deceived. But that, they tell us, is folly. Indeed, I shall not deny it; only let them, on their side, allow that it is also to play out the comedy of life.[8]

It belongs to scientific folly to reckon men more rational than they care to be. Such folly easily allies with political pride to make men the instruments of rational organization beyond their will. Sociology is soon conscripted to this task. Or rather, without self-knowledge sociology never comes to terms with the temptations of scientific folly. It is essential, therefore, that we investigate the nature of the conduct that is inquiry into the

8. Desiderius Erasmus, **The Praise of Folly,** trans. Hoyt Hopewell Hudson (Princeton, N.J.: Princeton University Press, 1941), pp. 37–38. Reprinted by permission of Princeton University Press.

lives of others. We must ask what it is—faith or method—that supports us in decentering our own life among others in order to make of it a dedicated focus of concern with the otherness of others. How do we accomplish this, what motivates its concern, how is it to be fulfilled? We are not to presume that it is the work of alienation: for it is not practiced outside of the umbilical ties between us and others who feed us, smile upon us, help, hurt, and puzzle us. Among men rationality is the incarnate pursuit of understanding that breeds in bodily presences. This is the sustaining bond of sociological inquiry. What would it mean to cut ourselves off from this union in order to make of sociology a science? If we could achieve such a distance, to what in the end should we apply sociology?

In the face of this question sociology attaches itself to scientific description. Yet in modern literature and science nothing is less certain than description. Or rather, there have been times and places where narrative was more of a settled attitude—or the very composition of a settled attitude. But today words come apart and leap from the sentences that try to hold them to literary conventions. Sense and nonsense are if anything rival sensibilities rather than the frame and limit of understanding. Thus nothing can be more passionate than the commitment to true social narrative, that is, to a narrative that is patient with the intimacies of ordered and disordered life, through which the body becomes flesh of the world and the world in turn is fleshed into the sense and nonsense of character and society.

Wild sociology acknowledges that it is born into the desperate circumstance of having to earn its living. For sociology is preceded by the marvelous acquisitions of commonsense living and pragmatic reasoning that make it impossible for sociology to begin, as does science, with a lack of confidence in man. Wild sociology has no other way than to assume its conventional debts to the great traditions of our senses, manners, and natural reason. Thus it has no other narrative allegiance than to the virtues and ways of daily living from which we build up the institutions of understanding and good will. Wild sociology cannot suspend the intimacies of need, of hope and injury, of tools and engines, of family and first love, nor of hate and broken friendship. These are never virtual engagements of ours attendant upon the commitments of speculative reason and its contracts of utility and profit. For our social life is not convertible to a thing of use, nor into an image of itself. Let this stand in the surrounds of abuse, utility, fantasy, machination, and contract that we bear, much as life holds against all its afflictions:

> The plainness and iterativeness of work must be one of the things which make it so extraordinarily difficult to write of. The plain details of a task once represented, a stern enough effort in itself, how is it possibly to be made clear enough that this same set of leverages has been undertaken by this woman in nearly every day of the eleven or the twenty-five years since her marriage, and will be persisted in in nearly every day to come in all the rest of her life; and that it is only one among the many processes of wearying effort which make the shape of each one of her living days; how is it to be calculated, the number of times she has done these things, the number of times she is still to do them; how conceivably in words is it to be given as it is in actuality, the accumulated weight of these actions upon her; and what this cumulation has made of her body; and what it has made of her mind and of her heart and of her being. And how is this to be made so real to you who read of it, that it will stand and stay in you as the deepest and most iron anguish and guilt of your existence that you are what you are, and that she is what she is, and that you cannot for one moment exchange places with her, nor by any such hope make expiation for what she has suffered at your hands, and for what you have gained at hers: but only by consuming all that is in you into the never relaxed determination that this shall be made different and shall be made right, and that of what is "right" some, enough to die for, is clear already, and the vast darkness of the rest has still, and far more passionately and more skeptically than ever before, to be questioned into, defended, and learned toward. There is no way of taking the heart and the intelligence by the hair and of wresting it to its feet, and of making it look this terrific thing in the eyes: which are such gentle eyes: . . . and they are to be

multiplied, not losing the knowledge that each is a single, un-repeatable, holy individual, by the two billion human creatures who are alive upon the planet today; of whom a few hundred thousands are drawn into complications of specialized anguish, but of whom the huge swarm and majority are made and acted upon as she is: and of all these individuals, contemplate, try to encompass, the one annihilating chord.[9]

Repetition is the ground of character and true narrative and it is in our ways and it is what sociology needs to settle in our daily living. But sociology need not know what it needs to know, and that is what is difficult in the narrative it undertakes. For it may forsake its task in generalities, failing to call upon the names of the things that are its poetic sources. Sociology enlightens us with talk of individualism, equality, progress, and environmental improvement. But character and place each have roots that hold against what scientific sociology has in store for us. Sociology lets self go free, without place, or past, or any injury of family. Yet these things return upon us. Sociology, to save itself, treats them as "problems."

Wild sociology abides in the daily necessity of having every day to make of necessity a daily thing and not tomorrow's mother. We know this and what we know of it is that it is repetition, the daily repetition of our lives, which is in our lives every day and in our talk and in all our senses, that is the conversable ground of sociology's way. For this reason wild sociology hides its own name. It is neither outside nor above the holy places it seeks to enter. It has no commanding voice, for it shuns the prescriptions of method and the forced entries of science. Wild sociology seeks therefore to persuade and to charm; yet not irresponsibly, for it is faithful to the poetry and prayers of mankind. Method presumes upon its own practice and in this it is careless and indifferent toward the particulars

9. James Agee and Walker Evans, **Let Us Now Praise Famous Men** (New York: Ballantine Books, 1966), pp. 290–291.

that fall under its rule. Wild sociology rejects the rudeness of method that lacks any respect for the community that suffers its practices. By the same token, it is not simply conservative; rather it imposes upon its actions and speech the obligation to bring our lives together.

Wild sociology is beholden to its community. For the sociologist needs other men, just as men make a family out of their happiness and their sorrows and do not bear these alone. No man really seeks privilege and exception but as gifts to be shared in the celebration of family and community in remembering our victories and defeats, welcoming our arrivals, and mourning our departures. Such community is rarely granted to us and is not to be usurped by the privilege of science intolerant of the ways of welcome. Thus wild sociology defends the community it chooses to inhabit as the place of its deeds. In this it solicits the community's own reminiscence and powers of repetition, which furnish the commonplaces of its reflection and self-appraisal. In this way wild sociology is obliged to observe and to listen for the bottom nature of things, where they are not ruled by passivity but rather launched upon the resolution to bring life together in work, in speech, in faith, and in understanding. Wild sociology is therefore without any method of its own beyond this very celebration that counts upon the labors of others to bring together our thoughts and speech, to offer us a chance of love and understanding. Thus in making sense together we appeal to the world as flesh, as an omnipresence that is never the material of science, for it lacks distance and indifference upon our part.

Many things then come out in the repeating that make a history of each one for any one who always listens to them. Many things come out of each one and as one listens to them listens to all the repeating in them, always this comes to be clear about them, the history of them of the bottom nature in them, the nature or natures mixed up in them to make the whole of them anyway it mixes up in them. Sometime then there will be a history of every one.

When you come to feel the whole of anyone from the beginning to the ending, all the kind of repeating there is in them, the different ways at different times repeating comes out of them, all the kinds of things and mixtures in each one, anyone can see then by looking hard at any one living near them that a history of every one must be a long one. A history of any one must be a long one, slowly it comes out from them from their beginning to their ending, slowly you can see it in them the nature and the mixtures in them, slowly everything comes out from each one in the kind of repeating each one does in the different parts and kinds of living they have in them, slowly then the history of them comes out from them, slowly then any one who looks well at any one will have the history of the whole of that one. Slowly the history of each one comes out of each one. Sometime then there will be a history of every one. Mostly every history will be a long one. Slowly it comes out of each one, slowly any one who looks at them gets the history of each part of the living of any one in the history of the whole of each one that sometime there will be of every one.[10]

The physicalism of scientific observation and reflection, by which I mean the presumption of distance, seems to me to lead sociology into an imperialism of method and rationality that undermines the ritual wholeness of the daily particulars which constitute the fabric of individual integrity and communal endurance. Every individual and community stands to us as a monument of human possibility expressed in the faces, the hands, the music, the food, dwellings, and tools that men endure against the earth and the twistings of man's own arrangements. The cycle of these things is born in an expansion of hope and possibility that is gradually simplified toward death. It is the burden of wild sociology and its imaginative power to cultivate this cycle, to follow its seasons, its shaping and its bearings of life. Scientific sociology cannot be faithful to this task so long

10. Gertrude Stein, **The Making of Americans** (New York: Harcourt, Brace & Co., 1934), p. 128. Reprinted by permission of Harcourt Brace Jovanivich, Inc.

as it is the instrument of the willfulness within modern society to deny the cycle of life, to subvert its repetitions by externalizing them into mechanical organs of production and reproduction.

Sociology's pride lies in its method of scientific analysis and unification, the aim of which is to make of the world a thing of construction through and through. We should not accept without reflection the physics built into the very notion of reflection's distance. What is the distance between men? How should thinking stand outside of greetings, comings, and goings? In short, is not everything **between** men, is not everything nurtured in the fold of their **presence**? Sociology's face is toward the world though it does not love the world in its nature, its houses, its food and furniture, its music and dance, its prayers and its terrors. Sociology is outward-looking, for it seeks to reshape destinies in the mold of environment. It shrugs off the weight of birth and family, the connections of blood, and the inevitability of death, in favor of reform and revolution. Sociology is democratic and progressive. Its method is the future via men's souls. It espouses the contingencies of love in order to write freedom into the chances of birth, family, class, and neighborhood. Sociology is convinced that what is difficult in its task is corrigible through the efforts of education, science, and politics to reduce all human arrangements to matters of rule.

Wild sociology needs time, for it deals with surfaces beneath which there lies the silent, wild being that is our lives made from the legacy of this body and family of ours and from the work of our senses and intellect where they have touched others and taken from them some kind of knowing that can never be refused and must always venture itself again. Wild sociology is governed by a profound respect for the particulars of place, time, and conduct from which men build their associations and the institutions of trust that sustain their communal lives. Its narrative keeps faith with this trust through a self-conscious artfulness, in knowing that things are not as they are in order to facilitate a superficial realism or to indulge an idle aestheticism. These are species of contemplative thought that fail to attach us to the awesome work of particular and local deeds which are the connections of social life. For true sociological narrative is not the empty iteration of how things are, apart from how it is we know them to be as they are. That is to say, true narrative is the soul's conversation with its senses through which we are engaged in where we live and live as we know we do. This is the real ground of sociological description and inquiry, and thus wild sociology is irredeemably a folk art. To keep its word it requires of us a holy vigil.

5
The Holy Watch

Wild sociology opens in the reversal of the look, in the seer who is seen in that moment of prayer that joins us despite our daily trespasses. For the trespass of hands and eyes, of warmth and rejection, is the bread of our lives together. Sociological distance is not an empty space between us: it is the reach for what we have in common through our mundane needs and their natural orders of commerce and ritual. To stand outside of these ancestral bonds, as does the observer, is to risk home and loss of faith.

Sociology is the study of man. How strange! For how does man become an object of study? What are the motives for such a practice and how does it coexist with the forms of daily life that come under the optic of sociological observation? What is the faith that supports the sociologist in his life? How does he live with the conscience of seeing men other than how they see themselves? To whom does he attribute the folly of difference: to the vanity of those whom he observes or to the vanity of the community of rational men that guides his own comparisons? Such questions are likely to be regarded as mere rhetorical flourishes, as disingenuous attempts to arouse interest in the long-solved practicalities of sociological work. Worse still, they might restore apathy, inasmuch as the difficulty of sustaining the direction of the inquiry they raise convinces us of the strength of the old ways to which we inevitably return.

And yet there is something uncanny in the sociological vision. It is not to be entered into lightly, nor, once acquired, should it be allowed to harden so that the care for what we see is no longer embracing. We cannot assume that our ideological, political, professional, or aesthetic faith will always be lively to **the collective focus of seeing and being seen** that is the ground of social life. Indeed, our politics may harden the original openness through which our concern for others irrupted into our lives and determined us never again to live outside of the mutual regard that shapes our joys, our sorrows, and our hopes for every human undertaking, whether it is the building of a bridge or the birth of a child. Sociological vision is in reality more a structure of care and concern than any literal vision. It is the care that orders the wild commerce of our daily talk, lookings, helpings, hurts, and angers. By the same token, it is the display of our shared lives, of our own growth, and the place others have in our lives without which we should be diminished and lonely.

> It is becoming apparent that concern is a normal dimension of everybody, including scholars, and that for scholars in particular it is the corrective to detachment, and prevents detachment from degenerating into indifference. . . . It seems obvious that concern has nothing directly to do with the content of knowledge, but that it establishes the human context into which the knowledge fits, and to that extent informs it. The language of concern is the language of myth, the total vision of the human situation, human destiny, human aspirations and fears.[1]

1. Northrop Frye, "The Knowledge of Good and Evil," in **The Morality of Scholarship**, by Northrop Frye, Stuart Hampshire, and Conor Cruise O'Brien, ed. Max Black (Ithaca, N.Y., and London: Cornell University Press, 1967), p. 16.

Sociological concern is not averse to scientific method. Indeed, much of what is called the scientific attitude turns ou' to be a moral attitude that most of us practice in our daily lives. For few men act without a certain detachment and objectivity, and most are unwilling to fly in the face of contradiction and failure. In this regard, the social sciences are no weaker than the physical sciences because the concern that infects them is not at all a subjective impulse but rather a general respect of natures and mutual regard that is a large part of our civic culture. No one will deny that even in the arts the direction has been toward detachment and objectivity properly understood as human concern.[2] Thus the tendency in the arts and literature is to shape subjective concern in the objective labor of a **craft**.[3] And this is a necessary direction, despite the ruin of things and language, so long as men refuse to alienate the labor of culture and its representative sensibility. Sociological concern is not the easy expression of political demands or of immediate social reforms. These may equally express the fall of sociological concern into indifference, that is to say, into a neglect of the integrity of sociological concern and individual care. For there is a tension of responsibility in genuine sociological concern. This is ingrained in our double commitment to the value of the individual and to the value of the society that enhances and yet unavoidably obstructs these values.

The wild sociologist needs heart, ideas, and ideology. He needs faith in the tissue of human time and the weave of human place in which he is caught more subtly than any notion of community can convey. Conventionality is the pulse of his life, stretching back into times and over distances he no longer

2. Leo Steinberg, **Other Criteria: Confrontations with Twentieth-Century Art** (New York, Oxford University Press, 1972).
3. John O'Neill, **Sociology as a Skin Trade: Essays towards a Reflexive Sociology** (London: Heinemann; and New York: Harper & Row, 1972).

recollects, resisting the ravages of his method, recalcitrant to organization. Wild sociology labors on behalf of an infinity of mankind bonded against everything that threatens, distorts, cripples, and injures the human family. The concerns of scientific sociology are irredeemably tied to the daily institutions of politics, ideology, and professional practice. For this reason the language of sociology is at times an orchestration of human love and at times a distortion or a characterization of average values that stylizes sociological concern without any surrender to the particulars of its practice. Today more than ever, sociology is bewitched by its own language, its imperious generalizations, its ambitions of control, its usurpation of relevance. Sociology seduces us because its subject, like the pool of Narcissus, reflects the shadow of man even in its least concerns, while at its best it rejoices the connoisseurs of humanity in their comfortable and learned distance from its everyday hopes and injuries.

In **Let Us Now Praise Famous Men** James Agee introduces us to one of the deepest meditations upon the nature of wild sociology that I know, and I want now to follow the path that it opens for us. The immediate concern of Agee's work is a documentary study of three families engaged in tenant farming and picking cotton. However, from the very outset Agee is concerned to guard against the sentimental and ideological distortions of sociological concern that are so often invited by the topics of sociological investigation. At the same time, he is deeply conscious of the set of relationships, the fraternal bonds, he is about to weave between himself and his readers, between his concerned public and the subjects of his study—and most agonizingly of all, between himself and the families among whom he lives and whose lives he observes, very possibly to their harm or merely for the peculiar enjoyment of a chorus of humanitarian readers and do-gooders. Under the weight of these considerations Agee turns at times to the eye of the camera but also for the same reasons to the compassionate icon of crucified humanity. And this is the way of wild sociology.

The risk involved in sociological work is that it will service ideologies far removed from the particulars of human purpose or else be received as an art to service the vague humanitarian aesthetics of its consumers, its lay readers and middle-class students. In the first case, the ideological reception of sociological work hardly begins to fathom the depths of human injury and comes far too soon to conclusions regarding the tissue of human connections and the viruses of relation, contract, and organization. In the second, the aesthetic perception of sociological work is disembodied from the intersensory and ancestral connections of mankind, whose infinitude defies dissection into science or art to such an extent that any observation risks obscenity and distortion. Moreover, the very aesthetic sensibility for which such risks might be undertaken has an awesome public ability to absorb injustice, beauty, rage, horror, and frivolity.

Thus anyone who is tempted to succeed in appealing to such a monster as the public must ask himself what has become of his first wonder at the lives of those human beings whose innocence of such "twistings" was his opening to the mystery of collective life. There is a certain obscenity about watching any human being, standing outside of his life when really the only place to be is at his side, sharing the same life. We cannot all do the same work. We are born at different times and under different circumstances. Yet the basic human desire to be in roughly the same condition and way of life has over time been built up in the institutions of the law and the church, of the Enlightenment, and of the liberal and social democratic philosophies of equality, to an extent that even when we find ourselves in the most different circumstances we nevertheless feel that we share or are working toward a common humanity. There are a variety of ways of reinforcing this bond with our fellow man. We can do it by simply sending money to the African missions. We may join a left-wing or right-wing party, or become urban planners. All these activities are motivated by the assumption that we know what others need, want, and are all about. Yet in working on a common project or to produce a common humanity, we find ourselves engaged in different ways of life. We are as much cut off from one another through the division of labor involved in working together as we are brought together. We find ourselves living possibly more intense but certainly more and more narrow lives. It thus becomes all the more important to establish ideological, political, and moral bonds with our fellow man.

Sociology contributes to the cement of these relations. Indeed, it is part of a whole range of urban man's vicarious experience. The more we separate from rural settings and move into industrial settings, the more we re-create the rural as nostalgia, in folk song and folk art. Thus we are conscious that there are people out there on the farms, or down in the slums, or out in the colonies. And we persuade ourselves that we are not entirely cut off from these people because we read newspapers, watch television reports, and drink orange juice or coffee to keep them in jobs. Or else we rationalize our charitable sentiments in the hope that our money will find its way into every crack and cranny of needful society. When we listen to folk and country music, when we pick up a book about the Cuban revolution, or when we read about the mill hands in the nineteenth century, what makes this a reasonable thing to do is not just that we happen to be music fans or students of revolution or of economic history fans but that we believe there is a common humanity that is made over, preserved, and advanced through just such activities, through our concern with other ways of life and their bearing upon our own living.

Such humanitarian concerns would be impossible if we were to hold on to solipsistic conceptions of mind or if we were to separate the mind and the heart in our understanding of sociological care. The care and concern that establishes our social life is an **institution** of sentiment and science that is manifested as much in schoolchildren's gifts to the missions as in reading the pre-Socratic philosophers or manipulating Keynesian variables to stabilize the modern economy. Sociological work belongs to this pattern of civilized sentiment and knowledge. Nevertheless, we encounter a paradox of sociological concern, namely, that its own activity adds to the differences among men another alienation that is simultaneously the basis for its search for communality and care. This is not the simple observation that reflection presupposes leisure and is therefore ultimately tied to social exploitation. It is the existential predicament of the thinker, the artist, the priest, and the visionary that their otherworldliness is strange to the only world for which they have any care. They therefore have to instruct the world in the very things they have learned from the world. But if sociologists are at all successful in this, they acquire a style of life and appeal to an audience whose way of life in turn aggravates the injury and injustice suffered by our common humanity. Yet there is no escape from this commonplace. It is the bread of our fellow men and we cannot refuse it. The questions we raise about the reasons for sociological concern, about its rights and its motives, must be shared in the common talk of the sociologist or the artist and his public. Ultimately, these are questions of mutual trust to which we must lend ourselves as the sole means of discovering our own motives as well as the public response to them.

Agee asked himself whether his own sociological report was

anything more than the expression of the impotency he experienced when he went out to help some people whose lives he found much richer, much more mysterious, than his own, but whom he had supposed in some way to be simpler, more comprehensible, more subject to alteration, and thus to justify the reasons he had assumed to be his purpose as a writer or social reformer. Thus he is concerned with the possibilities of obscenity, voyeurism, and betrayal as the real motives of sociological work. If this is at all true, then he fears he himself is more misshapen than the people among whom he moves, "all thus left open and defenseless to a reverent and cold-laboring spy." A good part of what we call social science is the study of individuals who are miserable enough to be the object of sociological inquiry. The wealthy, for the most part, escape sociological investigation, or when they fail to, the reason is evidently the alien designs of Marxists and muckrakers. They are generally allowed to pass through life altogether before any inquiry is made about their way of life. Or else they are kind enough to leave us memoirs. But the poor and primitive do not write memoirs. Their lives have to be documented, which means that their lives are the subject of ethnographies, questionnaires, and films. Thus the practice of sociology is entirely dependent upon the different forms of access to other individuals' lives, at the same time that sociology pretends to be a remedy for such inequality.

But wild sociology is not merely a fascination with the lives of others. It is a kind of **vigil** we maintain as much in our talk and shared experience as in the look and watchful concern for our neighbors and their children. The vigilance I have in mind is not simply watching lest certain things happen. It is the vigil in which things are encouraged in their form, in which, so to speak, things and the people around us seem to grow in us and we in them. Such vigilance is not easily assumed, and it is for this reason that we see Agee struggling with the scruples of cameralike realism or else with the image of the Cross in his search for a redemptive mediation of the holy particulars of human life.

For one who sets himself to look at all earnestly, at all in purpose toward truth, into the living eyes of a human life: what is it he there beholds that so freezes and abashes his ambitious heart? What is it, profound behind the outward windows of each one of you, beneath touch even of your own suspecting, drawing tightly back at bay against the backward wall and blackness of its prison cave, so that the eyes alone shine of their own angry glory, but the eyes of a trapped wild animal, or of a furious angel nailed to the ground by his wings, or however else one may faintly designate the human "soul," that which is angry, that which is wild, that which is untamable, that which is healthful and holy, that which is competent of all advantaging within hope of human dream, that which most marvelous and most precious to our knowledge and most extremely advanced upon futurity of all flowerings within the scope of creation is of all these the least destructible, the least corruptible, the most defenseless, the most easily and multitudinously wounded, frustrate, prisoned, and nailed into a cheating of itself; so situated in the universe that those three hours upon the cross are but a noble and too trivial an emblem how in each individual among most of the two billion now alive and in each successive instant of the existence of each existence not only human being but in him the tallest and most sanguine hope of godhead is in a billionate choiring and drone of pain of generations upon generations unceasingly crucified and is bringing forth crucifixions into their necessities and is each in the most casual of his life so measurelessly discredited, harmed, insulted, poisoned, cheated, as not all the wrath, compassion, intelligence, power of rectification in all the reach of the future shall in the least expiate or make one ounce more light: how, looking thus into your eyes and seeing thus, how each of you is a creature which has never in all time existed before and which shall never in all time exist again and which is not quite like any other and which has the grand stature and natural warmth of every other and whose existence is all measured upon a still mad and incurable time; how am I to speak of you as "tenant" "farmers," as "representatives" of your "class," as social integers in a criminal economy, or as individuals, fathers, wives, sons, daughters, and as my friends and as I "know" you? Granted—more, insisted upon—that it is in all

The Holy Watch   63

these particularities that each of you is that which he is; that particularities, and matters ordinary and obvious, are exactly themselves beyond designation of words, are the members of your sum total most obligatory to human searching of perception: nevertheless to name these things and fail to yield their stature, meaning, power of hurt, seems impious, seems criminal, seems impudent, seems traitorous in the deepest: and to do less badly seems impossible: yet in withholdings of specification I could but betray you still worse.[4]

Sociological vigilance is the care of things in their wholeness and integrity. It is neither an averaging nor an irony. It is a way of seeing things round, of celebrating time and place and the endurance of their human bonds. The saving of particulars and the frail connections of the human family is work that rests upon a variety of faiths. It may be the work of the ideologist, the political reformer, the social planner. But these perspectives easily lose sight of the particulars of ordinary life. It is for this reason that the images of the camera and of the Crucifixion are the instruments of Agee's concern with the epiphany of human events. The problem is how to see the eye seeing and not the recorded eye: how to see the eye and how to listen to what we hear in the sounding of human care. This comes from our openness to the belonging together of our senses and the community of being that is the possibility we have of learning togetherness and watchfulness. There is an obvious sense in which we may be counted among the community of mankind. But our humanity is properly our orientation to the community of being as our destiny or allotment. This community, our nature, approaches us in the involvements of care, not as a lacking but as a presencing of our situation.

Care, then, is the domicile of our being together.[5] But our

4. James Agee and Walker Evans, **Let Us Now Praise Famous Men** (New York: Ballantine Books, 1966), pp. 91–92.
5. Martin Heidegger, **Essays in Metaphysics: Identity and Difference**, trans. Kurt F. Leidecker (New York: Philosophical Library, 1960).

being together is easily subject to sociological rule. The division of labor and technology that subordinates human identity and difference to the confrontation of man and nature represents the reduction of care to need and domination. Thus, despite the intricate calculations and exchanges involved in sociological rule, it proceeds by challenging the framework or **institution** of human concern and solicitude for our corporate membership.

Agee remarks, as we have already seen, that he is writing about human beings who are not in any way concerned with the problems of the artist, or the musician, or even the priest or social worker. The problems of writers, artists, priests and sociologists are entirely over the heads of the people. Those who have such concerns are strange beings. They are monsters of concern. They want to do good, they want to save, they want to express, they want to celebrate. They experience themselves as above or outside the lives of those for whom they care. Their efforts are infected with a kind of superfluity, with doubts concerning truth and reality that have no counterpart in the lives of those for whom they intend help. And further, if the sociologist or artist is at all successful in resolving his problem of concern and alienation, his work will be taken up by others in the reading public whose lives make their concern with it a matter of good taste, education, liberal consciousness, Christian concern, so that the writer's work becomes a double alienation of the original suffering and beauty or whatever it was he saw in the lives of his fellow men.

These problems surround Agee's approach to the subjects of his study. The Mass is the canopy of the approach, entrance, worship, and return to the world celebrated through its own offerings of the fruits of its labors. The Mass is therefore the natural framework of Agee's report. Nor is this a mere literary device. It is the resonance of the **Introibo**, which is the approach to the holy interior of another life with whom we communicate through the efficacy of the Crucifixion. We are not, of course, dealing here with matters of religious certainty. What is at stake is the openness of human life to the approach of the other whose need is irresistible, even though its intent or consequences may lie far beyond our understanding. The approach makes us aware that human life is huddled about its own purposes, in its belongings, its families, farms, towns, and villages. To enter a town or to approach someone is to encroach upon their welcome, to seek a kindness whose offer must bridge the first strangeness, the searching eyes, and the beginnings of talk that make the human bond.

Agee relates three encounters in which he approaches first a group of Negroes enjoying themselves, a white family, and then a young Negro couple out walking. In the first instance, Agee and Walker Evans are introduced to a Sunday morning family gathering of visitors and children all obliged to assemble and sing for the landlord's intruders. Agee is agonized by the privilege that forces an intrusion into the lives of these people who nevertheless maintain an inner calm and dignity despite the injury they feel at having to treat what is of absorbing concern to them as something that must give pride of place to the curiosity and indulgence of others.

> Meanwhile, and during all this singing, I had been sick in the knowledge that they felt they were here at our demand, mine and Walker's, and I could communicate nothing otherwise; and now, in a perversion of self-torture, I played my part through. I gave their leader fifty cents, trying at the same time, through my eyes, to communicate much more, and said I was sorry we had held them up and that I hoped they would not be late; and he thanked me for them in a dead voice, not looking me in the eye, and they went away, putting their white hats on their heads as they walked into the sunlight.[6]

On another occasion Agee and Evans come to a fork in the road where Agee asks directions from a family sitting on their

6. Agee and Evans, **Let Us Now Praise Famous Men,** p. 30.

porch—a young man, a young woman, their children, and an older man. The family is silent, all the while watching the approach of the two strangers. But it is not an empty silence that hangs between them. Agee and Evans are already caught in the conversation of eyes that sustains and marks their approach. Already much has been said between the silently knit family, drawn together by the daily necessity of preservation against the invasions of injustice, cruelty, and misunderstanding, and the chance relief of these in good times and by occasional kindnesses.

> None of them relieved me for an instant of their eyes; at the intersection of those three tones of force I was transfixed as between spearheads as I talked. As I asked my questions, and told my purposes, and what I was looking for, it seemed to me they relaxed a little toward me, and at length a good deal more, almost as if into trust and liking; yet even at its best this remained so suspended, so conditional, that in any save the most hopeful and rationalized sense it was non-existent. The qualities of their eyes did not in the least alter, nor anything visible or audible about them, and their speaking was as if I was almost certainly a spy sent to betray them through trust, whom they would show they had neither trust nor fear of.[7]

Thus a passing inquiry may smell of danger and is not to be lightly made among simple people whose security rests in a natural knowledge of place and for whom the stranger opens the huge ambivalence toward him of fear and help. This is a visceral exchange. As the stranger approaches he is able to see more of the people on whom he imposes and they in turn read from his dress and bearing something of his intentions toward them. Between them there mounts the necessity of exchange long before any word is spoken. To tell all this would take so long and they, in any case, do not have the ability to articulate

7. Ibid., p. 33.

it. Thus Agee chooses to resolve the statement of their mutual relations and his relation to them through presenting them as statuesque figures, as though monumental in their sorrow and in their silence, molded by the pain of their labor, by the sparseness of their language, and above all in the way they stand over against the little part of the world and of human experience that belongs to them.

The third encounter that I want to describe arises out of Agee and Evans' coming upon a closed church that they want to enter. Again, the interest of this encounter is that it symbolizes the mystery of integrity and approach that throws back upon its spectator the look by which he seeks to inspect the secrets of persons and things.

> It was a good enough church from the moment the curve opened and we saw it that I slowed a little and we kept our eyes on it. But as we came even with it the light so held it that it shocked us with its goodness straight through the body, so that at the same instant we said **Jesus.** I put on the brakes and backed the car slowly, watching the light on the building, until we were at the same apex, and we sat still for a couple of minutes at least before getting out, studying in arrest what had hit us so hard as we slowed past its perpendicular.
>
> It lost nothing at all in stasis, but even more powerfully strove in through the eyes its paralyzing classicism: stood from scoured clay, a light lift above us, no trees near, and few weeds; every grain, each nailhead, distinct; the subtle almost strangling strong asymmetries of that which had been hand wrought toward symmetry (as if it were an earnest description, better than the intended object): so intensely sprung against so scarcely eccentric a balance that my hands of themselves spread out their bones, trying to regiment on air between their strengths its tensions and their mutual structures as they stood subject to the only scarcely eccentric, almost annihilating stress, of the serene, wild, rigorous light: empty, shut, bolted, of all that was withdrawn from it upon the fields the utter statement, God's mask and wooden skull and home stood empty in the mediation of the sun: and

this light upon it was strengthening still further its imposal and embrace, and in about a quarter of an hour would have trained itself ready, and there would be a triple convergence in the keen historic spasm of the shutter.[8]

The sociological eye is caught in that which it sees because it is beholden to the community of the body's senses and its labors which stand out against time and the sky as the monuments of mankind. Thus every perception of ours belongs to the labor of man, fashioning himself and the legacy he leaves in his children. The church that stands against the sky is a symbol of the body's architecture and the shaping elements in the lives of the community that built it. The eyes that follow the contours of the church and upon entering take inventory of its furnishings cast the visitor's whole body into a reverent and mindful posture and thereby join him to the community in which he is at first a visitor or stranger. This is an experience that is repeated whenever we regard things with sociological concern: the disintegration or harmony we sense around us enters into us and determines our mood and purpose in the community. Thus the community shapes sociological concern at least as much as it is in turn molded by the ambitions of sociology. But we are forgetful of this in method, while at the same time proclaiming our factualism or realism. The truth is, however, that every object, like the church or the families encountered by Agee, is never a mere surface any more than the eye is the naked instrument of vision. We are caught in what we see and what we feel and the path to the things and persons around us is paved with the story of our own lives, without which there would be no bridges in the moment.

The wild sociologist is obsessed with trespass; for this is his access to the lives of others. In their third encounter Agee and

8. Ibid., p. 37.

Evans, still trying to break into the closed church, notice a young Negro couple walking by. They decide to ask them whether the minister can be found to let them in. Since the young couple are fifty yards or so ahead, Agee follows after them, his eyes taking advantage of their beautiful and buoyant bodies in a way that at a closer distance would be improper. For a brief moment, Agee is filled with the vision of the young woman, her young man—the sway of their bodies, how they are together—yet afraid all the time that his presence will startle them. Worse still, Agee is agonized lest his admiration be read as malicious intent through the young couple's misunderstanding of why he is coming up behind them. Suddenly, they startle, he calls after them, and they set off in a frightened run, more terrified as Agee in great anguish runs after them to plead that he meant no harm. The whole incident is a passing one and yet it is central to the consideration of the nature of trust implicit in the intrusions of social life. Every day we must penetrate the lives of others, interrupting their thoughts, or getting them to pause on their way, or to set aside their work for a moment. We do this from a thousand needs and not because we presume upon their help or mean to encroach upon others without consideration for them. For these reasons we need to trust to the rituals of approach even where, as sometimes happens, they do not quite succeed. At such times, I think we have to rely upon one another's experience to mend things. Agee fails to allow for this deeper trust in the young couple, perhaps a while later, to recover themselves and decide he meant them no harm. Thus, although he has the highest respect for the dignity of those whom he intrudes upon, Agee on this occasion in some sense denies them the judgment that experience brings in handling the inevitable misunderstandings that arise in human encounters. If Agee sins at all against the couple, it is because he does not allow for forgiveness from them. He insists upon being the greater victim of the misunderstanding, whereas the young couple, despite all the times they have been chased and beaten, might on this occasion have realized they had been startled and that it was their fear that set the other man after them because of his own anxiety not to be thought ill of by them. In short, there are some human encounters that can never be brought to account even though they are remembered by us and shape our conscience.

Wild sociology is not a solo effort. One might even say that it is not especially an affair of the heart, however it may seem to involve the emotions. Indeed, it is precisely because of the emotions involved that wild sociology is not properly alive in us unless it begins in the deepest trust toward others to understand and reciprocate the care we intend. Sociological care is not paternalism. It does not righteously diminish the responsible growth and variety of opinion that it will surely meet. It is not parasitic. Yet it is nurtured only in belonging to others. It seeks community without wanting to dominate the community. Sociological care is mutual; it remains active only in giving and being given life. Sociological care is not simpering. It is not exercised from empty need, or from loneliness. It is a musical response, a dance. Sociological care is not burdened. It does not work from obligation. Nor from guilt or any self-abasement. Wild sociology sings the world. Yet it always has a particular task, a local need, a definite work to do, not wasted in vain generality or empty intentions. Wild sociology never ceases to learn from what it believes it knows.

Wild sociology shoulders a common task. For this it is beholden to the world of everyday use, of custom, of trust, of invention, of hope and memory, and of the countless and immemorial repetitions of the human family, which has tilled and irrigated the fields, sailed seas, built towns, villages, and cities, which has woven wool and cloth, carved wood and stone, written books, made music, song, and dance, and all in so fine a tapestry that none of us can ever find the first thread. Wild sociology faces the seamless web of human activity in need of its own place and without any magisterial claim upon men's time. By contrast, scientific sociology is impatient for success. It seeks identity through domination. Thus it is tempted to usurp the unfinished task of community as the proper work of sociology, to manage it and divide it into the spoils of science. For this reason method and role are the idols of sociology's usurpation. They make of work an assured thing and of persons a transparent collective. In this way much is lost in favor of saving the possibility of sociology.

Wild sociology assumes the secularization of the redemptive tasks of humanity given in our care for one another, in our talk and listening, in the exchange of our labors. We have nothing that cannot be taken from us; everything we give needs to be received. We cannot live without welcome. This is the work of our frail divinity, which belongs neither to science nor to religion. It rests in the eye of God, which is the eye of love and the light of a compassionate world. Thus the family is the shelter of our concern and deserves more than anything the care of sociology. To accomplish this, sociology needs to set aside its noisy individualism and daytime ambitions, just as the family itself must gather into itself everything that separates and isolates it upon this earth.

> This family must take care of itself; it has no mother or father: there is no other shelter, nor resource, nor any love, interest, sustaining strength or comfort, so near, nor can anything happy or sorrowful that comes to anyone in this family possibly mean to those outside it what it means to those within it: but it is, as I have told, inconceivably lonely, drawn upon itself as tramps are drawn round a fire in the cruelest weather; and thus and in such loneliness it exists among other families, each of which is no less lonely, nor any less without help or comfort, and is likewise drawn in upon itself:
> Such a family lasts, for a while: the children are held to a magnetic center:
> Then in time the magnetism weakens, both of itself in its

tiredness of aging and sorrow, and against the strength of the growth of each child, and against the strength of pulls from outside, and one by one the children are drawn away:

Of those that are drawn away, each is drawn elsewhere toward another: once more a man and a woman, in a loneliness they are not liable at that time to notice, are tightened together upon a bed: and another family has begun:

Moreover, these flexions are taking place every where, like a simultaneous motion of all the waves of the water of the world: and these are the classic patterns, and this is the weaving, of human living: of whose fabric each individual is a part: and of all parts of this fabric let this be borne in mind:

Each is intimately connected with the bottom and the extremest reach of time:

Each is composed of substances identical with the substance of all that surrounds him, both the common objects of his disregard, and the hot centers of stars:

All that each person is, and experiences, and shall never experience, in body and in mind, all these things are differing expressions of himself and of one root, and are identical: and not one of these things nor one of these persons is ever quite to be duplicated, nor replaced, nor has it ever quite had precedent: but each is a new and incommunicably tender life, wounded in every breath, and almost as hardly killed as easily wounded: sustaining, for a while, without defense, the enormous assaults of the universe:

So that how it can be that a stone, a plant, a star, can take on the burden of being: and how it is that a child can take on the burden of breathing: and how through so long a continuation and cumulation of the burden of each moment one on another, does any creature bear to exist, and not break utterly to fragments of nothing: these are matters too dreadful and fortitudes too gigantic to meditate long and not forever to worship.[9]

Like all creative thought, sociological thinking needs the rhythm of night and day. This is because the sociologist is caught in the everyday involvements of his fellow men, using them without thought, presuming upon their mixed kindness,

9. Ibid., pp. 53–54.

cruelty, and indifference. Every day he is witness to the differences of wealth, strength, intelligence, compassion, and beauty that mark the parade of his fellow men, shaping their homes, their children, and the news they have of one another. The wild sociologist breathes these differences, making them into the pulse and rhythm of his own life and family. At the same time, he longs for the unity and embrace of mankind, for the sheltering care that harbors the particulars, faults, and injuries of human life. For this reason the night thoughts of the sociologist swarm around the windows of the little houses men have set like stars in the earth.

Every thought of ours seeks shelter from the journey it begins and in its course remembers how life began well, enclosed and protected in the embrace of home. All our adventures, imaginations, and dreams are nurtured in the bosom of home, and however far they lead us they remain in the circle of the homeward return. And somehow every observation of ours bears this same caress and is not an aimless looking nor an empty stare. We see things and others in the shaping circle of our intrusion and embrace; the weight of bodies, the paper on the walls, the lamps and chairs, the sounds of mealtimes, are never bare particulars but warm animal signs that attract us even though we stand off because they are not our home but half remind us. Thus in his heart the wild sociologist pays the price of knowledge in the truancy of childhood memories and moves among men in search of his right home and his true family, to which he has no title but the price of love and sorrow.

Concluding Sociological Prayer

How should sociology keep its place? After all, sociology is powerful, men are in need of it, and the world is increasingly the instrument of organization. Why should anything keep its place; what, after all, is **place** in a world that is "going places"? We are now so accustomed to change and growth that we scarcely stop to consider the sources that feed the stream of our life. Indeed, the modern world gives us our lives in such comfortable surroundings that the question of self and its circumstance is likely to remain a residual anxiety, aggravated perhaps by our political responsibility toward those on the margins of modern ease. Surely, sociology is a permanent institution. We have built it up beyond anything that need remind it of its poverty. Where sociology holds the mirror to nature how should it see itself?

The commonplace nature of wild sociology will not be easily understood. Thus many will read what I am saying and not find in it anything like sociology. My concerns will seem to answer to no concrete sense of the conduct of professional sociology. But the lack here does not lie in what I fail to say of that sort but in the reader's lack of any need to inspect what authorizes his own concrete version of sociology as something to be found or to be missed in his reading. Sociology is not a literal fact to be discovered apart from the circumstance of its approach or how it is we are alerted to what we have to reckon with in looking for sociology. The task is to find our sociological bearings. This is not a problem of method. It is a question of concentrating upon sociology the salvation of self and circumstance as a connection of love as well as of knowledge.

We sense who we are and where we are mostly to be found from local habit. Let us say we are sociologists; let them say we are philosophers. The philosophers will only smile. It is enough, in any case, that we have found a path along which we can think. For we must know where we are at home if ever we are to be able to look elsewhere. We cannot distinguish other ways or see other places unless we know our own. We must bear in ourselves the tension between our own spot and the places that are distant and strange. In this, our knowledge of good and evil is like the difference between home and away, between where we can be ourselves and where we cannot abide or dwell.

> ". . . Anything is one of a million paths [**un camino entre cantidades de caminos**]. Therefore you must always keep in mind that a path is only a path; if you feel you should not follow it, you must not stay with it under any conditions. To have such clarity you must lead a disciplined life. Only then will you know that any path is only a path, and there is no affront, to oneself or to others, in dropping it if that is what your heart tells you to do. But your decision to keep on the path or to leave it must be free of fear or ambition. I warn you. Look at every path closely and deliberately. Try it as many times as you think necessary. Then ask yourself, and yourself alone, one question. This question is one that only a very old man asks. My benefactor told me about it once when I was young, and my blood was too vigorous for me to understand it. Now I do understand it. I will tell you what it is: Does this path have a heart? All paths are the same: they lead nowhere. They are paths going through the bush, or into the bush. In my own life I could say I have traversed long, long paths, but I am not anywhere. My benefactor's question has

meaning now. Does this path have a heart? If it does, the path is good; if it doesn't, it is of no use. Both paths lead nowhere; but one has a heart, the other doesn't. One makes for a joyful journey; as long as you follow it, you are one with it. The other will make you curse your life. One makes you strong; the other weakens you."[1]

Circumstance, reason, and love, joined in bringing each of the particulars of our lives to their communal and historical fullness, accomplish the salvation of sociology. Yet in making sociology an extension of our love of circumstance we do not mean that it may not be nourished on a rough and harsh ground. For there is no love that does not till the ground of circumstance. Thus circumstantial love is not moved by things to our own perfection but is rather a love toward the perfecting of things and others that saves our first need of them in their universal connection and plenitude. It is a love to be found as much in our own gatherings as in the gatherings of things, and in both of these what is saved is the opening and light of the world in which we are reflected and multiplied like Adam in Paradise, or any man anywhere beholden to the life around him. Circumstantial love is the perfection of common need and its uses. This is not a matter of proving oneself but of belonging and beginning again, which is the commonplace of daily living. This ancestral place does not yield to those who hunt it; it does not lie in achievement or status. The commonplace is approached only in the widening circle of care.

In his doctrine of the commonplaces Aristotle treats dialectic and rhetoric as separable modes of intellectual and moral persuasion.[2] But such a separation is precisely what made sophis-

1. Carlos Castaneda, **The Teachings of Don Juan: A Yaqui Way of Knowledge** (New York: Ballantine Books, 1970), pp. 105–106.
2. Aristotle, **Rhetoric and Poetics,** trans. W. Rhys Roberts and Ingram Bywater (New York: Random House, The Modern Library, 1954); **Aristotle on Dialectic, The Topics: Proceedings of the Third Symposium Aristotelicum,** ed. G. E. L. Owen (Oxford at the Clarendon Press, 1968).

tic dialectic the intellectual pride and danger of Greek political life. For dialectic may persuade at the expense of the moral community to which it appeals, thereby undermining the true place of rhetoric. For these reasons Isocrates sought to make rhetoric service the ideals of **paideia,** that is, to correct the alternatives of intellectual arrogance and Platonic spiritualism with the commonplaces of community and nation.[3] In this manner Isocrates understood that rhetoric's own seat is its place within the life of the community whose discourse it strengthens in order, in turn, to draw upon it for its own special eloquence. Thus the commonplaces of rhetoric strengthen the communal art of memory and the associations of civic knowledge. For rhetorical style is the embellishment of the way of life that it reinforces and not simply a matter either of the speaker's character or of his topic.

Thus, to address sociology is not to deal in the personifications of a backward art. It is simply to suit our speech to its topic, which is the place of our communal life. What we seek to diminish or to embellish in the practice of sociology is addressed in terms of extreme alternatives in order to gather its tensions. For our aim is not the victory of a virtuous sociology any more than it is to refuse the temptations in the ordinary practice and institutions of sociology.

It may be asked, then, whether a sociology of the commonplace can be radical. I shall answer that in the face of the bureaucratic and corporate rationality of the professional sciences nothing can be more radical than a sociology inspired by the love of human circumstance and its great conventions. Wild sociology rejects the ambition of the professional social sciences to assimilate themselves to the structure of domination that teaches the oppressed to see themselves through the

3. W. W. Jaeger, **Paideia: the Ideals of Greek Culture,** trans. Gilbert Highet, 3 vols. (New York: Oxford University Press, 1939–1946).

eyes of their oppressors, to sift the oppressor's language for some word the people can understand, to accept as charity the return of their own gifts. This is not to deny that the social sciences may intend help, justice, and betterment. But these expectations have been promoted long enough now to leave the poor cynical toward those whose own lives are all that has benefited from our subscription to the social sciences. The danger in this is that practitioners of the sciences will find the lay community ignorant of the complexity of reform and thus rationalize lay hostility toward its practice even where the people's anger is reasonably grounded in the experience of disappointment and failure. For social reformers prefer to judge themselves by their own intentions rather than by the results of the institutions they bequeath to the poor.

Wild sociology encourages a way of looking at things and saying things that matures with its own practice. It presumes upon no hierarchy of men; it does not command the first word, nor does it insist upon the last word. It is found in a dialogue that is entirely rooted in the aspirations of human development and political community. Thus wild sociology cannot thrive where some have the right to speak and others only the obligation to listen. For in such a situation no one truly speaks and no one truly listens.

> Human existence cannot be silent, nor can it be nourished by false words, but only by true words, with which men transform it. Once named, the world in turn reappears to the namers as a problem and requires of them a new **naming**. Men are not built in silence, but in word, in work, in action-reflection.[4]

Without community, speech has no duty to listen for itself, to seek address, and to respond to those whose listening addresses their own self-inquiry and mutual need. True dialogue

4. Paulo Freire, **Pedagogy of the Oppressed,** trans. Myra Bergman Ramos, (New York: Herder and Herder, 1970), p. 76.

makes men and it is only men who are partners to dialogue. But such speech is impossible where there is no love of man and of the world he is called to think and say. Nor is this a sentimental love, for it is the bond of freedom and humanity against injustice, darkness, and oppression. Such a love therefore must know its enemies as well as its own weaknesses in order to fight oppression.

Wild sociology will encourage radicalism. Yet it will be hard on its own radicalism, suspecting further evils from its own activity should it presume upon its relation to the lay community. It may well be that the daily practice of sociology encourages arrogance upon the part of its members, undermining the very resources of humanism with a numb professionalism or the shrill cry of ideology. If this is not to happen wild sociology must make a place for itself, and to accomplish this it must engage hope and utopia. Hope is the time it takes to make the place in which men think and talk and work together. Thus wild sociology is essentially engaged in the education of the oppressed.

Sociology is nothing apart from its attachment to the world. It is for this reason that wild sociology must be mindful of its own spectacle. It cannot stand outside of the collective focus of seeing and being seen that is the natural light of man. In this light the world is our circumstance, the surround of things and others, the time they take, the places they inhabit, so that we are obliged to know their ways by living among them, shaping our own lives, our talk, and all our senses to their community. The task of wild sociology is not to collect the world for sociology. Wild sociology gathers only out and about in the world, in the epiphany of city, family, work, path, way, manner, face, child. It is a craft with nothing in hand but its own willingness to become a shape of community, a house of being.

Society is the great body of sociology. In this body the sociological eye is not the eye of the scientific observer but the eye of human divinity, the mystery of the care in the human look, its holy watch. Prior to synthesis or analysis the sociologist's look dwells upon the particularity and universality of each human being, of his moods, his places, and his works. This indwelling is a connection of the eye, the ear, the heart, and the mind of the sociologist in the great body of mankind that heals its own wounds in the strength of its time. The vision of wild sociology is a celebration, a responsibility, and a humble task no greater than a mother's care for her children or a father's labor, and is entirely unredeemed if it fails them in their patience, in their hope, and in their endurance. Its vision is beholden to its sense of mystery, its anger, its thirst for justice. In this, wild sociology is ambivalently suspended between self-purification and social reform, between revolution and unending predicament, between betrayal and forgiveness. For sociology is bewitched by a power of order, by the hope of some plan or design in which the lives of men and women will not seem fleeting occasions of the failure of humanity. And this expectation arises above all from the warm presence of human beings, from their ideas, hopes, and fears, which admit the sociologist without the cover of strangeness and alienation, however much these seize upon him in his watchful hours.

The wild sociologist means to keep faith with the great commonplaces of human life, birth, marriage, work, and death, and to be faithful to what is strange and varied, brave and defeated, in them. He must therefore learn to understand his own curiosity and not place it above its proper human concerns. For in the great body of mankind, in all its times and places, in all its beliefs and visions, the sociologist's own activity risks monstrosity in its pretended freedom and in its rootless possibility. Sociology is the poorest of the sciences, for it is brother to man unless it tricks him with the power of politics or the promise of history. Scientific sociology, however, is not always sure of its own work and is thus tempted by other enterprises as models of power and accumulation. These possibilities consume much of the energy of sociology in the effort to force its bread in the unseasonable factories of method. The way of ordinary men is infinitely more patient; it is repeated upon their lives in countless labors, monumental in the movement of fingers, eyes, and hands; in bending, lifting, folding, sowing, and cutting; in hauling, shipping, mining, flying, weaving, and baking; in watching, digging, planting, selling, and buying; in eating, drinking, sleeping, and living; in reading, writing, praying, and singing; in burying, marrying, mothering, and learning. And each of these is so finely wrought upon the bodies of men and women and of their children and families, in their homes and fields and in their factories, schools, and churches, in their markets, their streets and parks, that they are all so much music to the shaping circle of our being, our joy and sorrow—all in their endless epiphany.

It is in the midst of these things that are the world's blessing and instrument that we assume the common cares of sociology. For the concern of wild sociology is not just the encouragement of order in others but the very shape of our own life. It is for this reason that the commonplaces of social life are the occasions of our thanksgiving.

THE AUTHOR

John O'Neill is a graduate of the London School of Economics and Political Science and of Stanford University. He is now Professor of Sociology at York University, Toronto. He has lectured widely throughout the world and is an editor of the journals **Philosophy of the Social Sciences** and **The Human Context.** He is the author of **Sociology as a Skin Trade: Essays towards a Reflexive Sociology.** John O'Neill has edited **Modes of Individualism and Collectivism** and **Phenomenology Language and Sociology: selected essays of Maurice Merleau-Ponty.** He has also translated Merleau-Ponty's **The Prose of the World** as well as Jean Hyppolite's **Studies on Marx and Hegel.**
    All these titles are published by Heinemann Educational Books.

83